A Journey within the Self

Contents

FROM REVIEWS AND READERS

. . . Told with unusual frankness . . . meticulous accuracy . . . without any of the conventional inhibitions . . . In the best yogic tradition . . . corresponds to what certain advanced yogins have gone through. (Passages) conform to identical experiences of mystics both in the West and East.

The voice of Truth has its own unmistakable authenticity . . . a model of non-appropriation.

M P Pandit
The Hindu
Madras, India

Journey is a true and unusual account . . . unputdownable.

. . . Likely to gain wide acceptance and recognition. A straighforward manner and speaking of other-worldly matters in a down-to-earth fashion . . . explicit and reader-friendly.

Sheer experience . . . makes compelling reading. The words flow like poetry and the reader revels in them as much as in the content . . . holding out a promise that glimpses of eternity are within the reach of everyone.

The Independent
Bombay, India

Such extraordinary collection of experiential memoirs . . . remarkable in the magnitude of their assertions, expressed vividly. Has already received admiring responses.

It is the intellectual rigour that is extraordinary . . . as extraordinary perhaps as the candour in her writing.

Not a dead wisdom, but an understandable, live idiom . . . as much Indian as it is instantly universal . . . a vista that can be simultaneously investigated and experienced.

Shilpa Kagal
The Weekend Observer
Bombay, India

. . . An account of the authoress's sudden and spontaneous spiritual enlightenment which, since its publication, . . . has been making waves in spiritual circles.

Saaz Kothare
Saturday Times
The Times of India
Bombay, India

A book of rare experiences . . . fascinating . . . so much self-assurance.

M V Kamath
Mid-Day
Bombay, India

. . . Rarely has anyone fathomed into the day-to-day yogic experiences with such utter frankness as Deepa Kodikal . . . so vividly that the reader's mind is engrossed from cover to cover . . . Here lies the uniqueness of this book . . . she discusses over sixty different aspects of the road to salvation.

. . . It is no doubt an expression of a highly elevated soul, full of humility. This book is a must for every Sadhaka and non-sadhaka, it is a unique experience beyond mind.

S P Udyawer
KSA Magazine
Bombay, India

Deepa's experience teaches one great lesson that spirituality is the birth-right of every human heing, householders and sannyasins, of women and men. The style is beautiful and narration runs smoothly.

Swami Ranganathananda
Ramakrishna Math
Hyderabad, India

. . . Shows us the art of living. Many books have been written about different types of Yoga and spiritual experiences. But this book is different. It shows the path through which she received spiritual knowledge and enlightenment . . . in a language that is simple yet effective . . . a good book.

Ms Lakshmi Venkatachalam
in broadcast of Book Reviews
over *All India Radio*, Bombay, India

. . . A marvellous book with a record of her own soul-thrilling experiences. It is a book of great inspiration . . . of wonderful spiritual experiences.

It will be of immense help to those who wish to ascend to the great heights of spiritual wisdom and knowledge . . . will be the source of great strength and a guide for the adventures in spiritual life.

Swami Devarupananda
Ramakrishna Math
Bombay, India

. . . Splendid book . . . the transparency of (the) extraordinary experiences has made the book unique. It captivates . . . it is a rare kind of inspiration. To anyone it is a marvellous journey, the only journey that matters in life.

Swami Muktirupananda
Mayavati, U.P., India

I am too overwhelmed . . . I have not read such (spiritual) book more than five or six times during last 45 years!

Ashwin Mehta
(Well-known photographer of the Himalayas and Nature)
Gujarat, India

It is very rare to find such books of experience . . . correctly showing and demonstrating that sadhana is a spontaneous process activated by Grace, not something that we can control with techniques, something on the contrary that goes quite beyond structured approaches, a gift from the Divine.

I am enriched and encouraged by reading (the) book and I am grateful for that.

Alberto D Formai
Pondicherry, India

. . . Simply wonderful, breath-taking . . . her language is so poetic and original. To read her diary is a deep experience in itself . . . this unique document, full of divine revelations.

Mrs. Harma Orshoven
Holland

A splendid spiritual odyssey . . . a breathtaking and unending voyage, which opens vista after vista of splendour of the inner world . . . a fascinating story of awe, fear, pain and ecstasy . . . rare, mystical experiences.

Extraordinary diary . . . rich contents . . elegant, graceful style . . . leave a lasting impression. Stokes the fires of detachment and dispassion.

A rare book that should not be missed by spiritual aspirants.

S M
Prabuddha Bharata
(A monthly journal of the
Ramakrishna Order, started
by Swami Vivekananda in 1896)
Almora, UP, India

What a wonderful book . . . I know it had some profound effects in me. You really see the spectrum of this spiritual evolution from her descriptions . . . it humbles one.

Colleen Engle
Oregon, U.S.A

The very thought that someone like you exists is so consoling and highly motivating as well.

Shanta Kelker
Mumbai, India

. . . fascinating . . . I am particularly charmed by all the deep spiritual experiences described; they are glorious and amazing . . . great examples.

William J Eddy
Fairfield, Iowa, USA

. . . just wonderful . . . I feel happy just by reading it . . . I am almost losing interest in reading any other book after this.

Mohan S Divekar
Bangalore, Karnataka, India

. . . inspired by your spiritual progress.

Y S Rama Lakshmi
Hyderabad, A.P, India

. . . wonderful and enlightening book . . . beautifully explains in simple understandable language . . . one of the best books I have read.

Deep Suvarna
Mumbai, India

. . . most amazing.

Ray Napolitano
Bloomfield, New Jersey, USA

. . . marvellous spiritual diary.

From *Mystics, Masters,*
Saints and Sages
Ed. Robert Ullman &
Judyth Reichenberg-Ullman
Berkeley, California, USA

You can't believe the pleasure and the attention I took to read the wonderful path taken by your soul to merge with the Divine . . . I was eating your words.

Milou Van Migem Lepage
Mortsel, Belgium

I am still in awe of Deepa's spiritual experiences and depth of spiritual awareness. What blessedness. So inspirational . . . leaving one awe-struck.

Colleen Engle
Fairview, Oregon, USA

I have found your book very inspiring . . . this lovely book, it will always be an important part of my spiritual library.

Phyllis Goldsmith
Alberta, Canada

. . . indeed a remarkable chronicle of the spiritual journey. Few have left descriptions of their actual experiences . . . the book illuminates. We are in great debt to Mrs Kodikal for keeping this journal.

Drs LM & MB Jerry
Alberta, Canada

Thank you for such an inspiring book . . . supremely excellent work. I have thousands of books on spirituality and many by Indian authors but nothing to match your book. I simply could not put that (sic) book down once I had begun to read it, slowly, meditatively, pondering its truth . . . first of many readings. I carry it whereever I go. This book really inspires me to accelerate my sadhana. The experiences are given in such a lucid style with so much truth given . . . wonderful, wonderful, wonderful book.

Your book is a special contribution to that legacy (of India). Thank you profoundly for a most extraordinary spiritual book.

Louis (Jim) Ponti
Oglesby, Illinois, USA

Yogis rarely write their own stories. There is a famous work *An Autobiography of a Yogi*. Now it is yours. Both are excellent experiences.

K Vijayan
Mudappilavi, Kerala, India

The experiences . . . a great source of inspiration.

C S Visweswaran
Chennai, Tamilnadu, India

. . . after many years, I think, I read something so authentic . . .
so factual.

Dr Diniar Mistry
Solapur, Maharashtra, India

Your book is worth a million dollars.

P S Rajkumar
Adyar, Tamilnadu, India

Your book was of great assistance . . . and inspired me to resume
my sadhana.

A A Rajan Iyer
Riyadh, Saudi Arabia

I was deeply moved by . . . Mrs Kodikal's experiences.

V M Rao
New Delhi, India

I have read your extremely gripping and interesting book ... with
great awe and delight. Written very lucidly and with sincerity

Minal Devi Solanki
Mumbai, India

Really a good book, full of clarity, profound significance for the
person who is spiritual, and acts as 'ghee for agni'.

Deepak Sethi
Jammu Tawi, J & K, India

. . . a gripping adventure of a vibrant inner awakening into the
spiritual unknown . . . dramatic para-psychic events . . . spell-
binding spiritual journey unfolds a saga, amidst family duties,

where the actor, the action and the audience are one, Advaita, and in this oneness is contained all.

Prof K S Ramakrishna Rao
The Mountain Path
Sri Ramanasramam
Tiruvannamalai, Tamilnadu, India

I was thrilled and actually overpowered by its style and contents. It truly deepens faith in God and enriches the cultural and spiritual life of our people. Hence it is a must for Sadhakas and non-Sadhakas.

Dr V R Talgeri
Mumbai, India

I was absolutely fascinated by it.

Dr M M Karande
Mumbai, India

A very profound work and a great gift to others on the path.

D Rajan
Kapaa, Hawai, USA

. . . a spiritual transformation at the deepest, pure advaitic level . . . an extraordinary diary of yogic revelations . . . most inspiring. Highly recommended.

Deva Rajan
Hinduism Today
North American Edition
Concord, California, USA

. . . honest, sincere and without a trace of presence of ego . . . such experiences are rarely written and published. It gives a message of hope to the mankind. It also gives man a firm belief in God—in Self.

Kanubhai Mandavia
Junagadh, India

Wow! What a book . . . truly excellent . . . written very plainly, very well and also very honestly. You have the experience and also the language to express it appropriately . . . a profound book.

Dr Prashant Shah
Baroda, Gujarat, India

Editor's Note

A vast body of writings is available about the experiences of the seekers of True Knowledge; of the practitioners of spiritual disciplines, such as, different types of yoga; of the saints seeking the Lord in love and compassion; of the mystics; of the sufis; of the renunciates practising the rigours of penance or hatha-yoga or self-imposed isolation. These writings are mostly 'post-facto', in that the spiritual practices and experiences are recollected at a later date and written down either by the seekers themselves or by their followers.

Rarely does one come across a spiritual saga of the seeker's trials and tribulations, his innermost thoughts and mystic experiences, written down by the seeker himself *whilst he is actually going through them*, during his spiritual 'apprenticeship', and on to the revelation of Truth, of God, in whatever form or aspect it is vouchsafed to him.

A jotting down of every thought, every experience, as it is lived, with no diluting on subsequent reflection. No emendation in the light of later experiences of a more advanced level. No filtration through the minds of the followers, and thus no distortions or misconceptions.

Rare though such memoirs of mystic events and spiritual adventures are, still they are mostly by seekers of Truth as it is revealed in the form of their favourite deity, the Lord in an incarnate form; or, of Truth revealed in manifestation of primal light, or primal sound, without an ascribable source. Still, these are revelations of Truth in duality . . . the experiencer is distinct from the experienced. On the one hand, the spiritual practitioner, the devotee, the yogi, or the saint; on the other, the Lord. The seeker and the sought. The lover and the beloved. This distinction is maintained.

However, the rarest of all are the writings of those beings who are blessed with the 'becoming' of oneness with the Lord, the non-dual 'experience' of One-ness, of merging one's identity with the Universality.

And these extremely rare, as-it-occurred memoirs of a non-dualistic 'experiencer' are to be treasured, as they give us a glimpse of the ultimate in spiritual attainment, at least insofar as it is understood by man in his development so far.

Having pointed out the rarity of an advaitin's 'experiences' being made available to posterity in first-person accounts, one must now look at the statistical odds of a person being the witness in person, in continual attendance, at the 'advaitic' flowering of, at the non-dualistic 'experiencing' by, a spiritual seeker. The odds could be one in millions?

It so happens that I was given the perhaps unique opportunity of being literally the bedside witness of the tribulations undergone by a human being in the attainment of 'advaita', of one-ness with the Lord, of the merger of the subject and the object, of the annihilation of the individual ego and its dissolution into the Universal. I was the witness to the hardships, yes, and the pain endured with extreme fortitude by both the mind and the body of the person so 'chosen' to be blessed with such an exalted, blissful spiritual state. It was all an inseparable mixture of discomfort and helplessness combined with indescribable ecstasy and bliss, according to the author.

My wife, the keeper of this day-to-day account of her state of mind and thoughts and 'experiences' during a period when she was first vouchsafed the 'advaitic' state, had, surprisingly, never aspired for anything even remotely resembling 'advaita'. On the contrary, for her, the rightful place for God was as a deity kept in the household altar, to be remembered with love and worshipped.

The reader will agree that it is most unusual for a person who had never read scriptures or philosophical treatises or undertaken any rituals or penances or yogic disciplines to be made the recipient of not just the more prevalent dualistic revelations but the extremely rare non-dualistic, 'advaitic', self-realization.

Through all this period, which is described in detail in the following pages, I was by her side most of each day and throughout each night. Being myself a voracious reader of the lives of spiritual seekers and of mystic accounts and spiritual literature, and having practised 'sadhana' with the blessings of and initiation by my Sadguru, I could appreciate and, to a certain extent, evaluate the author's thoughts and 'experiences' narrated in her writings. I was 'there'; I had the ring-side seat. I was the Sanjaya of *Mahabharata*, in our bedroom, as each day, each night, the author went through both the bliss and the pains of her extraordinary spiritual transformation.

I could witness for myself, admittedly from the outside, the beginnings of a never-ending spiritual adventure, and its profound accumulating effect on the life of an otherwise ordinary though highly multi-talented housewife; how she battled to maintain her equipoise and win mastery over the mysterious forces bestowing upon her, though unasked for, the divine boon of one-ness with the Lord, the awareness, the realization that God is within man, and that, in truth, man himself is God.

The author did not show me her diary during the time she wrote it from the copious notes she maintained on a day-to-day basis. On being allowed to read it later on, I immediately realized its immense value as a contemporary, first-person, authentic document of a person going through a spiritual transformation culminating in 'atma-dnyana', self-realization of a non-dualistic 'advaitic' nature.

The author was averse to the idea of her diary being published. She had been totally factual in her writing, leaving herself vulnerably open to possible misinterpretations. For, finally, spiritual yearnings and aspirations can only be fulfilled experientially, in a manner unique to each individual.

Fortunately, I was able to convince her of the importance of her spiritual log-book for aspirants in all walks of life, irrespective of their religion, caste or creed. I am confident that this journal about the author's journey within the Self will be a beacon of encouragement to the many who, with faith and hope, sit in meditation, or worship before the altar, or contemplate upon the mystery that is Life and wonder at its origin and its purpose.

The author and I would like to acknowledge the tremendous encouragement and help given to both of us, at various times, by several of our friends who are travellers on the spiritual path, as also by others, in the course of getting this book ready for publication: Among them, our special thanks to our friend and mentor, the late Kisanbhau Nemlekar; to our cousin, Vasanti, for patiently making sense out of the hand-written text and diligently typing the first draft; and to my colleague, M. Gopalakrishnan, for preparing a faultless, final typescript.

To attempt to render thanks to my Sadguru, we feel, would be inadequate in any words.

March 1992   **Raja V Kodikal**

Komal
15th Road
Santa Cruz (West)
Bombay 400 054

Preface to the Third Edition

Despite a continuing demand for it, *A Journey within the Self* has remained out of print for the last several years.

Then in 2005, the author's latest book *Teachings of the Inner Light* was published. It is steadily acquiring an increasing repute as a book of excellence for the experiential authority, simplicity, lucidity and the persuasiveness of its blueprint for right living. It inspires the modern reader to a secular pursuit of spiritual development. One need not wait to encounter an enlightened personality for spiritual guidance to embark on a journey of self-improvement, that, over a period, automatically transforms life and living for the better.

The increasing popularity of *Teachings of the Inner Light* has also led to a fresh, wider demand for *A Journey within the Self*. Recognizing this, Viva Books, the publishers of *Teachings*, have come forward to bring out an enlarged third edition of the *Journey*.

A fresh chapter, 'The Years Roll by', has been added to this edition, acquainting the reader with the author's further spiritual development subsequent to the period from 1981 to 1986, when events narrated in the main body of the book took place. It re-emphasizes the main theme of both the books, namely the relationship between Man and God.

Introduction

This journal is a day-to-day account of the unfolding of a saga where the actor, the action and the audience are one. In this oneness is contained all.

In this journal is contained the truth of and the reasons for our existence as was revealed to me step by step.

I had not read any scriptures prior to my experiences outlined here, nor had I any yearning at all for Knowledge of the Divine. Life was perfect for me. I needed no change. Desire for this or hankering for that was unknown to me.

Then one day I began perceiving a new dimension to life, stark and spread everywhere. I began to wonder how I had been blind to it when it was all-pervasive and so obvious. How could I have been so insensitive to all this divine grandeur?

I began writing down every thought, every feeling, every event, as it occurred to me, as it was revealed to me. It was an urge I could not suppress. Impelled by an inner force, I put my pen to the paper. I have not striven for a literary style. I have not strained for any particular effect. I could not have possibly done so because the words would just pour out of me and the hand would rush across the page.

In communicating, one makes use of the language one is familiar with. I too have done the same. Even at the cost of being unoriginal in style. I did not want to break the stream of Knowledge that was pouring out merely to be original.

When the stuff is one's own, one has the leisure to coin clever phrases and new words, but when one is conjoined to a hidden source of Knowledge and does not want to either miss or hinder the flow, explaining with the familiar words and phrases is the wiser thing to do.

Words which had no meaning to me, profundities which I had not grasped before, presented themselves with a clarity that only an inner experience can give. All that I experienced, all that I perceived, all that I gathered, I wrote down daily, even at the risk of being repetitive. It is not that I underestimate the intelligence or the grasp of the reader. But this is a faithful chronicle of my state and my feelings at the various times. Besides, I feel that the repetition, wherever it occurs, has come in the right context and makes a point complete and clear. In any case, the subject being profound, repetition will, in my opinion, make certain points sink in all the more deeply, which will be all to the good. The unfolding of the Knowledge led me from one discovery to another and held me fascinated constantly; and the same points were shown in different lights and connected to various others so precisely that a grand pattern emerged through this very repetition.

This fascination and this grand pattern I would like to share with my readers and hope that they too surge forward in their own discoveries and investigations. A lot of people will find that they too have experienced similar things, perhaps without fathoming their importance.

There is neither anything new nor my own in this journal; everything in these pages is purely that which was revealed to me. I have only been an instrument to jot them down.

The diary covers a period of my life starting when I was forty-three years of age. Educated in the best of schools and colleges in New Delhi, I have been in Bombay since my marriage at twenty-one. Groomed in a life of relatively easy accomplishments in education and other activities, such as glider-flying, dance, drama, painting, I was, after marriage, deeply involved in being the wife of a successful executive (who later became an industrialist). My husband Raja and our three growing daughters, Nandita, Aqeela and Akshata, with our friends and relatives, formed my charmed circle. Then along came our fourth child, Tejaswi, the Shining One. She was less than three years old when the narrative commences.

Since childhood, I had been experiencing things differently from the way others normally do. Of course, at the time, I was not aware of the exclusive nature of my experiences. I took them for granted, imagining them to be natural and common enough. I was also, naturally, not knowing that these were perhaps the fore-runners of such experiences as are narrated in these pages. It is only now, on checking with a cross-section of people, that I have found that very few have had similar experiences, at least not as consistently and over such a long period as myself.

Early in life, when I was eight or ten, I realized that I could direct my dreams. Ordinary dreams or nice dreams were, of course, a pleasure to have; but, during nightmares, of which I had a generous quota, this gift of directed 'propulsion' acted like an invincible armour against any fear. I was a timid child and was always petrified at night. In my nightmares, I would be perpetually followed by a band of gypsies, or find a big feline stalking me or trying to enter the house, or I would have encounters with ghosts. Haunted thus repeatedly, one day I mentioned to my mother that I was scared at nights. An off-hand remark by her, to make light of my fright and to reassure me, changed my life altogether. She said, 'There is nothing to be scared of. It is your dream. Only you can see those creatures. They can't see you.'

I was stunned. How true, I thought. If the creatures peopling my dreams cannot see me, then if I were to stand still where I was, they would bypass me. I would be safe! With a herculean effort of will, I put this to the test at night, in the nightmare that followed. I was being followed by the same band of gypsies. With all the courage I could gather, I stood my ground and did not flee as I normally did. And, to my utter disbelief, I saw the band moving on from either side of me, oblivious of me. I was invisible to them. They could not see me, they could not feel me, and, what's more, they walked through me as if I was not there. I stood trembling in the middle of the road a long while, digesting this incredible occurrence.

The marvel of this discovery never really left me. A new vista of what is possible had opened before me.

Now I was my own master. Fully armed thus, nightmare

thereafter became, after the initial fright and a slight uncertainty, a challenge from which I would come out unscathed.

From hereon, it was only a matter of time before I concluded that I could do all sorts of impossible things in a dream. So, when the gypsies arrived next, instead of willing myself invisible, I jumped like a blob of flubber and landed on a branch high up a tree. Now nightmares were fun. Any time the gypsies or the tiger or the lion appeared, I would become invisible or become a piece of flubber, or would just take off on a sortie. Now dreams became flights of fantasy.

Pleasant dreams I would let be, to see what they had to offer me. Besides, it took tremendous effort, at least in the beginning, to will myself to do such bizarre things. Of course, I need not have gone to all this trouble, as the gypsies could not see me in any case. All the same, I learnt a thing or two about flying and that was worth it.

Soon I found out that I was conscious in my dreams of the fact that I was dreaming and that it was not a reality. One day, I dreamt of a whole lot of skeins of wool in brilliant colours stacked in shelves as in a shop. I was all a-flutter because I could not choose any colour for myself, as each colour was so vibrant. I was greedily looking at the colours and wishing I could make up my mind, when my sister seemed to say, 'What are you getting so excited about? This is only a dream. You won't find all this in the morning.'

I realized that what she said was true. No point in choosing non-existent things. But, nevertheless, I chose a colour, reasoning that, if I were ready with my choice, I could avoid a similar frenzy of uncertainty the next day when we were actually going to the market to buy wool. Right enough, the next day, I made a quick buy of the same colour and came home happy and excited.

From that day, the indecision involved in any choice departed. I simply knew exactly what I wanted. From then on, I was always conscious in a dream that I was dreaming. This reduced my fright as also my disappointments in the mornings.

When I was about six, I heard about the grandeur of the Mediterranean Sea. That night, I dreamt I was in a liner cruising through an ocean and I knew intuitively that it was the Mediterranean. It was a normal black-and-white dream, and I saw that the much-heard-of gorgeous blue of the ocean was missing. I fancied that either this was not the Mediterranean, or that the elders had exaggerated. At once, the ocean turned a spectacular blue. And since then, all my dreams have been in colour and in vista-vision. The blue of the ocean, the white of the foam and the super-liner, and the black of the slicing of water by the liner, are as vivid today.

I began bringing the objects of my dream into sharper focus. If a tree was far away, I would adjust the focus as one adjusts the binoculars or a microscope. Now each vein of each leaf, each flower, each insect, each grain of mud could be seen. The view could be brought forward or pushed back, the vision made sharp or blurred, the colours made dark or light. All at will. It became a big fun game with me. Now, it was not restricted to dreams alone. Even when I was awake, I could close my eyes and conjure up any object or a scene, and repeat similar exercises. I could manage it perfectly.

Often, if I heard of, say, a temple on a hill, and wished I could see it, at night I would be allowed a glimpse of it. And, not only would I see the deity in a magnum size, I would also be shown the entire hill and the elaborate ritual of 'puja' and given the sacred 'prasad'. All this to the accompaniment of the mellifluous tolling of the temple bells. I began seeing temple after temple, with deities as large as mountains, beautifully carved and alive. And I would always be travelling, not by any modern mode of transport, but by transmigration.

Often, I would foresee a coming event in my dreams; or sometimes get to view it after it had occurred, if I had somehow missed it. In this manner, I saw many weddings and other functions which I had not attended, and the events in them would be found to be matching the actual happenings when I would check them out with the right persons.

Along with this, even at that young age, I became aware of a state of perfection in all that made up life. Life was so perfect, as it was, that even to crack a smile was to disturb this perfection.

So, I would often look at people, even acquaintances and friends, without giving even a flick of a smile. I would stare at them like an onlooker would, not participating in their talk or their excitement, not empathizing with them. I would be aware that they would be taking me to be anti-social or frozen-face. However, try as I might, the smile or the excitement would not come. There seemed to be a lock within, which would not open. And that was because, deep within me, there was calm and peace of such stillness and depth that it held tight the ripple that could have ended in a smile. But, surprisingly, I did not lack in friends, and frozen-face notwithstanding, I was still much sought after by my friends. Perhaps, the peace, the quiet and the inner joy were somehow transmitted to them!

A trio of deities, Lord Krishna, Shri Ram and Maha-Vishnu, held me captive day and night. The nectar I derived from thinking about them was not a meagre quantum. Very considerate to a young devotee, they never left me alone in my thoughts. Although strictly an outdoor girl, full of play and mischief and always in company of friends, I still led a private and intimate life with my beloved gods, even amid school and studies.

I slipped into matrimony without a ripple of excitement. The ripple still would not come. I was still an onlooker. But there was no revulsion or regret either. Thrown into a whirlpool of socializing, I adjusted instantly to the new life of a large joint Hindu family. School and college activities had yielded to painting, badminton, swimming and bringing up my babies, and entertaining and being in turn entertained to a lot of luncheon or dinner get-togethers. But although there was a lot of activity and laughter in my hectic new life, deep within me another life prevailed which was serene, and to me, more real.

Each pregnancy brought in its wake a radical change in me. I was normally very active, indulging in various hobbies, but, during pregnancy, a lethargy would come over me with force, and result into such a stillness that the body would hardly move. I would just sit and stare at nothing and have no reactions to life. I often wondered if I looked like a zombie; but, no, there was a reassuring intelligence and an ethereal contentment behind this stillness, which I did not want to exchange in return for anything.

I was in a thought-free and desire-free state, and went about my chores with an effort. As suddenly, these moods would depart and I would be active again. These were recurrent moods. I would get a burst of energy only when I just could not avoid doing a particular bit of work. Then again I would lapse into this serene somnolence.

Now I recognize these as samadhi-like states. At that time, of course, I did not give it a second thought, taking these to be normal pregnancy traits. But I spent a lot of time staring at the sky, gazing at the sun, enjoying the landscape, getting lost in the setting sun and enjoying the ocean, the breeze and the temple bells. And only mythological stories would hold my interest.

I had three daughters one after the other. I was happy and content. They began growing up, and life was spent in bringing them up.

Around 1976, Raja met his Sadguru. He became a highly conscientious disciple. I could not understand why anybody needed an outsider to obtain solace and guidance. There was an inner guru, I felt, who could give all the strength and help required, if one sought his help, sincerely and calmly. Raja and I would have lots of arguments about it. I told him that he was weakening himself, running every time to an outside agency to get solace. But he was adamant, and asked me to join him. I felt no need of outside help. All the help I desired was within me. Develop the inner guru, I told him repeatedly.

But Raja was insistent. For years, he went alone on his visits to his spiritual mentor. He also began meditation. He would get up early in the mornings and meditate for hours at a time. I thought it such a waste of time to sit in one place and do nothing; I would rather paint or do something more concrete and useful, or even spend my time thinking of Lord Krishna and sip the nectar. When the heart was full of Lord Krishna, I was sure, meditation and worship were redundant.

At that time, of course, I did not realize that Raja was earnestly in quest of this inner guru, and that he was only following the path he knew best, that of seeking outside help. He did not believe in idol-worship, so he did not find Krishna-worship either appealing or very effective. He found in his Sadguru an anchor and a guide, and progressed rapidly in his spiritual odyssey. The all-pervasive, formless Brahman, the immanent Paramatman, is more appealing, more satisfying to Raja.

When my children grew up and I had more time on hand, I went with Raja one day to meet his Sadguru, more out of curiosity and still more for the pleasure of a long drive. The Sadguru blessed me in profusion and said that he saw me as Lakshmi, the goddess of wealth. He blessed Raja and me again and again, and said that a lot of happiness and luxury were in store for me. I wondered if he knew my real feelings about gurus in general, and, despite it, was blessing me. Anyway, never the one to shun blessings, I bowed at his feet and reverently offered flowers to him.

Thereafter, occasionally, I would accompany Raja to the place, thirty kilometers away from Bombay, where his Sadguru lived. Again, it was more for the pleasant outing that I went; and, besides, who doesn't feel nice being blessed! Though I did not feel any real need, I think I wanted to play safe, and not miss out on the blessings. One never knows, I thought!

One day, the Sadguru said to us both: You are destined to have one more child, a male one this time. It shall be a child blessed with divine grace. It shall come into this world blessed with Sadguru's divine grace. It is destined to achieve great things in life. You will ask me: What things? I will not limit the child's destiny by spelling out anything specific. It will be a child of freedom. Free to distinguish itself in whatever field of activity: spiritual, intellectual, artistic, even political! You must both seriously consider having another child. This is my boon, my spiritual blessing to you both.

For over a year, we hesitated over his urgings. I had three daughters, fairly grown-up, and life was again settling down to an even tenor. I was happy and content; I did not want to get bogged down again with drying nappies and supervising studies.

Besides, where was the guarantee that, this time around, we would have a son. To ensure that our three daughters were married into good families and settled down amicably was enough of a responsibility. I did not want any added responsibility. Our daughters were growing up nicely, and I was feeling free again.

So, I stopped going with Raja to his Sadguru. But the pressure from Raja was building up as, repeatedly, he was offered the blessings of his Sadguru's 'tapas', his spiritual force. Forget about a son; wouldn't it be wonderful to have a divinely blessed child in the house? he asked repeatedly. I was still sceptical and reluctant. Life in Bombay was becoming more and more expensive; could we afford the luxury of a fourth child?

The blessings and the promised rewards accompanying the fourth child were escalating. Total strangers who had uncanny intuition, such as, astrologers, 'nadi shastris'—who could, by touching the pulse, predict the future—and others, by some strange coincidence, began visiting us and predicting the birth of an extraordinary son. We could not avoid a fourth child, they said. If not now, some years later, this would be inevitable.

My resistance was melting away. Was I being unfair to Raja, to the unborn child, and to myself? Wouldn't it be nice to have such an extraordinary child? Wasn't it worth taking a chance?

One day, we were asked, if we were really not interested, then the Sadguru would give the spiritual blessings to someone else. That did the trick. Piqued that such an illustrious child should be born into some other family, I took the plunge, and, praying fervently to the Almighty to guide me and to stop me if it was a foolhardy step, I agreed.

We were asked to bring a coconut and flowers one day, and, amid recitations of mantras and manifold blessings, and in an ecstatic mood, the Sadguru handed back the coconut and flowers to me. With joyous laughter, he blessed Raja and me again and again.

I went to sleep that afternoon. I felt pleasantly relaxed. Raja too had his brief afternoon siesta. I fell into deep, almost a drugged sleep. And I dreamt of long continuous streams of light entering me. I saw that there was no ceiling to our bedroom, it was open to the sky. I saw light from the brilliantly sunny firmament pouring down on to me. I was lying down on my bed and gazing up at the sky and gigantic beams of light cascaded down and disappeared into me.

The drugged feeling increased. I could not open my eyes. My body was heavy and I was in the tenderly protective depths of Mother Earth. Was I awake or asleep, I could not make out.

I forced my eyes open. I was, without a doubt, in our own bedroom, ceiling and all. I slipped again into another divine stupor. Again, there were those dazzling beams of blinding light and the blue sky behind them.

I slept on, and was shown the lane outside our bungalow; it had turned into a broad gushing river. A turbulent muddy river rushing past our house with great speed and force. Along with this rush and speed was an ethereal calm about it. The buildings on the opposite side stood in their places as usual. No one, other than me, was aware of this sudden river. Nothing else stirred, I stood at the gate pondering over how the street we had used a little while earlier had turned into a swollen river, and how the river could manage to combine this calm and poise along with its gushing turbulence. And it slowly dawned on me that the very orderliness which seemed to govern the fervour, the turbulence and the haste of the river lent a strange aura of peace to the atmosphere. And nature all over moved, jumped, stormed, burst and flounced, but cradled in the same equipoise and having an order of its own. The still eye of the storm seemed here to have expanded to contain the storm itself.

I observed the red of the muddy waters, the green of the moss and slime, the white of the foam, and the various shades of green and grey and blue of the river, and marvelled at the fluidly complex mosaic that was being formed. I stood there gazing at the awesomeness of the river, and slowly turned towards its source. Ours is a blind alley. From where could the waters have come? As I watched spellbound, I saw, further down, not the source but a huge undulation in the waters. Something was moving ponderously in the river. Something huge. I could not take my eyes off it. It moved again. I could see the slimy green and grey, slippery, slithery sheen of the undulation. It was a gigantic snake. I wondered if all the snakes of the world had joined in to form this one snake. Its girth alone was half the width of the street. It never showed its head or its tail. Should I rush in and call Raja? I wondered. But more and more of its body came into view.

Slowly, it was moving past our house, oblivious of me, maintaining its slow undulating movement, unaffected by the elemental haste of the river. The glint of the afternoon sun made it almost luminous.

I searched for the right word to describe this incredible vision. Regal? Majestic? God-like? Mystical? Something definitely worthy of worship. Something radiating unquenchable power, unquestionable force.

The serpent had so completely taken charge of me that I had forgotten to panic and flee. It held me in a deep thrall. I stood there engrossed, forgetting to get surprised or frightened or even to call Raja. There was this rippling plateau, almost submerged in water, showing only its blunted peaks, quietly heaving and gliding by with a hint of meandering. There was an air of auspiciousness about it all, and I felt very humble. I must have gone into an oblivion, because when I came to my senses, there was only the usual dry street, and a feel of the huge serpentine movement within me. I stood there a long time wondering in the dream whether I was dreaming.

I woke up with a tinge of regret for not having called Raja to witness this strange, mystic sight, and found my body vibrating and with a feel of deep lassitude. But there was an air of enchantment in the room and a strange brightness in the air. And I became aware that there was an unspoken prayer in my heart.

This was just the beginning. All through my pregnancy, day and night, sleeping and awake, I experienced many wondrous visions, engrossing in their content and vast in scale.

I would be on a cosmic swing, deep in outer space, oscillating from one end of the sky to the other.

I would see stars floating by me during both day and night.

I would see light rushing into me from even the chinks in the door and the windows. Columns of light would beg of me to open the door, so they could rush unto me; but, finding me as if drugged and reluctant to move, they would themselves forcefully push the door open and seek me out.

I would see star-studded gigantic 'sudarshan chakra'—the divine, all-powerful discus-like weapon of Lord Vishnu—majestically whirling in the sky like a wheeling galaxy. This cosmic wheel would be covering the entire expanse of the sky. As I watched, it would slowly, almost gently, descend upon me where I lay on the bed.

I would see clusters of stars exploding and forming themselves into the Sanskrit letter 'Shree' in the Devanagari script, and the sacred Letter would rush flaming into my body.

Day and night, I would see bullets of light streaking towards me and penetrating me.

Snatches of Sanskrit hymns would arise on my lips—I who had not studied the language. The sacred seed-word 'AUM' would, on its own, come forth from deep within me.

Sages, yogis and rishis of the ancient times would appear in my sleep and announce themselves and worship me, as also bless me.

At times, even in the night, I would be surrounded by either surging waves of light or a deeply silent and still ocean of light. And many more similar phenomena I would witness even when awake.

Raja would visit his Sadguru every week and report on my experiences. No doubt, the child being carried in me, would be an extraordinary one. More blessings, with even loftier predictions, would follow for the son to come.

Favoured as I was with such propitious omens and dreams and happenings, I wondered if the son, to be born amidst considerable comfort, would one day renounce it all and turn into a wandering ascetic. All the predictions would come to naught, I thought, as, in these modern times and fast-changing society, one has to face the world and be part of it and move with the times, and, within its ambit, do something impressive if one wants to leave a mark on it. No one had time for renunciates any more, perhaps, not even in India.

I gave birth to a baby-girl, our fourth daughter. Amid concealed disappointment and embarrassment came the verdict from the Sadguru that even girls could reach great heights of achievement. What about Indira Gandhi and the like! The list was endless. There was hope still.

Quietly, everyone sought out some extra lustre in the baby—Some unusual signs? There were none. She was a normal, adorable, cuddlesome, lovely baby, with not one but three cute dimples on her cheeks.

It was expected that the moment I was delivered of the baby, I would stop having these supernal experiences.

But my experiences did not stop. After an initial, post-natal rest period of two or three months, they in fact escalated in both frequency and intensity. Each night, each day, brought with it a new experience. Sometimes, I would find my throat muscles straining as though to bring out words, even though I was in a quiet sleep. Strange utterings and guttural sounds, measured intonations of chants, and a deep humming sound would emanate from me in spite of myself. Raja interpreted the deep hum to be the mystic 'Omkar' sound that vibrates forth from yogis during particular advanced meditative stages of their sadhana.

I would see myself engulfed in incense smoke, or sleeping on a bed of nails, or levitating, and flying without wings, among other things.

My experiences at this stage were attributed to the delayed impact of the coming of the baby. No one conceded or guessed, except Raja, that I myself, in my own right, could be heading for something rare, something mystical. It was nobody's fault either. I had never talked to anyone about the strange experiences I used to have even in the pre-marriage days. I had unknowingly always lived in the ever 'present', the 'now' of this moment. Past had always been forgotten in the all-enveloping present. It is only now when I look back and reflect that I know that I was all along rushing headlong towards an implosion into divine felicity.

As I experienced more and more, the past got erased instantly and the mind remained ever clear and receptive, till one day I woke up and found myself slipping into an altogether different dimension, and, I perceived a world stark and beautiful. I wondered how I had been so oblivious of it, just as I now wonder how others are so oblivious of it.

And it is this stark and beautiful world in a different dimension that I have tried to portray before you.

My mystical education has been gradual and in monitored doses. I have brought together and tied up the loose ends and presented before you, among other things, a few short sketches, each on a particular aspect of my experiences, even at the risk of being at times repetitious.

I feel that these brief details about my background are sufficient for the reader to start with.

The journey on which I have been made to embark is not ended. By its very nature, it is an unending voyage. It does not really matter much as to where one is on the path; what matters is that one has been made aware of being a traveller along the most royal avenue of mystical self-awareness, self-knowledge, 'atma-dnyana', one-ness with the Lord, call it what you will.

March 1992   DEEPA KODIKAL
Bombay
India

1

Man and God

It was the eve of Christmas. All of us at home had planned to stay awake for the birth of Christ. Though ours is a Hindu family, we do celebrate festive days like Christmas for the fun and joy of it. After a heavy dinner, we put some music on in the living room and settled down for a long wait. One by one, each one made for his own room. Finally, only Akshata, our third daughter, and I were left. It was 11.30 p.m. on the twenty-fourth of December in 1983. Akshata was determined to sit up and I decided to give her company. With the melodious Beniamino Gigli on the record player, the dim lights and the anticipation of the birth of Christ, the atmosphere in the room was charged with a rare sense of expectation. Expectation of what? Looking back, I realize now that there had been a feeling of merging with Christ. To feel his presence and to feel it pervading us. This happens to me during all the festivals. One gets an irresistible desire to merge with the presiding deity of that festival. And what better time than the solitude of the night when the angels descend, to invoke the blessings of the divinity?

I was sitting up straight on the sofa with folded legs and closed eyes, slipping into meditation. Meditating on what? Was it on the music of Gigli? On the stillness of the night? On the permeating fever of Christ? Or on nothingness? Perhaps on the all-encompassing spirit of the night. Whatever it was, it was beautiful and peaceful. Soon I must have become oblivious of everything. I was blank, yet I was aware of everything, of the music, the stillness and the beauty of the night. Everything in its entirety, I suppose, culminated into a void, as all colours in uniting become white.

Soon it was midnight. The music ended. Akshata and I wished each other a Merry X'Mas. I felt myself enveloped in a blanket of peace and well-being. As I went upstairs towards my bedroom in our duplex apartment, I could sense an aura of enchantment, tranquillity and permanence. There seemed a definite purpose to life and the world seemed stilled with an inner peace.

Each night after that, the day's work done and Tejaswi, our youngest daughter, gone to sleep, I would get an urge to meditate. I had often tried earlier to meditate, but there were always obstructions. Of late, whenever I tried to meditate, Tejaswi, who was not yet three, and who would be fast asleep at that time, would promptly get up and not go back to sleep till I had abandoned the impulse to meditate. When I had become aware of this phenomenon, I tried to meditate at different times during the night. Just after she went to sleep; at midnight, at 3.30 or 4.00 a.m., or at any odd time I would sit up with the idea of meditation, and, as if on cue, Tejaswi, who would be in deep peaceful slumber, would instantly get up and cry and sometimes even shriek. Raja, my husband, and I decided that the bond between her and me was too strong. Cutting off the placenta is only a physical act, not adequate for the strong mystic bond that might be existing between the two of us. I had to give up the .idea of meditation for good.

Only once, about fifteen years back, when Aqeela, our second daughter, was two years old, had I sat for meditation on an afternoon, inspired by Swami Vivekananda's words. After making Aqeela sleep, I sat up in the meditating pose next to her. How long and on what I meditated I do not remember, but after some time, I had apparently got into a state of oblivion. Suddenly I became aware of a far-off place of utter solitude, and from somewhere very distant, I heard a child calling out to me. But as if in a coma, neither my mental nor physical faculties could function and cognize the fact that I should respond. I remained in that state of oblivion, continuing to hear the distant cry and yet not responding to it till I was nudged by Aqeela herself. Then I became aware that Aqeela was actually yelling away at me for attention and had crawled over me as I was not responding to her crying.

This incident of getting into an oblivion thrilled me to no end. I was convinced that, for that short spell, I had gone into samadhi. That is why I could not hear Aqeela yelling away. I waited for the whole day, excitedly to narrate this episode to Raja when he came home from work. One remark from him put an end to my scheme for regular meditation. He said matter-of-factly, 'You must have fallen asleep!'

It was much later that I came to know that if one falls off to sleep whilst still retaining the erect meditating posture, it is not an ordinary sleep. Anyway, the fact that our four daughters were growing up and the fact that Raja's remark had punctured my enthusiasm kept me away from meditation all these many years.

And now after fifteen years, this Christmas night put me back into the mood for nightly meditation. However, to my consternation, I found that within no time, my head would slump forward and I would be fast asleep. I knew that it was not quite right to try to meditate after a long day of tiring house-work, but there was no other suitable time. So I persisted. But the pattern continued. No sooner did I assume the erect posture, I would fall off into a deep slumber. For half an hour, I would struggle with myself to keep awake but to no avail, and then would decide that it was more practical to sleep in a normal, comfortable lying-down position than make a pretence of meditating.

But the quandary continued: nothing much was done by me by way of worship and altogether nothing by way of meditation. In this age of a revival of diverse modes of worship and meditation, I realized that I was perhaps the only one in our circle not doing either. There were days when there was no inclination to go through even the most elementary and rudimentary gestures of worship that are normally done in any Indian household. Such spells of 'spiritual' lethargy had come upon me often, earlier. They were in fact lengthening in time span. For instance, in 1981, I had not gone near the household altar for nearly five or six months after the Ganapati festival and had not felt any need to do so.

I had often looked at this altar as one would at meaningless things in a strange house. Not that my respect for the various deities had diminished, but the urge to worship was not there at that point in time. I knew it would come back with renewed fervour as it had come back so many times earlier. I could wait.

On the twenty-ninth and thirtieth of December of 1983, there was no trial at meditation. One of our two servants had left us, and after the day's heavy work, I could not bring myself to go through the futile motions of seeking one-ness with God. I went to sleep early these two days and enjoyed deep and peaceful sleep.

On December 31, Nandita, our eldest daughter, took upon herself to make Tejaswi sleep in her own room. I settled down to watch the TV for the New Year's Eve telecast. It was a bore as usual, so I gave up the idea and went to bed. Aware that after Tejaswi had fallen asleep I would have to shift her back into her cot in our room, I decided to keep awake. .

Suddenly, I found myself sitting up for meditation. I had no prior thought of meditation. I had not at all planned for it. There had been no such urge either. It was as if the body was acting on its own.

After some time, I found my head gently vibrating and at the same time nodding to a mild rhythmic hum. Though I was vaguely aware of this, it had not registered in my mind as being connected in any way with meditation. The subtle flutter was akin to the vibrations of a poised, winged insect that produced a mild buzz. This buzzing or humming bee sound brought about an unadulterated peace and bliss. It also brought the meditation to a focal point. Till this time, apparently, the mind was blank. No thoughts had come. I tried to recollect the trend of my thought, but no tell-tale marks were there to indicate any thoughts had been there at all. This buzzing sound and the vibrating of the head could be stopped at will by a slight tightening of the neck muscles. The relaxing of these muscles would start these vibrations again. It was a pleasant sensation. To cognize this took hardly a couple of seconds. Soon I forgot all this and went back to a pleasant blankness and the humming sound.

I stopped the meditation at midnight, wished everyone in the family a Happy New Year, brought Tejaswi back into our room and went into a deep sleep.

Sunday, January 1, 1984, 11.00 p.m.:

Again I sat for meditation. Nandita had taken on the responsibility of making Tejaswi sleep. Within moments, I found my head nodding rapidly. Not violently and not even in a wide arc. A gentle but distinct up-and-down movement. Though the awareness of the movement was there, it did not bring with it any awe, wonder or memory. It was there only for enjoying it. No thought concerning this nodding entered my head. My focus was solely on the enjoyment. I meditated thus for about twenty-five minutes but found that the baby was restless and so gave it up.

Monday, January 2, 1984:

Sat for meditation after Tejaswi went to sleep at night. The nodding movement started immediately. There was a rhythm to it, and it was not confined tonight only to the head, but was from the base of the spine upwards, with me sitting up cross-legged. The movement was from the hip joint or from the base of the back. What's more, the back moved sideways and the head moved up and down like the movements of two interlocked gears, one horizontal and the other vertical; constant, uniform, unopposed to each other. It gave a pleasant, gentle feeling, and though more pronounced than the two earlier days, still not jerky or wide in span. I felt the body was in a state of vibration. I recalled now that on the two previous nights also I had experienced similar vibrations. These vibrations excluded any thought. There was no awareness of the body, only of this rhythmic vibration. I found that it could be stopped simply by not desiring it.

Slowly, the whole body tuned into this silent beat and the nodding turned to rocking. Very gently, as if the body joints were lubricated. Concentration was on rocking, and nothingness. A feeling of permanence set in, and a feeling that this should go on and that nothing mattered in the world except this rocking. I got so absorbed in it that I do not know when I went to sleep. Again it was a deep, deep sleep.

I must mention at this point that whenever I sat for meditation, I could not recall to mind any mantra or any of the numerous names of the Lord (nama) or forms attributed to the Lord (rupa). Try as I might, my mind would be blank. Any forced recall of the name or form of any deity or the chanting of any mantra would bring in some sort of an agitation in the mind.

Once I had mentioned this problem to Raja's Sadguru, his spiritual guide. He had smiled and said that this total absence of recall of either mantra or nama or rupa was the best form of meditation, if it occurred spontaneously, without effort, as in my case. He told me not to get worried over this and only to remember the Sadguru just once before sitting for meditation and then let the thoughtless meditation continue on its own. But I found to my surprise that remembering the Sadguru even once before meditation brought in the same discomfort and restlessness of the mind. It was as though the mind resisted any thought at all. At my next meeting, sheepishly, I told the Sadguru about this. Again he reassured me that this should be no cause for anxiety. On the contrary, he said, it was excellent because it looked as though I was heading straight for the highest states in spirituality—namely, the Nirvikalpa stage. He was overjoyed and told me that, whenever I could, I should just close my eyes and sit and simply forget the world.

This I found most conducive, and, whenever I sat thus without thinking, an ethereal bliss descended upon me instantly. No thoughts ever entered my being and I could continue to be in a state of nothingness. I could not describe what this state was like, as it was beyond words and beyond thought. Only after concluding my meditation would I become aware that my mind had been blank and it was all peace and tranquillity.

Tuesday, January 3, 1984:

Now a pattern had emerged. Even tonight when I sat for meditation, no name or form of any deity or any japa or mantra at all would come to mind. No thoughts. A feeling of deep and great contentment descended upon me. I was on my side of the double bed, with Raja on the other side. Tejaswi was fast asleep in her cot. The lights were off. Within minutes, slowly, the body began bending forward from the hips and there was an urge to rest the forehead on the bed in front, while continuing in the sitting position.

It was very comfortable thus bent over, but then I thought it was again the confounded sleep overtaking me, as I had heard some time back that the difference between going off to sleep during meditation and the true meditation was that, in the latter, the body remained erect. So I snapped myself out of this seemingly sleeping posture and started all over again. Again, very gradually, the torso moved forward from the waist and eventually from the hips. The bending of the body was peaceful, intoxicating and promising of inexplicable comfort. Any effort to stop the movement ruffled the calmness of the mind. Repeatedly, the bending movement began!

Of late, I had been feeling like doing something to reduce my weight. But what with hardly any time available during the day and the many interruptions a housewife is subject to, I had not been able to do anything. Now all of a sudden, there was a flash of an idea that, during meditation at night, (the only free time available to me), I should try out some of the prayer-mudras (gestures or movements) which would serve the double purpose of toning up the muscles and of doing meditation. Hitherto I had been sitting for meditation in the casual meditative pose with legs folded and hands resting on my lap. The stiff lotus pose was uncomfortable for me. So now I concluded that this compulsive urge to get this particular yoga-mudra was either an auto-suggestion or the onset of sleep. Anyway, as the initial wonder of the puzzling movement was wearing off and it was now more of just an ordinary experiment and it did not seem to bring to mind any remembrance of the Lord, I decided that I had enough of the play and went to sleep.

Wednesday, January 4, 1984:

Discussed the experience of the previous night with Raja. He told me that as one advances in spiritual practices, various mudras (yogic gestures) take place of their own during meditation without any volition on the sadhaka's part. Postures which are very difficult to get into during the normal course of life are attained with ease and comfort in a state of meditation. Great rishis of yore, in a state of deep meditation, were inspired into these positions and a complete knowledge and understanding of these positions and their effects on body and mind were unfolded to them. This knowledge and practice have been passed down to aspirants through the ages.

Raja told me to expect various mudras and asanas and even contortions of body and face to take place during meditation. As there are eighty-four hundred thousand yonis (stages of evolution and species) to be undergone before one is born into the human race, these yonis are re-lived during meditation, so the man behaves like and may even temporarily imitate various birds and animals and reproduce their sounds and movements. Not all the millions of species he has passed through, but only those necessary for his own spiritual progress. In short, man undergoes a vastly speeded up evolutionary course during meditation. As one advances along the spiritual path, one may also expect, during meditation, an urge to express oneself through one of the performing arts like dancing or singing. So, independent of him, various movements and sounds of a particular art may flower out. An aspirant may even find himself writing poetry or devotional treatises or turn into an orator. An advanced adept may achieve the ability to tap unknown sources of knowledge, of art, of self-expression that are in the universe. And even a layman in that field, at a particular stage of his advancement, could perform or display art or knowledge of the highest order.

This is yoga; yoga means unity; unity with the highest knowledge, with all knowledge. This is how the divine classical music, dance, any art form or revelations about the universe have welled out of the great ancient masters. Intuitively, as against the empirically gained knowledge of today. This is a very simplified explanation but it served my purpose at the time.

Nevertheless, Raja was a bit taken aback by my progress as I was but a beginner in the path of this quest and hardly seeking anything from it and hardly serious about it. Only on an impulse had I taken to meditation and that too never meditated for any significant length of time. Anyway, he encouraged me to continue.

Again at night, I had an urge to meditate. So as on the previous nights, the chores done with, I sat down to meditate in a casual pose on the bed.

Within minutes, the body eased forward and a yoga-mudra was assumed. After enjoying the mudra for a while, I sat up again. Instantly the mudra repeated itself. Now fully enjoying the mudra and totally reassured by Raja's talk and in a spirit of high expectancy, I relaxed completely and let go. I felt venturesome, an adventurer into the unknown!

After a few repetitions of this mudra, when the body was back in the sitting position, suddenly, instead of it moving again forward, I began getting a feeling of 'shrinking'. The feeling began creeping over me, gently and gradually, that the body in the sitting position was slowly elongating, that is, it was becoming taller but slimmer. The width of the body was shrinking and thinning. Slowly, the arms began drawing closer and closer to the body, crossing each other near the chin, the shoulders lifted higher and higher and the entire torso became long, narrow and still shrinking. At the body level it felt fine, comfortable and exhilarating. The mind felt sublimated, peaceful and calm. At a still deeper level, I felt almost as if there was no mind, no will, no one, no past, no future.

Slowly, the hands raised themselves and the lifted shoulders spread out. The hands continued to lift and spread, much the same as the wings of a mighty eagle lift and spread in slow purposeful motion before a leisurely flight. I felt I was about to take off into the grim darkness. A sudden fright gripped me in the solitude of the night. A feeling of space, loneliness and a fright of the unknown seized me. Quickly I woke up Raja, and with a thumping heart, told him with a finality that the path of meditation was not for me and recounted to him my experience. Patiently he explained again and reassured me that this was something divine and that I should consider myself extremely fortunate that I was being given such divine experiences so early in my quest and that I should completely relax and enjoy whatever came my way. These experiences were called kriyas and had nothing to do with ghosts or being-possessed state. He said that I should continue and that he would keep awake to give me courage. But I had enough of yoga and meditation and still in that terrified state I went to sleep. Inspite of the fear, my sleep was a deep one.

Halfway through the night, I found my head turning from side to side on its own on the pillow. Bewildered, I woke up Raja and almost crying told him what was happening. He explained that as I had resisted the yogic power which had been awakened in me earlier in the night, it was still active and would continue so for some more time. Again he assured me that he would keep awake and suggested that I should give in to the yogic power. He said that it never brought any harm as it was divine, and he again urged me to relax and enjoy and allow myself to be one with the primal force of the universe. On a strict promise that he would keep awake and to prove so would continue to talk, I let go. My head rolled, rotated and twisted on the pillow in a definite pattern and yet seemed without a pattern, without any let-up. It was soothing to the muscles and to the mind. Raja again suggested that I sit up and enjoy. But so much dare I did not possess. The head rolled, twisted, rotated in all sorts of contortions and patterns, progressively gathering speed. After allowing this movement to go on for some time, I decided it was enough and went to sleep.

Thursday, January 5, 1984:

By now meditation was an admixture of fascination, adventure, want, yearning, as also shivers and a slight dread. It was fairly early in the night. I was free as Tejaswi was asleep by eight o'clock. The house was still awake. My other children and Raja were bustling around in the various bedrooms. Only Raja's reassuring talk was making me go on.

Within moments of sitting down and closing the eyes, the head went into a quick spin, rotating, twisting, rolling. The base of the neck formed the fulcrum. Up and down, round and round, sideways, as if the head was fixed in a ball and socket joint. Now there was no dread, only enjoyment. When in such a state of relaxation and enjoyment, I would always be pervaded with a feeling of contentment and as if the joints were lubricated and were being massaged. The eyes would be closed and drawn inwards, giving rise to a screwing up of facial muscles. It felt as though all the muscles of the face were being pulled or drawn within the eye socket. A deep feeling of time being non-existent, of will being superseded, of the rest of the world whisked away, would pervade me, all in the midst of the noisy activity of a large family.

Slowly, the body started rotating from the waist in much the same way and along with the motions of the head. Now the shoulder joints, waist and head were all following their own respective movements, sometimes in counter directions. All the joints felt well lubricated and massaged. After half an hour of this spiritual rock and roll, I decided to stop and go to sleep. Sound sleep as usual.

But even in the deep sleep, I realized there was an urge to begin these movements. If I allowed myself, these movements would begin again. If I decided against, they would not start, or even if they started, they would stop.

Friday, January 6, 1984:

Any time during the day I relaxed, I would get into these kriyas, these involuntary actions. For example, if I was lifting a cup and I relaxed the muscles of my hand, the hand would go into an orbit of its own. All my limbs by now were waiting to catch me napping. The whole day I was either swaying or rocking or doing my chores in a ballet-like fashion. The previous day, my body had been unconsciously taut, apparently to instinctively ward off this involuntary ballet. Today, I quite enjoyed myself and went about weaving my own choreographic movements. But any time I had serious work like cooking or I was distracted, the balletic movements stopped of their own. If need be, they could be stopped voluntarily.

10.30 p.m.: Now a deep fascination for meditation developed and a spirit of high drama and adventure. With a firm promise from Raja to keep awake and reading, and with full lights on, I sat down for meditation. I suppose the word meditation was inane by now. I just sat down, ready and relaxed. I did not have to wait. The head began twisting in all sorts of funny movements with the nape of the neck as the fulcrum. Soon, from the waist, another movement started. Shortly, the shoulder joints joined in. Now there were various movements in the body simultaneously going on. The hip, the waist, the shoulder joint and the nape of the neck; the various parts began rotating, twisting, rolling and rocking. The movements became more and more rapid and pronounced but were never jerky or uncomfortable. Each part of the body, in addition to the general, overall body movement, was also involved in an independent local movement of its own. The body now resembled a complex machine in high gear with various parts flashing at a tangent to each other, following different movements, ever-increasing in tempo, a mass of seemingly haphazard and confused movement and yet following a bigger grand pattern. The span of the movements was increasing fast. The waist movements were taking wide circles and bending forward, almost touching the bed sometimes.

The fright had gone by now. I had learnt that complete relaxation brought with it more enjoyment. I also learnt that I was the master and any time I decided I had enough I could stop with no repercussions. No forced continuation of the movements took place and it was my will that 'that force' was obeying.

After about forty minutes of this madcap movement, I got bored with it. The thought that it was boring put an instant brake on the movement. The 'force' apparently had a high sense of self-respect! I decided, then and there, never to hurt or humiliate its sensitivity.

Each day Raja would narrate to me the experiences of other yogis and discuss with me their spiritual aspect. We would talk late into the night and finally fall into deep slumber.

Saturday, January 7, 1984:

The urge to reduce my weight was getting a bit stronger. Today being Saturday, there was no hurly-burly of sending Tejaswi to school. The others too would be getting up late. So, in the morning, found some spare time and decided to do some physical exercises. No sooner had I started than the 'force' took over and made me do the most fantastic of exercises possible. Exercises I would never have normally managed; exercises I had never even heard of or seen performed! And the beauty of it was that I was doing these difficult movements with such supple ease and grace. I had only to think of the stomach and the stomach exercises would take place; think of the thighs and the thigh exercises would commence; and so it went on. It was beautiful and I was excited beyond imagination as though I had a jinn who would obey all my commands. This was the first time I sort of woke up to the potential the 'force' had. All these days, with all these experiences, I had no feelings of awe, wonder, joy or surprise. I took them all as a matter of course and never speculated about them. Now I realized what a force it was and what the implications of it were. It was the primal force awakening in me!

10.30 p.m.: Same place, same scene, same time. It was always the bed, the night and an urge to meditate. Ours was a double bed, and, next to our bed stood Tejaswi's cot, painted yellow. A dressing table in the front and two steel cupboards to the right. The decor of the room was daffodil yellow and cream. There were yellow, cream and fawn striped silk-cotton curtains hanging in the windows. There is an attached bathroom. There is a floral motif on the wall, painted by me, against which stood the dressing table. The table lamp next to Raja was on. Raja was reading. Tejaswi was fast asleep.

Again the movements of the neck, shoulders and waist began. Again a lot of swaying, twisting and turning of the body.

Nothing mattered in the world any more except just 'being'. Though I was fully aware of everything in the room, I was totally withdrawn from it. I knew and I did not know. I was aware and I was unaware. I existed and I did not exist. The world existed and the world was no more.

The movements increased in speed and degree. Raja quietly put off the lights and went to sleep. I knew and I did not bother. The movements continued. I was fully aware of the movements and yet I had lost the awareness of my body. I did not exist yet I knew all. Gradually, the body began bending forward and backward, ever-increasing in span, now almost touching the bed in front, now the pillows at the back. Now the forehead touched the bed in front, now the head rested on the pillow at the back. The legs which were crossed now slowly stretched out and repeatedly the head touched the knees and then going back rested on the pillows.

Finally, the body did not lift any more. There was a feeling of complete relaxation and a most sublime feeling of just 'being'. I was now in a half-reclining position with a few pillows piled up behind me. My body was still and calm and unmoving. Not like a stiff log of wood but completely relaxed and soothed. Each joint felt well-massaged and now resting.

There were no thoughts entering my mind and there was no intrusion of knowledge. Only a feeling of bliss and contentment.

Nothing mattered in the world but just 'being'. There was no future, no past.

Only a void.

Only *that* moment.

Time must have elapsed, but I had no knowledge of it. The world must have spun but I had no knowledge of it. Suddenly, I found myself praying: It was not I who was praying, but I knew these were all my innermost prayers. My lips were not moving and no sound was coming out, yet the prayers were loud and clear in a deep rumbling voice.

Yet I knew I was not praying; I had no thoughts entering me and there was no identity of myself with my body or with my family. The mood was so sublime and pure that even prayers would be intruders.

Then who was it that was praying? These prayers were my innermost prayers alright! Yet I was sure that it was not me praying at that particular time. It was definitely someone who knew me thoroughly, who was within me and who was a part of me, because clearly I was different to that being. I was positive it was not me. The prayers were coming forth inspite of myself because my mind was blank. I had no knowledge, and no thoughts were mine.

Then who was this being within me who, in a clear deep tone, brought forth such loud, distinct prayers?

Was it indeed praying? No. In fact, now in a voice full of authority, the inner being was blessing me and forecasting that all my wishes would be fulfilled. A continuing shower of blessings poured forth in such glowing terms that, though these could be my innermost desires, yet I would not have thought of their coming true in my wildest dreams. Yet the inner voice was going on like a runaway engine, without brakes, without let-up, heightening its blessings, becoming more eloquent in its predictions of achievements in ever-more brightening language.

My only contribution to all this torrent of eloquence was to remind this inner voice of the various members of my family, one by one, and it would start again in the most glowing terms, like a wound-up spring, about each person.

It said, 'Stop bothering about the house and the chores. Concentrate on the Lord. I have assumed the responsibility of your house and your chores. I shall see to it that everything will be done for you according to your wish. You find that you have no time to pursue your hobbies, but I shall see to it that you write and your writings will go far and wide. The words and the knowledge will well out of you, and you will wonder whence all this is coming. Each word will be luminous and inspiring. I shall give you the will and the time to write. Writing will be your mission and you shall accomplish great things.

'Your daughters are your manifestation. They will carry out your work for you. They will bring lustre and fame to your family.'

To my silent query about Raja and his business, the voice said, 'Do not worry about Raja's business. You and your family shall be bestowed with all things divine in life and contentment, which is the most valued of all.'

Thus it went on. The above is just a summary of it all, and in mild words at that. It was as if a silent dialogue was taking place between 'it' and a part of me. While it went on with its blessings and these predictions, another part of me was praying to God to make it all come true; even if a portion came true, I would be happy, I said. On the one hand, I was praying; on the other, I was listening to the inner voice. Now I was begging God to explain what was happening. How much of it to believe and how much to discard. The voice was now more authoritatively assertive and was talking faster, repeating its assertions in ever more glowing terms.

A thought had just to occur to me, and the answer followed immediately. I realized that the one who was praying, the one who was blessing and predicting and the one who was watching it all, the three were existing together, were expressing themselves together.

The devotee and the Lord had merged. The prayers and the blessings had merged. The doubts and the answers had merged!

It was beautiful, yet unbelievable. It seemed true but beset with doubt. It was exciting, still I knew it was a mirage. It had all merged and yet all were separate. There was a duality and a non-duality.

It was convincing, and yet smacked of make-believe. It was heavenly as much as it was ridiculous. It was divine; it was crazy.

I thought I had lost control of my mind. I knew that it was only my innermost feelings finding an expression, though in an unexpectedly forceful manner. Though I had never asked for so much in life, in fact, had never prayed for anything in life, all the natural desires of any housewife were now surfacing.

I attributed all this to my half-asleep condition and putting a firm lid on it and thinking about it no more, went to sleep in the same half-reclining position.

Sunday, January 8, 1984:

I made breakfast and partly finished cooking for the day. No one had yet stirred and Raja was at his meditation. Tejaswi was in the garden with the maid. I locked the bedroom door to do my physical exercises.

My concentration was on the exercises. There was no thought as to the previous night's experiences, no plans for the future. Only the present existed and the exercises. Hardly had I begun them when various mudras started of their own. My hands, wrists, fingers, face, neck, torso, all were taking part in divine dance

forms; the most stylized namaskars, salutations. I was bowing
down again and again to the Lord Almighty in a most graceful
dance-like manner. Different forms of dance 'abhinayas' and
'mudras'—the most beautiful of expressions hitherto unknown
to me, I could feel flitting across my face. My heart was in raptures.
And yet through all this, I was also an observer, noting every
little detail with clinical detachment—the ecstasy, the almost
delirious state, the strong waves of sensuousness creeping over
me, overwhelming me. It was like having sex but multiplied many
times over.

I was delirious with intoxication, every cell of my body melting
into an unbearable though totally joyous ecstasy, when the deep
rumbling and by now familiar inner voice again intoned: 'This is
"turyavastha". You are in "turyavastha". You have merged with
the divine! You have become one with the Lord. This is
"turyavastha", the highest state of exaltation and this will be
your permanent state from now. Do not underestimate this nor
doubt it. You have merged with the divine! But you see that you
are fully conscious of your surroundings; that is because you have
a perfect mastery over yourself, like Lord Krishna had. Not in the
future, nor in the past has any one had such a mastery except
Lord Shri Krishna. All have had to lose body consciousness or go
into samadhi for at least a short while, partly or wholly, but
because of your full mastery over yourself, you have full awareness
of the outside world. Going into samadhi or losing control of
oneself is of an inferior nature as compared to the state you are in
now. Yours is of the highest order, achieved only by Shri Krishna,
and now you are the next to get it. Do not underestimate or
doubt it. This is "turyavastha", the highest, with perfect mastery
and it will be your permanent state from now on. You are higher
than the highest, next only to Lord Krishna. You are not an
avatar because an avatar comes with a mission. A mission mighty
in stature for the benefit of humanity, but you are born only to
enjoy this "aishvarya", this resplendence. Aishvarya of the highest
order. Neither the aishvarya of a tycoon, for that is only money
not true aishvarya, nor the poverty of a beggar, for that means
hardships, but the true aishvarya of total contentment. The Lord

wants to enjoy this aishvarya through you. You are the highest, but remember you are the most humble. You are the greatest, but remember you have no mind. You have all the powers, but you have no will. As you are no avatar and have come only to enjoy this aishvarya, you have not to use any weapons, any powers. Your only weapon will be your rage against others but that too only occasionally. You have come to enjoy, so the demons or the evil that dare face the avatar will be restricted in your case to such minor agitations as minor insults or ill-feelings of others towards you. Remember to be as humble as the Lord. Remember, you and the Lord are one.'

Then this inner voice went on to repeat its blessings, now in even more glorious terms than the previous night. With authority that left no room for doubt, it predicted the highest of rewards for my children, my husband, our business, and my writings. The Voice reminded me of a mother encouraging her child taking its first faltering steps, infusing it with confidence and making it feel special. Later on, I realized that the exuberance displayed by the inner Voice was due to its self-discovery and that it sobers down eventually.

Through all this inner verbosity, this cascade of blessings, this ebullience, there lay another mood in me. This mood was of a rare, deep stillness, a sense of permanence and stability. All the ecstasy was controlled and contained in that stillness and calmness. I was the ecstasy and the intoxication, and yet I was apart from it all, the intoxication cradled in the watchful, still calm. This, I suppose, was the stabilizing factor giving at once a sensation of conviction and disbelief, intoxication and mindlessness, exaltation and a sense of total humility, the divine and the ordinary.

If my hands moved at all, they moved in namaskars and mudras. If I relaxed my body muscles, I would go back into that 'bhava', that divine exaltation. Tighten the body muscles, once again I was the housewife of all the past days. If I willed that voice to stop, I would have no mind. Allow it freedom, I would be that divine being proclaiming things, knowing things, understanding things. It was that simple to switch into the divine or to remain out of it.

Through all this, I was fully conscious of what was going on in the garden and on the road. I could hear the car horns and the laughter of children. One part of me was spouting all this grandiloquent rhetoric and the other was listening to it, unable to make out what it was all about.

I now remembered clearly the happenings of the night before. It was the same deep, resonant, rumbling voice coming from deep within me, holding forth in English. It would roar like a lion in between, hurting my throat. My facial contortions would be like a lion's at such times. Especially, when a flicker of disbelief occurred in a corner of my mind, the lion would roar; and the roar would issue from my throat, and my eyes and my whole face would be lion personified. The inner voice would again and again admonish me not to doubt or underestimate it, and again that growl and that roar!

This went on till Raja knocked on the bedroom door. I was not sure whether to recount the whole episode to him or to dismiss it as a mere play of the mind. I had never read about anything of this sort nor heard anyone tell such things, so I was at a loss to know how much of all this was true. Yet it was all very convincing. Further, I had never coveted nor hankered for nor striven towards anything spiritual in the remotest sense, so definitely I was not building it up. Here was no question of deceiving myself into a particular, peculiar state of mind, for I did not at all know of any spiritual or mystic or occult states. I was debating as to what was to be done when the inner voice came on again, forceful and authoritative.

I told everything to Raja, admonishing him not to doubt or underestimate my state. It was me talking to him and yet not me. Though I was the instrument of speech, it was neither my voice nor my style of talking that came out.

The word 'turyavastha' had a sobering effect on Raja, as he had read a lot about such matters. He told me to come downstairs and give him breakfast and to be very careful near the cooking gas. He also gave me a few tips on what was to be done if I was totally overcome by the exalted mood. I laughed at him; by that, I mean the divine in me laughed as I was still in that exaltation.

I told him he had not yet grasped the extent of my avastha (state) which was very rare as it was accompanied by full control of body and mind.

Right through my daily chores, I was in the exalted state. By now all my doubts were dispelled. It was physical, this feeling of exaltation and this knowledge that I was higher than the highest because of this mastery of mine. It was not my ordinary mind or my intellect telling me, but the very body infused with knowledge, exaltation and 'knowing'. There was no mind and no intellect. The feelings and the words were coming from somewhere I could not fathom. I was talking, walking, doing things on impulse, without my intellect or mind taking part in them. I had somehow discarded my mind. Out of this blankness would spring forth words and knowledge and this exalted feeling. A number of saints and yogis flashed across this blankness to tell me that, because of my mastery over myself, I was of a higher order. Again and again, I was told to be humble and not let 'ahamkara' (ego) develop in me but to dwell in this state of purity where the mind is always merged with the Lord and hence has no separate existence of its own and so is kept away from the baser emotions and feelings.

I felt that I was vast, limitless in size. A feeling of all-pervasiveness swept over me. I was everyone, and everyone was me. There was one continuous principle pervading everything. Everything was one. I felt love pouring out of me. Compassion streamed forth from me. No one was baser or inferior to me. There was no sin, no badness, no punishable instinct.

I saw only innocence all around me. I saw clearly that man behaved as he did due to his innocence and not due to any badness in him. Is he to be blamed for his wrong understanding of things? Compassion was the dominant feeling in me, seeing man cling so dearly to this illusory world.

This was an altogether new world to which I had awakened, where purity, innocence, permanence and bliss ruled the cardinal points. There was no sin, no anxiety, no ugliness. This was a world of deliriousness, springiness, buoyancy, love and generosity.

Throughout this, the inner voice insisted that the superior

nature of my state lay in my complete simultaneous mastery over both the states—the divine and the ordinary—retaining control over the self and the body, and not going into samadhi; in other words, being in full command of my mental faculties as also co-ordination of physical body, even in the state of the divine. Again and again, it stressed that this was very rare and of the highest order.

I could switch out of this state instantly! All I had to do was to pay more attention to my routine duties, not to do them mechanically. With my concentration being more on the chores, the inner voice's explanatory preaching would dim down a little though the exalted mood would persist. The two states, the exalted and the ordinary, were now running parallel within me, in equal measure, with equal emphasis. I could do my work perfectly, think and co-ordinate, and as well be in that exalted mood and be a partaker of superior knowledge. To switch from one state to the other, all I needed was to concentrate a little more on one, then the other would become a shade dimmer but would continue to make itself felt with effective force.

Confident now that I could control this mood, I thought of making one more attempt at my physical exercises; so after Raja's breakfast, I came back to my room and started them. As I lay down on the bed and bent my knees in an attempt to do some abdominal exercises, I had a sudden intense pleasurable sensation as of sexual enjoyment. Of its own, my left hand gripped my right hand at the wrist and guided it to the lower parts of the body. The four fingers of my right hand began tapping at them in unison. I was lying down on the bed, my knees drawn up and lifted up. It was a very comfortable posture and the tapping there by my fingers gave me immense pleasure. The fingers had a life of their own and were weaving an intricate pattern of tapping, probing, advancing, retreating, following a rhythm which I could not identify, still less direct and control. A thrill ran up my spine, of an indescribable sensual pleasure. Ecstasy effused out of every pore of the body. It was like being at the height of climax of an intercourse, but the pleasure was more ethereal and, I felt, fully divine. There was no lust in it, no passion, only a deep pure pleasure, infused with an intoxicating adoration of the Lord. It made me feel sublime.

I watched myself perform this little dance of the fingers and derive ecstasy out of it and with a candour startling to me wondered if it was sexual excitement I was indulging in! But instantly the same inner voice was in the ear again, 'This is not a sexual urge. This is something divine. You are not exciting the sexual organs. You are invoking Lord Shiva. This is not merely a sexual organ. This is the sacred "yoni". This is a sacred "linga". A linga of the highest order. You are invoking Shiva Himself. Shiva that is life! Shiva that is linga! Shiva that is continuity of life!

'This is a sacred temple, not a sexual place. You are invoking Shiva to enter you.'

At once, words of adoration and worship of Lord Shiva started within me. I began to spontaneously utter 'Om Namah Shivaya'... 'Om Namah Shivaya'... 'Om Namah Shivaya'... (Salutations to Thee, O Shiva) repeatedly. The fingers continued to follow some strange dictate and moved in a particular rhythm and pattern. The salutations to Shiva and other Shiva mantras, unknown to me, poured out of me faster and faster. The inner voice was gathering momentum and volume. I knew that only I was hearing this voice and that it was flowing out of me of its own and that it could not have been audible to any one else even had they been in the same room. My tongue moved, my throat muscles strove to keep pace, but my lips moved not.

I knew I could stop all this, but did not. It was happening to me of its own, but still a part of me searched through the deep recesses of my memory to scan if I had read or heard of such a thing previously and if it was possible that I was reliving it or play-acting it, prompted by some deep buried memory. No, I had no previous knowledge of this, and as I watched myself experiencing all the pleasure and ecstasy, I was more and more convinced that this was happening to me inspite of myself and that I was not doing it of my own volition. All this was unplanned, unthought of and had taken place so fast that I could have hardly thought it out on my own.

The movements of my fingers and the chanting of the Shiva mantra 'Shiva Shiva Shiva', and the fervour were indeed intense now and I was in a state of delirium when that inner voice spoke again, 'Shiva is entering you now! Shiva is entering you. You are allowing the force of Shiva to enter you. You are merging with the Divine. Shiva is entering! Shiva is entering.' Then, 'Shiva has entered ... Shiva has entered you ... You have merged with Shiva. You have become Shiva!'

I lay staring blankly at the wall. There was an inexplicable bliss now. A feeling of fullness and completion. I knew the divine intercourse was over. I felt at peace with the world. A deep stillness pervaded me. My feet came down slowly. My arms fell at my side and I was limp and satisfied. If contentment was heaven, I had glimpsed it.

I lay on the bed for a long time, wondering what had happened. The mood of stillness and contentment still pervaded me. I was fully aware of the magnitude of what had happened, yet my mind was blank and calm. I felt that I was vast and all-encompassing, even unto eternity, yet I was conscious of one point, the point on which my eyes were fixed. I knew I had become divine, yet I also knew I was a mere housewife. There was no thought in my mind, and so no wonder, no joy, no feeling of greatness or any sense of achievement. Everything seemed absolutely natural.

I looked at my watch. Just a few minutes had passed since I had come up to my room. All this had taken only a few moments. I was fully awake. It was not a dream, as I was fully aware of my surroundings all the time and my eyes had been wide open.

I did not know what to do. To allow myself to continue in this mood or to get on with my normal work. Suddenly I remembered it was a Sunday, and, as such, might be a busy day. I got up and had a brisk bath, but the state of exaltation continued. I got dressed and made for the kitchen. But I found myself walking to the bed instead. I sat down in a regal pose, and my face assumed the expression of 'Bhavani', the divine consort of Shiva. From deep within me, a deep leonine roar emerged. My eyes, the slant of my head, my posture, everything now resembled the Durga idol that is worshipped during the Nava-ratri celebrations!

All of a sudden, I felt I was the primal force that sustains the universe, the primordial Being of whom is born the cosmos. I was the female component of the born and unborn energy that has made the universe and sustains it. I was Durga. I was Bhavani. I say 'felt' because one part of me was still observing all this.

I knew my eyes were not the eyes of moments ago. They were radiating a force of the highest degree. They were emitting an intense light. I felt the span of all the distances within me. A deep laughter, springing from the knowledge that all the mysteries of the world were within me, springing from effulgent kindness, from unquestioned greatness and an all-encompassing love, forced itself out of me, welled out from somewhere deep within me. I laughed mightily. I knew there was only kindness in me, over-flowing kindness. Love, outpouring love. Knowledge that I had all the knowledge. I felt that I had all the power of the universe in me; the force of all the arms within me. I knew I could be as swift as lightning, and even faster than light. Yet there was no body consciousness. I sat there waiting for humanity to come and feed themselves on the love and kindness flowing from me. Divine kindness, divine love, which saw no sin or ill. I felt I was the universal mother, a cosmic mother whose children were the entire humanity. I wanted one and all to come and partake of the eternally flowing celestial love and kindness of this supreme motherhood.

A bizarre thought flashed across my mind that Raja as the husband was in the unique position of being able to consort with the cosmic force, the primal force of the divine, the force of the universe! I laughed and wondered if he would realize that and appreciate it. In this exalted state, I persuaded myself to go down to the kitchen to finish my work. Amid a continuing smile of joy and laughter of ecstasy, I prepared lunch for the family.

Monday, January 9, 1984:

Now the two states—one of the divine and the other, ordinary—were being experienced by me simultaneously. Relaxing the mind and the muscles would instantly put me in the ecstatic mood and 'mudras' would start and 'bhavas' of ecstasy would light up my face, no matter where I was or what I was doing. The next instant, by slightly tightening the body muscles and getting immersed in some routine work, I would be my normal self. As I could not wholly immerse myself in either state ignoring the other state, the two states ran simultaneously and in equal measure. A slight additional concentration to one side would tilt the mood a little more to that side. Otherwise, I would carry on with all my chores, fully co-ordinated and efficiently, remaining at the same time in that divine mood. I understood that this would be my permanent state now, already proclaimed, and now confirmed by evidence.

I got up in the morning, calm and collected. There was no past, no future, no memory, no plans. Only the present existed.

Just to *be*, in the present. This would be my permanent state now.

I was totally composed. There was no mind. I searched for my mind. It was not there. I searched for some joy, for elation. I searched for awe, for any doubt; a sense of wonder, some surprise. Nothing. There was only an awareness of deep internal peace, still deeper calm, further stillness. In those depths, there was stability and permanence. Permanence without a beginning and without an end. I was doing my chores, but it did not seem to matter. Nothing seemed to matter any more.

Unthinking, I went to my bed and sat down on it. Overcome by an intense sensuousness, I had to lie down. Once again, as on the previous day, my hands acquired a life of their own, both the palms cupping myself in a tight, almost protective gesture. As the intensity increased, I held my breath and pressed my palms down harder. There was such intense pleasure and pain, intoxication and delirium, ecstasy and numbness, and yearning spread all through the body, but, all the same, concentrated to such a point within it that my breathing came to a stop. My palms pressed further, my body tightened up and I thought my eyes would be sucked inwards. I prayed feverishly to God not to let me enter the spirituality through this path as advocated by some gurus of modern times. I prayed for guidance.

But prayers gave way to an intense yearning for my beloved Lord Krishna. There was an overwhelming urge to merge with

Krishna. I began calling out to Krishna. I knew this exaltation would end only by becoming one with Krishna. The anguish of separation was too much, too much. Pain and pleasure were transmuted into a rare ecstasy. Suddenly I felt being infused with tremendous energy. I felt the force of the cosmos entering me. Force, power, energy, light! Words, mere words.

My hands relaxed; so did my body; and I got the feeling of total abandon, of total satiation, of absolute freedom. I was limp with sensuousness. Would I melt today with this love? Was the energy entering me or bursting out of me? My eyes were closed, but I saw light everywhere. I felt a current passing through me. My body was in a state of vibration. Would my body burst today by so much infusion of energy?

Power was emanating from me. Song was flowing out of me. Dance was springing forth from me. There was joy scattered everywhere. The universe was dancing with me. I had merged with Krishna. I had become Krishna. Krishna was me. I was Krishna. Love for Krishna welled out of me, and yet I was Krishna Himself. Was I Radha, His consort? Nay, I was Krishna adoring His Radha. I rejoiced! I was Krishna. I danced and I sang. There was spring in the garden and a glow to the world. I saw lustrous splendour in the air. Was I feeling light or was the force of the universe sustaining me? There was spring in my gait. I marvelled at so much joy in the world, so much love suffused all around. I was feeling cosmic. I wanted to shout and tell people to open their eyes and look around. Krishna is everywhere. They are Krishna. Why can they not see such a simple thing! Why can they not comprehend such a joyful thing! Opening of the eyes was all that was required.

I rejoiced! There was bliss in my heart! If enlightenment meant perceiving you are the Lord, I had been enlightened. If realization meant understanding the Lord is in you, I had realized. If experiencing meant confirmation, then conviction meant authority. I was certain now. The Lord truly resided in every heart. One need only open one's heart to partake of that love, joy, bliss and ecstasy. God was truly love and joy. I felt serene. I felt one with the Lord and at peace with the world. It was so simple. Why were people so blind?

I looked at the flowers. I seemed to know them. I smiled at them. I knew we were of the same stock. I felt one with them. I smelt the flowers, and I knew I lent that scent to them. I too was pervaded by the same scent. I looked at the butterfly and felt one with it. I felt its flight, I was flying along with it. I looked at its beautiful colours, and I knew the colours had come out of me.

Divine knowledge poured out of me. I began comprehending profundities which earlier had baffled me. Pieces of a vast puzzle started falling into place. The inner voice intruded again. 'Yes! You are Krishna. You were always Krishna.' Again it blessed me a hundredfold. It blessed our children, it blessed our business and our life ahead. It showered blessings on Raja. It revealed to me that just as Bhagavad Gita came forth from Krishna, a book on the Lord would come from me. But in a language as plain and simple as the essential nature of the Lord is. Just as, by His wondrous simplicity, the Lord can permeate every nook and corner of the world, so by the very plainness of the words, the book should tug at every heart.

From the sublime to the ordinary was a moment's job. All this divinity was alright but I had put on too much weight which had to be got rid of! I looked at my watch. Not much time had elapsed. I resumed my exercises again. My hands, on their own, began massaging my body. Systematically, rhythmically, and with expertise. Portion by portion, the hands went over the entire body as if they were guided by some expert. There was technique there and power and ingenuity.

The inner voice came back again. It seemed to know everything. It told me that there was no need to do my regular exercises, as the massaging would work as well. It showed me the principles of massaging and told me one month was all that was required to tone up the muscles. Remember, it said, through this massage the cosmic force is working on you. It also revealed to me that only my lower chakras had been opened, the merging with Shiva was opening of this chakra. (Later, I came to know that this was called the 'swadhishthana chakra'). The inner voice continued. Chakras are very sensitive and subtle nerve centres in the body; opening or piercing of these results in certain spiritual experiences and sometimes gaining of certain occult powers or 'siddhis'! Swadhishthana chakra is very near the generative organs and the piercing of this important chakra produces certain sensual and sublime experiences. Krishna had to enter that way. Eventually, when the other chakras open up, Krishna would enter through the entire body. The voice was leonine.

I got up for a bath. During the bath, the inner voice was very active. It was potent and powerful. It went full blast like a speeding truck without brakes. Vigorously, it blessed me again in the most dynamic terms. It told me that it was the purity of my heart that had made God reveal Himself to me. I had led a life of perfection where the baser emotions had found no place to thrive. Purity of mind and total involvement in God was required to see things in a different light. That purity of mind I had attained.

It also said that it was not for nothing that the golden lotus was shown to me a few days earlier. One night, prior to all this experience, I had seen in my sleep a beautiful, softly-glowing, bright-yellow lotus with the edges of its petals of a rich golden hue; the lotus was three-tiered, with the bigger petals in the outermost circle. The petals were thick, smooth and succulent. The lotus was without a stem, placed flat on the ground with its petals fully opened out. In the centre of this open lotus was an 'agnikunda', a vessel holding sacred fire, meant for holy oblations. The lotus seemed to be placed right at the top of my head, just under the skull. This, I came to know later on, was the place of 'sahasrara chakra', the thousand-petalled lotus. After that day, I was often conscious of that part of my head, and many a time I would get a tingling sensation there, or a gentle throbbing or vibrations.

The voice now told me that this golden lotus, this sahasrara chakra, was about to be fully opened. It would bloom in its full glory. There was a profound meaning in showing me the lotus that night. When the Lord reveals Himself, all that remains is purity and joy. Joy of the highest order, and total 'aishvarya', or contentment. It said that the joy, the comforts and happiness that I had hitherto experienced were as nothing compared to the joy and 'aishvarya' I was to have in the future. These things would come with such force and in such abundant measure that I would beg the Lord to exercise some restraint. I was Lakshmi incarnate, it said. So 'aishvarya' would dance attendance on me. There will be such joy, contentment and ecstasy in me that Lakshmi would dance at our threshold, it said. Money will pour in; business will thrive and this house will be the abode of Lakshmi and 'aishvarya'. 'Aishyarya' that spelt glory, splendour, riches, contentment, knowledge, bliss—all with an underlying feeling of renunciation.

With more blessings and predictions, the voice changed into a roar. I looked at myself in the bathroom mirror. I thought I looked like the MGM lion, rolling his impressive head sideways while roaring. But there was no trace of ridicule in my thought, no wonder, and no joy. There was only a serenity and a conviction that all this was true. The conviction did not express itself in words but there was a deep silent knowing it was true. There was no mind to question, to doubt; there was only some deep inner peace and tranquillity which I knew would not be ruffled any more, nor would it ever sublimate into nothingness. There was a sublime bliss where words as ideas would be intruders.

The whole day passed in this bliss and in the simultaneous consciousness of two states. (This consciousness of two states, that is, duality even in non-duality, never really leaves me.) At night I did not sit for meditation. I was distinctly made aware that the chakra in the head (the sahasrara chakra, the thousand-petalled lotus) had not yet opened. I went to bed early. Even in my sound sleep, there was an awareness of the dual state of mind. One, of the worshipper, and the other, of the worshipped. The two had merged and yet retained their identities. Prayers and blessings were one. One led to the other, and that led it back to the first. But there was no first and second as they both sprang together, from the same source.

I was told I need not worry about the house, household chores and the children's studies, for just as the gods were the Lord's 'indriyas', sense organs, to look after the world for him, my daughters and Raja were my 'indriyas' and would look after my chores for me. The fulfilment of my innermost desires was the Lord's responsibility, and I should surrender everything to Him and devote myself to being with Him and to concentrate on Him.

In my deep sleep, I was told that I was being taken from 'turyavastha' state to the 'Parabrahma' state—the Absolute. In this 'flight' from 'turyavastha' to 'Parabrahma', there was no self-identity. Neither of being the divine, nor of being the ordinary! But there was another being along with me, not having a separate identity from mine, yet separate from me, contradictory though that sounds—which was educating me and guiding me. Both of us almost formless, a wispy smoky trail, the size of man. We 'flew' together into the infinities, in one form yet separate. I was being guided, yet I seemed to know the 'path' already. All I was conscious of was of being existent and in motion. Motion of a flight, of an ascent. Ascent into the 'Parabrahma'.

I felt I am nothingness, I am just 'being'. There is nothing to see, nothing to tell, nothing to smell, hear or touch. Yet there is total bliss. There is no light, yet there is no darkness. There is merely existence. Only an awareness. Nothing beyond. Nothing before. Time is not there. I *am*, that is all. And an awareness of motion. An awareness of duality in me. Of duality, as also simultaneously of oneness with this 'other' being. But after the flight into the 'Parabrahma', I am suddenly alone. The two have merged. The residual form has gone. It is I alone that exists, that pervades. Now there is no motion, no light, no darkness, no ascent. Only an awareness and stillness, an all-pervading awareness, all-inclusive, ever-present. Only existence and awareness and a total bliss!

Tuesday, January 10, 1984:

Next morning, while doing my exercises, all sorts of yogasanas and namaskars manifested from me automatically. The mood slowly gave way to ecstasy. As I lay there limp, motionless, mindless, suddenly I saw in a tremendous flash that, my God! I am the Lord! The Lord God, creator of the universe, of the cosmos, of the multiple universes. I was aghast. I had never discerned such a simple fact. How was I so blind and so dense all this while, even when I am the Lord God! As if swept aside by a magical hand, all the veils were removed, and I saw with limpid clarity that I am myself the Lord I am trying to merge into. I saw things distinctly now and in their minutest detail.

I stood up. I felt that the Lord had awakened from a deep slumber in which He had forgotten all the past. Only the present remained and the renewed knowledge of who He is.

I felt pure, cleansed! Crystal-clear, stark, cleared of all the veils of ignorance. And I knew this is the original nature of man, and me; and it was going to remain thus for me from now on. I found myself free, above the universe. Light—above time, space and causality. I felt 'karma' slipping away from me. I was out of its clutches. It was not going to affect me any more. I saw with clarity that I sustained the universe and am not bound by it. In all its fullness, I awakened to the knowledge that I am the Lord. That every being is the Lord!

I saw another dimension added to the world. Now, this world was free of causality. Free of karma, I felt above causality. I felt space and time interpenetrated within me. This world was stark and pure. Sin did not exist here. I was free of sin. This was the abode of love, affection, compassion, tenderness and knowledge. Only innocence lay spread out here. Love poured out of me. Compassion poured out of me. Knowledge poured out of me.

Thoughts got suspended, and along with them vanished the joy, the pain, the query, the wonder. Only an awareness existed, of peace, of knowledge, of sheer ecstasy. There was no marvel at what was revealed and no query as to what was not.

Only a bond existed. Bond of oneness with all. Bond of their source within me. Bond of all source being in me. Knowledge that I sustained the universe, but am free of it and not bound by it.

No pleasures of the world could have matched the inner peace that I had, and, this fullness, this peace, this ecstasy, this feeling of purity, of immaculateness, spread a glow of well-being through me. The realization that the Self was divinity brought an equanimity and tranquillity like the still, clear waters of a lonely lake.

That I was indeed the Brahman—encompassing as well as pervading the cosmos, without change, without difference, and of the nature of Reality, knowledge and bliss—added a glow to this ecstasy!

My gait was different now. The feet trod very lightly on the ground. The earth did not seem to have its dense mass about it any more. Not that it would give way, but it somehow felt ethereal (reliable nevertheless) as did my body. My body too did not seem to be real or solid and weighty as it used to be earlier. As if it did not form a part of me, though I was using it to see, to watch, to comprehend things, and to move about. I could feel my body, but somehow that sense of feel belonged to someone other than me. I felt that, though I was using my body, I was free of it—independent. That I could slip out of it at will. I had the sensation of immense space, a feeling of limitlessness, of eternity, of all-pervasiveness.

However, my body was weak and wobbly. I lay down on the bed. Suddenly I felt a surge of energy entering me with overwhelming intensity. I knew it was the cosmic force rushing into each pore, each cell of the body, a force mighty in dimension and coming from the infinite. I basked in this energy. Waves of heat emanated from me. Yet I was not warm. I was Radha, and I was Krishna. Krishna was entering me with overwhelming power. I felt energy racing through my body as if storms were raging within me. I almost heard the rushing sound of the energy.

I felt the anguish of Radha separated from Krishna, and the mischief of Krishna teasing Radha. I was pining away with the grief of Radha and shaking with Krishna's laughter. Ecstasy was sapping my energy. As much as I felt infused with energy, so also I felt limp. It was not an unpleasant sensation though it left me incapacitated. There was no will to move or to think. Only the desire to sip the nectar that was the communion with Krishna.

How long I lay on the bed I do not know, but I had to get ready and go and pick up Tejaswi from school. I got up to go for a bath. There was a feeling of deep gratification in me as if I had at last found my true identity. As if the coin had fallen into the right slot. There was a naturalness in this state, a certainty of truth and of oneness with the world, of sameness throughout. I was pervading in all the creatures and they in me. The same principle suffused in all of us. They originated from me and I from them. A common origin in all. The same sky, the same space beyond and the same infinite permeated through me as well as through all. I wanted everyone to experience this continuity, this oneness, and what intrigued me was the simplicity and the obviousness of it glaring at us in such stark nakedness and which we all failed to see even when it was so easy and natural to see. Nothing miraculous, only a will and intent to see and recognize would be enough. How simple it all was!

There was divine mirth in my heart, again and again. I was surprised at myself for having so long failed to see the Lord that is in me, the Lord that is myself. I was astonished beyond words how such an obvious fact could be overlooked. In fact, now I perceived that there was nothing else to see, nothing else to feel but the presence of the Lord everywhere.

Again and again, in a tremulous voice, I implored Raja to try and behold with renewed eyes, to transcend ordinary vision and see the truth that lay all around. If I could see it, so could he, I encouraged him. What confounded me was the conspicuousness of the Reality and the obtuseness of man that inhibited him, all because of his stubborn refusal to believe, and transcend. What a beatific realm lay on the other side! What a fabulous panorama it unfolded; where the display of the cosmic was such a commonplace and where the vista culminated in a cosmorama beyond infinity. Where love and joy lit up every countenance and where sins and ills had no bearing. Where the purling laughter gurgled in the deepest recesses of every heart and where everything merged into the infinity and the eternity that are the Lord. The Lord that dwells beyond existence and non-existence, beyond the manifest and the un-manifest, creation and destruction, and Who is imperishable, eternal, undecaying and kindness. The Lord Who is the primal force, and Who is the mover of the worlds.

I found I could not open my eyes fully. A force radiated from them. There was an intensity in them, and they could observe inwards as well as outwards simultaneously. They were heavy-lidded, veiled, a light ruby-red and emitted a glow. The force of the primeval was in me, the power of all creation, born and the yet to be born. The force of the mystery that shrouded this power was overwhelming.

As usual, during bath, one part of me watched and listened. I saw myself going into ecstasy and assume all the aspects of the Lord. I was exalted. There was jubilation in my heart at this rediscovery. The full impact of the realization dawned upon me. Layers and years of ignorance and delusion had been removed, and the true self, shining in all its majesty, was revealed. Having surrendered my will at the sacred feet of the Lord, the glorious true self had shone forth and had taken charge of my being, and things were happening to me on their own, guided by that superior force. Realization dawned that the true self within me was none other than the Lord Almighty. The Almighty that pervaded and permeated every being and every atom. The Lord Almighty that had love and bliss as His aspects. The marvellous Almighty Whose manifestation was this stupendous world and all its suns and the stars and the wheeling galaxies.

I was watching, ecstatic yet serene. The ecstatic and exalted mood was revealed as an inseparable aspect of the Lord. This mood must touch any being that perceives the Lord. Contradictorily, I was also composed. This part of me that remained unruffled was my subdued mind—negated and surrendered at the Lord's feet. I was a watcher, an observer. I was alert to what I perceived, what I heard and what I performed, as these things were being done through me.

The vociferous roar of the inner voice was heard again. As if anticipating a doubt, it started straightaway with a warning not to undervalue all that I was witnessing. All that was happening, all that I was perceiving, hearing and feeling, was nothing but the truth, it said. Truth of the highest order, to be shown to the very few.

It went on to bless me and my family a hundredfold and said

that the golden lotus of my 'bhagya' (prosperity) had opened. All the 'vighnas' (obstacles) coming in the way of business were being removed. Mark this day on the calendar as the golden day of your life—the tenth of January—see how it will turn your fortune. Now you doubt all this and think it might be your wishful thinking and as such you do not want to announce it to the family, lest it should not come true and you become the laughing-stock. But with authority I tell you, shout it out without hesitation and mark this day. It is a golden lotus that is opening. Not ordinary wealth, but sublime wealth, wealth of contentment and glory will be bestowed upon you. The voice roared on, and my throat ached with this silent roar. My face was awesome to look at in the mirror.

For a while, my head and body swayed to some hidden rhythm. I began my bath. Suddenly, Gayatri-mantra, the holy incantation to the Sun, gushed out of me. My mood was supernal. Other mantras in the ancient Sanskrit language issued forth from me, even though I knew no Sanskrit. I began offering 'arghya' (oblations) to myself. I was doing my own 'abhisheka', the way one bathes an idol. My mood was spiralling into the celestial. I knew it was self-invocation that was being performed. Invocation to the Self that had blazed forth.

I poured water on my head amid chanting of mantras, and with oblations in adoration of myself, and I knew I am the creator and the creation. The highest praises, 'stuti', for the Lord burst out of me, and I knew it was all directed towards myself. Again and again, I felt I am greater than the greatest and yet humbler than the humblest. Repeatedly, I was warned not to fall a prey to ahamkara—ego—even though I had now perceived that I am the Lord, and to remain always the most humble of all, which is also the true nature of the Lord. He too is free of ahamkara. Ahamkara, the inner voice told me, separated man from the Lord.

Instantly, I felt I pervaded everywhere. Every soul was me and I was in every soul. All that the others could think, I could think; all that they could sing, I could sing. It was as if suddenly all of us were conjoined by some unseen web. All interconnected and all-knowing. I began singing a most difficult song sung by the famous Lata Mangeshkar, note for note, effortlessly. Singing is something I would normally never ever hope to do. My exaltation soared. I sang on, and I experimented. I prayed to Almighty that this gift would be permanent.

I could feel what others felt. I knew what they thought. I was one with them and they were me, and we were all one with the Lord. He was us. I tried to make Raja comprehend such an obvious thing. I could not get over the wonder of it that if I could perceive this why couldn't he when he was sitting right next to me? But I understood with sadness that a transformed vision was required to perceive this seemingly simple truth. Was this the opening of the third eye that is shown in the centre of the forehead, I wondered!

That entire day, I felt a terrific cosmic force entering my being, akin to a continuous current of electricity. The vibrations were most powerful.

Throughout the day, I was in this exalted state, the 'turyavastha' —the fourth state of being, the other three states being, the waking, the dreaming and the deep-sleep—with full awareness and full control of both the states, the divine and the ordinary. I had only to choose which state I would like more to be in. Repeatedly, I was told that this mastery over the two states from the beginning was rare. To a silent query as to why I had received this infinite grace, I was told that I had, from childhood, unknowingly led my life according to the ideals laid down by Shri Krishna in the Gita, that is, leading a life without attachment, without the desire for the fruit of my actions, and with full devotion to the Lord. And when done unknowingly, such an attitude had greater significance as it only went to show that such attitude was natural to me, and I need not strive further towards perfection. And for this, I was to be blessed with 'maha Aishvarya', the highest grace.

2

'Vishwarupa'— The Universal Form 1

Throughout the night, I was in deep meditation. I was in meditation inspite of myself. Henceforth, my sleep would be my meditation, and my meditation my sleep. In deep meditation I was again told I was in 'turyavastha' and I was being led to 'Parabrahma'. And then I saw the 'vishwarupa' as is described in the Gita. That is a visualization in anthropomorphological terms. What I saw was the universe as it is. In its entirety and in its universality. The 'vishwarupa' as it is.

I saw the entire span of the sky as seen from the earth. I was shown countless luminous stars scattered across the sky. Some of these were twinkling, some were static. Each was an independent star, each spinning round its axis as also swirling in its orbit. Some were moving as constellations, in groups. There was enough room between the stars to steer comfortably without colliding with each other. Each star knew its path, took enjoyment in its movement, was aware of the grand spectacle, the cosmic picture, obeyed the laws of the giant and the tiny star-systems of the universe and accepted its being part of the whole.

I saw that these myriad stars, seen and unseen, receding into the unknown, together formed a galaxy, girdling the heavens; and I saw this mighty galaxy receding to tiny star structure, then appearing as a single star among another group of a mightier galaxy, where each star was a galaxy itself. Each galaxy and each star within it was spinning around itself and in its own orbit, and this super-galaxy itself, as a whole, was swirling around in an orbit of awesome dimensions.

This mighty ocean of star-clusters, composed of galaxies within a galaxy, was now but a lone star amidst yet another giant star-system wheeling in the depths of space. The stars, the star-groups, the star-systems, maintained their own axial and orbital flights, tiny and mighty, resembling interwoven galactic wheels. It was a galactic tapestry in motion.

This went on, each galactic super-system eventually forming only a part of a bigger group. Revolving, gyrating, vista upon vista unfolded, unfurling giant star-systems, each composed of hundreds of millions of stars and galaxies wheeling in the depths of space. The span of the cosmodrama, the immense orbits, the stupendous speeds, the immensity of the universe, the stars compassing it, was awesome and beautiful.

This went on endlessly into infinity. Suddenly, I found I was not on the earth watching this busy, hurling universe. I was at a point beyond the endless complex of galaxies, beyond the outer lonely galaxies girdling the fathomless depths of inter-galactic spaces. I was at a point where I found this entire endlessness and infinity as a single star, and, this endlessness and infinity, now compressed and comprehended as a tiny star, was but a single star in a sky full of such stars in countless numbers . . . !

Each star-universe was in itself an endlessness, infinity, and was composed of stars and galaxies of a different kind. The space beyond the galaxies was composed of such star-universes of various sizes and colours, some barely moving, some oscillating, some vibrating, some hurtling across the sky, some huge, some like decorative lanterns, some like discus. Stars mighty and small, all in motion and twinkling like diamonds of various hues. Each star was endlessness and infinity.

Slowly, I perceived this sky acquiring depth. Deeper and deeper, farther and farther it went, and I saw this deep space studded with deep-sunk star-universes, all endlessness in themselves, of various colours, of various shapes and hues, and of various movements.

As I beheld this magnificence, I found the grand vista was not only to my front but also behind me, and, in fact, all around me.

I was now the centre of a circle whose frontiers were simply not there.

All this time, I was huge enough compared to the stars to have a span of vision encompassing the entire field of the firmament. My proportion to the stars was as is man's in relation to a gnat. Huge! The stars too were distant. But as I observed the star-studded sky, the distance between me and the sky suddenly dwindled and the star-universes were all around me, encircling me, floating by me.

I found myself becoming smaller and smaller till finally I became non-existent. I was snuffed out.

Now I was everywhere! I was everywhere at the same time! All-pervading. Any point and every point was a centre. There was now nobody excepting these heavenly bodies floating gently by, and me—all-pervading and all-seeing.

Every point was the centre of this vastness, and the frontiers from any point were fathomless. Each point was in itself an endlessness and all around was endlessness.

The sky was chock-a-block full of stars, but with adequate room for them to move with no panic of collision. And I was everywhere.

The star-universe systems in their movements were passing through other star-universe systems, effortlessly, as one slips through one crowded compartment after another in a moving train. What's more, these star trains were moving not only horizontally, but also vertically, radially, in all possible directions much the same way as would a sky full of divine bursting fireworks.

Each star-universe system was slipping through many star-universe systems at a time, and, in turn allowing many other such systems to pass through in larger groups, yet managed to retain its own size, identity, movement and rhythm. That is, each system was moving from and through system to system yet was in its allotted place in relation to other systems, moving or oscillating within its own span of movement.

Now, the entire process was reversed as if a powerful lens had been inserted, and I saw that these star-universe systems, each an endlessness in size, were not like a tiny star but were a construct of super-galaxies; each part of this construct in turn splitting into the galaxies of which it was composed. And this entire complex intermingled with other complexes, yet retained its size, shape, identity and form.

Each super-galaxy again broke up into a system of galaxies, each one passing through the others; and so on and on. It was endless.

Thus each star or star-cluster appeared to be merging in or forming a part of other clusters flung in different directions, all at the same time, yet retaining its place in its own cluster.

Each star, each galaxy, each super-galaxy, moved around its axis and around its orbit, yet managed the above merging. Thus each star, each system, whizzing through the other, formed a part of a bigger whole, inseparable from the other groups and the even bigger grand pattern, yet retaining its own identity.

As each star or star-system spun on, retaining its place, its relative distance, its perfect placement in relation to the bigger groups, it appeared to be hardly moving. The firmament appeared to be in an equipoise, and, each of its components in perfect equilibrium. And yet I knew the firmament moved.

The lens was now removed: The stars regained their forms concealing their complexities of galaxies, floating gently in endless emptiness and endless time. . . .

This was only one aspect of the universe. There were universes within universes, invisible universes, visible ones, universes lying side by side, in one place, 'existing' through each other simultaneously in 'different' dimensions of time, in different spatial dimensions; it went on endlessly. . . .

These were the manifest universes. Then there were the unmanifest ones. Only in their potential. . . .

This was a glimpse of the universe !

I began by seeing the universe as one sees the sky from earth. Slowly, my individual identity was broken down, and, when my limiting individuality was totally demolished, I assumed the universal form. I was everywhere at one time, seeing everything, the micro, the macro, from the closest quarters, from the furthest range. I was everywhere, all-pervading, formless, omnipresent, all-knowing and all-enjoying.

I was omnipresent, all-knowing and all-enjoying. But I was not the universe. I was totally free of it, independent of it and uninvolved in it. I spread everywhere, but formlessly and unencumbered by attachments, an eternal witness not bound by the universe. I was pure and intelligent consciousness, seeing all and knowing all, but not depending upon the universe for sustenance.

I felt light, free and unmoving, yet I was at all points, all at the same time. Witness to everything.

Uninvolved, free of emotions, free of thought, pure and vast, I remained poised in eternity and in infinity, in quiet enjoyment, still, composed, calm and in repose!

3

Man–God

Wednesday, January 11, 1984:

Woke up in the morning contemplating on the 'vishwarupa'.
Raja has got into the habit of inquiring about my overnight
experiences. As he is well-read in practically all the subjects, we
would discuss these experiences with respect to various fields of
human knowledge, specially physics and astronomy.

Now I found that when my mind alighted upon a mystic or
philosophical or spiritual topic, knowledge about it would unfold
before me in clarity and in depth. This had to come about on its
own; if I forced this process and took it upon myself to delve
into this knowledge, I found that it would be subject to error,
reflecting my own previous, perhaps erroneous, impressions, my
own views, and biased by my prejudices and conditioning. The
knowledge that came to me was profound, and it welled not
from my previous learning, for I had almost no such grounding.
When occasionally in the past I had tried to go through such
'serious topics', I had failed miserably in either holding my interest
in it or in understanding even a fraction of this vast body of
specialized literature.

Now I understood in a flash things which were previously
utterly beyond my comprehension. Knowledge came about
absolute truths and other unfathomable profundities in a steady
flow as if some obscure dam had burst within me. Knowledge
came about mundane things, about scriptures, about mystic
matters, philosophical conundrums; knowledge came about the
Lord. It was as if some magical lamp had been lit within me. All
the ignorance and obtuseness had left me, revealing what was

perhaps an ancient wisdom inherent in every human being.

In a flash, I understood what was meant by profound words like 'Sat', 'Chit', 'Ananda'. (Existence, Knowledge and Bliss). In a trance, I saw who or what were the gods—who were Vishnu, Brahma, Shiva, and who the Sadguru. Knowledge poured out. I had only to sit still and subdue my own thinking and reasoning. Like a tap being opened by unseen hands, knowledge, staggering in scope, full of conviction and authoritative, would flow forth. Sometimes I would just know intuitively. At times, the inner voice would educate me. It was as if all the knowledge was already there, waiting only for each successive sun-burst to reveal a different facet, a new aspect, each sun sparking off the incandescence of the next sun! And all this in words I could understand, simple, direct and easy.

After bath, I walked to the bed, heavy-footed, reluctant, yet drawn there by irresistible force. I already felt limp with love, with anticipation and fervour. By the time I sat down on the bed, I was in transports of love and rapture. Joy inexplicable made me breathless. Ardour and adoration crushed my being. All of a sudden, I felt ecstatic. Each atom of mine dancing with joy; each pore singing the glory of the Lord; each hair pined for the Lord. A terrific pressure began building up in my head. I was losing my identity. The pressure increased into ecstasy. I was weak with intensity of the ardour. There was an inward pull on my eyes. My body felt weak. I was being sucked into a world of enchantment. Ecstasy and intoxication, I thought, would tear me apart. I was intoxicated to those ethereal heights where I saw myself as Radha waiting in ecstasy for Krishna. I pined for the Lord till I thought I would disintegrate into nothingness, when suddenly I felt a burst of energy of astounding magnitude pouring into me. Energy of stupendous power.

This was no ordinary energy . . . this was Krishna entering me. The Krishna force penetrated me with singular vigour through the whole being. The energy thundered through me, rousing each particle of mine into an extravaganza of joy. A thrill passed through me. The pining wove into fulfilment. Marvellous joy spread through me. Unsurpassed bliss. Wondrous blessedness.

An inordinate feeling of well-being pervaded through me. I tasted heaven in the union with the Lord. I felt His love seep through me; felt His enduring touch caressing me. The cosmic force continued unabated.

I was basking in this celestial union when someone opened the gate to the compound of our bungalow. As the watchman was not there, I got up to see who it could be. Immediately, the ever-alert inner voice informed me . . . 'Do not forget this house has become a temple now. The Lord has made His abode here. No bad man will enter this house henceforth; and if he does, he will do so only after leaving his bad intent outside. Delve into the Lord with a free mind. No harm will come in the sacred precincts of the temple.'

I remembered a strange incident that had taken place when Tejaswi was to be born three years back. A male servant, about sixteen years of age, had come to work for us. He was perfect as a servant. Whatever one could consider as an ideal in a servant, he qualified for that. Because of some complications during pregnancy, I had been ordered complete bed rest. This boy looked after me like a nurse would. A few weeks before Tejaswi was to be born, he left us without a word. He came back shortly, seeking his job back. But from previous experience, we had found that if we took back a servant once he had left, he invariably caused trouble. So we did not re-employ him. Some time later, the police came inquiring about this boy's behaviour during his stay with us. We learnt from the police that this servant had decamped with a lot of cash and jewellery from his subsequent employer. Later, when we were cleaning our bedroom, we found a butcher's knife hidden away near the tube lights, up on the pelmet. With what intention and by whose hands the knife came to be there, we do not know, but definitely the Grace of the Lord had sheltered us; with all his bad intent, the servant had not been able to bring himself to actually committing any crime.

The cosmic force was still entering my being in its fullness. I had merged with Radha, and through her yearning, had lured the bewitching Krishna. Krishna had come, unstinting in love, bringing with him the elixir of total contentment. I felt satiated.

There was a stillness in my heart, an awareness of knowledge and permanence.

I began to feel I was in existence from the beginning and would be there for eons to come.

My gaze became one-pointed and I realized there was nothing to feel, nothing to see, nothing to tell. Bliss that was unutterable descended on me. Silence of the eternities spread around me.

Only awareness remained. Only existence.

There was nothing before and nothing beyond and suddenly I realized I am 'That'. I am 'That' which had created the universe. I am that universe.

I am the beginning; I am the end. I am Time; eternity; infinity. I am knowledge; I am bliss; and I am pure consciousness. I know I am all and all is me.

I am the Lord.

The world that spread before me was magical. There was spring in the air and music in the ears. Joy danced in attendance. I got up. The state of Godhood and non-Godhood . . . that of being an ordinary mortal . . . were running side by side separated only by a flimsy veil, that too with a conscious effort of will. It was easy to let go of either state and yet hold on to both simultaneously.

At the height of this state of 'turyavastha', I was told to pay my humble respects to Raja's Sadguru, to our spiritual friend Kisanbhau Nemlekar, to Swamiji, who is the religious head of our particular community, and, to our 'Kuladevata', that is, Lord Shiva, the presiding deity of the Kodikal clan. I was reminded again to be humble and to follow the Lord's way—in spite of being the greatest, He was humble to the extent of being non-existent. I was told that great glory is in store in being humble.

I looked around. I saw the world with the Lord's eyes. These eyes saw things different from those seen by ordinary mortals. These eyes were liquid rubies and they emanated rays of a peculiar radiance. These were only half-open, they could not be opened full. Behind them was the knowledge of being the Creator. The Great Lord God, the Almighty Creator of this astounding, marvellous universe; He in whom exist all the gods and deities;

He of whom are born Lakshmi, Bhavani and Saraswati! From whom cascade forth knowledge and divine bliss, to permeate the known and the unknown universes. The Creator who is the eternity and the infinity; the cause and the effect; the supreme manipulator of destinies!

I got up and started moving. My head was heavy, and I thought my eyes would burst out. My walk was slow and measured. My mind was still. No thought came into it except for the awareness of having all the knowledge in me and the awareness of sublime bliss and ecstasy which are the attributes of the Lord. I heard only silence amid the bustle of the morning.

I came out of the bedroom to the altar across the small connecting lobby. I stared at the various deities on worship there. A queer mixture of feelings arose in me. Today these deities failed to move me to ecstasy. The fervour of devotion did not well up in me. Instead, I saw them emanating from me. I saw them existing in me and sprouting forth as my offshoots . . . they were my vassals. And then suddenly I remembered what these deities stood for. A whole tradition of myths and legends stood behind them with the full force of thousands of years of devotion and faith poured forth by countless generations of men and women. This massive tradition of fervour and devotion now surged through me, and, I found myself prostrating before these deities, my own vassals, and thanking them with gratitude. The ecstasy of knowing who I was, the ecstasy of self-revelation, of humble gratitude, mingled with a rare jubilation. Again and again, I prostrated with a prayerful heart, and simultaneously I was listening to the inner voice that told me that I was myself all that they represented. I had become them. They had merged in me.

As a housewife, I had more important chores to attend to than indulging in such ecstatic moods. I tore myself away from the altar and proceeded towards the kitchen.

This 'turyavastha' state lasted the whole day and night. All the while a powerful cosmic force was coursing through me and I seemed to be in a state of deep meditation.

Then I was told that meditation and worship had become redundant for me. They were a prerequisite to lead one towards the goal, but if the goal itself had merged with one, where would the path lead to? Henceforth, the very act of living would be meditation for me. Leading a normal life and taking life itself as meditation would be my worship. And writing would be its manifestation. I was again told to guard against ahamkara, ego, and to remain as humble as the Lord and as plain as Him.

The whole day, knowledge about various subjects welled out of me. It was a non-stop gush. I could stop it of course, but if I allowed it, it would flow on. This force, I found, was very obedient and uncommonly considerate, anticipating events and adapting to situations. It never embarrassed me. It would appear and disappear with the most benevolent gravity. It did not hamper my activity nor acted as a hurdle to any chore. It was there all the time now, day and night, educating me, informing me and guiding me, disappearing when appropriate and reappearing when sure of no interruptions.

In no way did it change my outward life. No one came to know of my changed inner life, as I could get in and out of this mood at will. Nor did I announce this to anyone as I found this state most natural. There was no awe, no wonder, at what I was experiencing. There was nothing to announce.

In the afternoon, a fountain of knowledge was let loose. I wished I could jot down all the points before I forgot them. Immediately, as if on cue, I was made to get up, taken to the altar and made to prostrate. Amid other mantras, 'Gayatri mantra' and 'Ganesha Stuti' (in praise of the presiding deity of Wisdom) welled out of me. After repeatedly bowing down and reciting 'Aum Ganeshaya Namah' (I salute thee, O Ganesha!), I was led to the writing desk in the children's room and made to begin this book, first writing on the fly-leaf of the notebook the words 'Shri Ganeshaya Namah' and the phrases of 'Gayatri mantra'. Do not underestimate the power of 'Gayatri mantra', I was cautioned.

Though I did not know what I would be writing, I began to write. I was doing no thinking. Words flowed from my pen, not out of any reading or information previously acquired, as I had never read any philosophical tracts or mystical treatises or any of the holy scriptures. In fact, I had always considered all these books a deadly bore and could never interest myself in them or in discussions. But I was now writing with clear ideas marching out sequentially. I did not have to change or modify them. These thoughts came from some hidden source, the padlock of which had suddenly been opened.

Sometimes I wrote as the Lord; when I was not in that exalted mood, I wrote as a devotee referring to the Lord as separate from me, jotting down all that was welling up in me. The flow came in a singular, clear, uncluttered stream, a most regulated and perfectly monitored flow of thought. None of the ideas were my own. I had only a propelling urge to write. This flow of thought has continued since. All that has been written is purely experiential.

In the evening, I was Lakshmi, the Goddess of Wealth. I wanted to be in reds and pinks and was told to wear henceforth such auspicious colours more often. I left my hair loose. Try as I might, I could not tie it up in a bun as I usually did. Tying up was a hindrance and I wanted complete freedom. Freedom to expand and pervade all over. Where I sat was the centre of the universe, and through my closed eyes, my gaze reached out far and wide, scanning the universe. I was in ecstasy, surrounded as I was with wealth . . . of riches, of glory, of supreme contentment. My aura was brilliance. It streaked across the cosmos. My halo was glory. It winged through the worlds. Wealth was my attribute. It poured out of me. 'Aishvarya' was my reflection and it pulsated out of me. Kindness, compassion, and love emanated from me. I sat there, the knower of all, the seer of all. The consort of the Lord and yet his most humble worshipper. It was I myself sustaining the universe. It was I who moved the world. I sat there in a state of meditation, gazing at one point, knowing the worlds were within me.

I got up and walked around in a half-daze, attending to my chores, still wrapped in this mood. Half-closed eyes of mine were laden with knowledge and contentment! The whole night I was in extremely deep meditation. I was told I was in 'Brahmavastha', the state of identifying with the Lord.

The inner voice used to guide me day and night, even in deep sleep, which would be a state of deep meditation henceforth.

Suddenly, the voice stopped, and I was no more myself. I had no identity of my own. I was the expanse of the universe. I spread across the length and breadth of the cosmos. The cosmos was me. Each star, each galaxy, was me. I had no identity, I had no name. I had no form, the universe was my form. I was aware that each distant star was me. Each distant galaxy that stretched into the infinity was me. I felt the most distant star as I would feel my fingertips and I knew it was me. The eternity was me and the cosmos was me. It was I alone from eternity to eternity. It was I alone from infinity to infinity.

The experience lasted but a short time. The feel of it, the memory, still lasts. I was led into an oblivion. Oblivion of the deepest silences.

Oblivion of the deepest recesses.

4

God and the Path

God is nothingness. God is just 'Being'. There is nothing to see, nothing to tell. It is just nothingness. And yet this nothingness is total bliss. Bliss divine. Bliss that cannot be described, that cannot be conveyed. It is nothing, yet It is everything. It is a void, yet It encompasses everything. There is no light. There is no darkness. There is mere existence, pure and simple. Only an awareness. Nothing beyond. Nothing before. Time is not there. 'I am' . . . that is all. This is the Reality. This is the Lord.

The state of Godhood and non-Godhood, that is, being divine and being an ordinary mortal, can run side by side. Only a flimsy, thin veil separates the two. The veil of ignorance. It is so thin and practically non-existing that when one crosses this, one is not even aware. The transition is smooth and casual. It is not accompanied by any fanfare. To enable one to enjoy this state are the gods and the deities made in the image of man. To convince man that man is made in the image of God, not in form but in essence. That God and man are one. That man can become the Lord.

The fabulous number of deities or gods and goddesses are all essentially the same. They are identical. They are all manifestations of the same Reality representing different aspects or facets of the Infinite. They are all omnipresent, born of the same Reality, and ultimately the same incomprehensible Brahman! Brahman, the Absolute, is non-personal. But the heart finds it appealing to approach the divine through the worship of a personal god or goddess. This intimate worship helps in leading man to exalted states of sublimation and a feeling of merger in God, however transient such a mood of unity might be, thereby helping him to lose himself and his identity and transcend to greater heights of purity so essential for his spiritual progress. This personal deity represents the personification of the fullness of the Brahman.

To enjoy the ecstasy of Godhood, these deities are evolved by the individual according to his inner nature, his inner being, conducive to his exaltation. One can make this deity in any form and name. When the Eternal Lord encompasses everything, even this form and this name are His. If this symbol, this representation, of God leads man to a higher state of consciousness, then, by all means, let man evoke it and give it a name. It will surely lead him to the main spring, being born of the main spring. It will, like a pigeon homing in to the roost, lead him to the Lord.

The gods of the Hindu religion are most appropriate and appealing. They are scientific in their conception, catering to every need of an individual and catering to individuals of varying needs. Finally, it is for the upliftment of the 'jivatma', the embodied soul. Whichever is the god found to be of help to an individual in invoking this 'atman', he is the best-suited for that individual. Man can progressively identify himself with the chosen deity and through this merger, enjoy the Lord Eternal.

These gods also bring the message of the Lord. The prophets are also doing just that. They are telling man that God and man are one. God is man, and man is god. Without form, without identity. All one and the same. What connects the two is the 'atman'. This 'atman' has to be invoked; and invocation culminates into man becoming one with the Lord.

The gods are there, and not there. They are essential to lead man to higher consciousness. To lead him to Godhood. But once there, they are not needed; they become non-existent. Man surpasses them. Because 'atman' is the greatest, as it is continuous with the Lord or the Brahman and thereby it is the Lord itself. Man becomes the Lord and these gods get contained in him.

The Supreme Reality—the vibrant and pure 'existence', the intelligent and all-knowing consciousness, the eternal, unchanging, ever-fresh knowledge and the supreme bliss—this is the Reality, this is the Lord. Eternal, omnipresent, omniscient and compassionate, love itself.

The Supreme Reality, the font, the sustainer and the soul of the universe, and of man.

The Path to Godhood:

The path to Godhood is through bliss. To be blissful at every moment and to enjoy bliss without being aware of it and without making an effort, leads one to the eternal bliss. To begin with, one needs to cultivate the habit of being in bliss. Then it becomes totally natural to be in bliss. Without being aware of this minute bliss, the eternal bliss eludes you. Because this minute bliss and the eternal bliss are one and the same. One originates from the other, and one leads to the other. Just as by knowing the alphabet, one knows all the words, so also, only by comprehending this minute bliss can one comprehend the eternal bliss. Till then, just as without knowing the alphabet, all words are a blur, without the proper assimilation of this bliss, the eternal bliss is but a myth.

Forget the past, negate the future. Be in the present. Enjoy this present. Enjoy this moment. Be in bliss. Enjoy the bell of the temple, the gurgle of water, the laugh of a child. Seek enjoyment in small things, in the little happenings. Every moment will have some enjoyment to offer. Hold it. Get lost in this enjoyment. Get submerged in this moment. This moment to moment enjoyment will lead you to greater enjoyment and ultimately to bliss. This minute bliss will finally lead to the eternal bliss.

Enjoy every moment. Working, resting, sleeping, playing, meditating, let any moment be a moment of bliss. Eventually this state will be effortless and natural.

Thousands of tiny moments of bliss pave the path to the eternal bliss.

Who are these gods in the image of man?

These gods are my 'indriyas', my senses and my limbs. I work through them. They look after the world for me. Deities are existent and non-existent like me. They have a form and they do not have a form. I have no form. But I can take on any form. All forms are mine.

The gods are my officers who leave me alone to be in deep meditation and in eternal bliss. The form that tradition lends a deity represents deep profundities. It represents an aspect of life, of the divine.

These gods are my manifestations, born of me, inseparable from me, having their origin in me. They lead you to me.

If you require them to have a form, they acquire a form. If you transcend them, they have no form. They merge in me just as you merge in me. It is me all the way. It is man all the way.

5

The 'Sadguru'

Thursday, January 12, 1984:

Raja and I went to his Sadguru in the morning. We wanted to tell him what I was passing through. The Sadguru was in a state of ecstasy anticipating our coming. He had already heard from Raja about my experiences. He asked me a few questions to verify whether it was only the arousal of 'Kundalini', the semi-dormant cosmic power in every individual, that had taken place; or I was in a much higher spiritual state. My answers seem to have satisfied him, for he roared with joyous laughter. He was simply jubilant. He clapped his hands and, with a blissful expression on his face, amid mantras, blessed me manifold. He went into ecstasy and 'shlokas', mystic couplets, poured forth from him.

He exclaimed that he was the Shiva and I the Shakti, Shiva's manifestation. He blessed both Raja and me and our family and gave me advice as to what to avoid and what to cultivate henceforth for further progress. He told me that I was on the right path and never to forget that the grace of the Lord and the blessings of our ancestors were upon us. He pointed out the pitfalls I might face and how to look after myself and how to remain on the right path. He rejoiced that one more in his own image had been born. I told him that my sahasrara chakra had not yet opened up. He laughed joyfully and said, 'Right! Right! Henceforth you will know everything yourself. Knowledge will come to you of its own and things will happen on their own. Do not worry. Now it is not your responsibility. Continue with faith in the Lord and in your Guru.' This was the beginning, he said.

The beginning of a new path. A path of enchantment and glory. Remain humble and have faith!

I had no way of finding out whether the sahasrara chakra had opened up or not. But I just knew intuitively that it had not.

Also, when the Sadguru was questioning me earlier to check if it was just the arousal of Kundalini or the manifesting of a higher state in me, I was in the mood of I myself being the Lord 'seeing' things in a different light. I knew nothing about the Kundalini shakti, the cosmic power in man, but I was certain it was not merely the Kundalini being aroused. This certitude or intuitive knowledge is the hallmark of that exalted mood as also an equanimity and peace. There is a deep feeling of humility, and love and compassion flow from the entire being.

The whole afternoon, there was a constant, powerful inflow of energy. I felt the movements of the cosmos within me. At dusk, I went to the altar to light the evening lamp. Looking at the various photos and idols of deities, a fond thought flashed in me whether the other gods too would visit me the way Krishna had? Fondly, and with a prayer in my heart, I called upon them to visit me; instantly, a scandalized counter-thought surfaced: How could I invite them when only the lower or the swadhish-thana chakra had opened up so far? Promptly, another voice joined in: Alright, so you want all the gods to visit you, so be it. I shall open your chakra now. See your head chakra is being opened. See! It is opening . . . opening . . . now it has opened . . . opened wide for all the gods to enter. Now your head chakra is wide open. You can invite all the gods to enter now. But remember, while all the gods will enter through this chakra, only Lord Krishna has the liberty to enter through any chakra, even through the entire body. Only He has this supreme liberty!

I was staring at the altar all this time, witnessing, though nothing was happening outwardly. However, I knew instinctively that my sahasrara chakra was indeed wide open. I felt a slight tingling sensation at the top of my head, and that was that. I had opened the chakra in that split second!

I prostrated myself before the altar. Now an invitation in words seemed redundant. I knew my invitation had reached the deities.

I lay prostrate for a long time in a mood of ultimate surrender and prayer.

In this state of devotion and worship, as I finished my evening puja, I became acutely aware of an intense yearning for the union with Krishna. This yearning was physically painful. Tearlessly, I pined for him. Shortly, I felt the union and the ecstasy. In that union, when I merged with him I felt his ecstasy and the love he bore for me, and my love for him increased many times over. Bliss and contentment wrapped in supreme ecstasy pervaded me, and I went into a deep meditation.

Now the dimensions of space and time were revealed to me. I was shown how to travel back and forth in time and in space. How to go into the future and retrace back into the past.

The illumined inner voice was now becoming dimmer. Its function was over and it was withdrawing. More and more, I knew things intuitively or knowledge came to me as a revelation. This intermediary voice was no longer needed. Now it was often a silent dialogue with the self, and, oh, that certainty.

6

Dimensions of Knowledge

When our own mind has been silenced, that is, when our brain gets silenced along with our emotions, ego, accumulated knowledge, earlier impressions and associations, in short, when the state of our mind has been thoroughly wiped clean and there is no mental activity, our perceptions become sharp. Knowledge pure and true from some eternal source comes flooding in. There should be no effort or activity from our side, then the flow is uninterrupted and clear. The moment an effort is put in, the process gets contaminated by our emotions, biased knowledge, prejudiced mind, preconceived ideas and the all-too-human trait of erroneous interpretations, and the purity of the knowledge gets diluted.

Knowledge includes the dimensions of thought, time, space, feeling, etc. and how to 'travel' in them.

Dimension of thought:

Imagine concentric orbits in grooves. Imagine each groove to be a groove of thought. As thoughts are innumerable, imagine these grooves spreading out into infinity; endless concentric grooves. As the mind hooks on to a thought, it gets lodged into that particular groove, and while chugging along this groove like a tiny wheel, the mind perceives more and more knowledge about that thought. New vistas are opened up. Deeper meanings are unfolded, allied information is supplied, and like an encyclopedia complete with illustrations opening up its pages, a complete picture gets unfolded before you with the required information. As new thoughts come in, no matter how far a distance, the wheel very smoothly changes tracks and begins travelling along the new thought in the new groove. The new groove that it gets hooked on to slips closer and gets into sharper focus whilst the previous thought-groove recedes in the background making place for the new thought-groove. This shuffling of grooves is smooth and a perpetual affair, and the distant thought-grooves and the closer ones keep changing positions. The groove in operation is always in sharp focus. The knowledge it unfolds is true and pure.

The tiny wheel of the mind can travel forward and in reverse, and fast and slow. It is instant travel as in flashes of revelations, when the knowledge of centuries can flash through instantly, or it can be a full stop as in a blank mind.

When a person advanced far in yoga allows the mind to ramble on undirected and without interfering with the process, the knowledge that unfolds is true, and the change of tracks smooth. This is also called contemplation, when his mind is calm and in repose and acts only as a screen to receive clear and true images. But when he consciously thinks of something or tries to change the course of the flow of thought or tries to answer a question suddenly flung at him, his own effort comes into play. He now takes upon himself to change the course, to lift the wheel and put it in the right groove. Unless there is perfect mastery, there is every chance of his positioning the wheel in a slightly off-the-course orbit. As this is a task of precision of untold perfection and the system delicate and highly sensitive, every possibility of error, however small, looms ahead. That is why, no matter how advanced a yogi, he can sometimes foretell wrongly or give a wrong opinion or answer; and, if he grants a boon, it might fail; or, if he tries to achieve something, it might not fructify. All this is because he has failed to put the wheel in the right orbit due to his personal involvement.

Whenever knowledge comes spontaneously, or a boon is bestowed on a genuine impulse, the chances are greater that such knowledge is true, and such a boon will fructify because this impulse is untainted by personal involvement and hence by human error, and has come from some higher source.

For this reason, it is often said that it is unwise to interrupt a great yogi or saint or seer in his discourse or ask irrelevant questions. It is difficult for the speaker then to go back to the right groove, because the grooves are so subtle and sensitive that in fact they are not there! A master in his field, of course, should find no problem shuttling among various grooves.

This is the dimension of thought with imagined grooves of concentric orbits all in one plane.

Dimension of time:

The dimension of time also works in similar concentric grooves in another plane of equally subtle, sensitive and, in fact, non-existent grooves. One travels the same way as with a thought, backwards or forwards in a flash, or comes to a dead halt, all processes of course being highly complex.

Dimension of space:

Space travel as a mental process also works the same way. When a yogi in meditation travels through the cosmos, he travels through a similar groove, changes track and goes to infinity and comes back. As the grooves go as far as the universe can stretch, which is endless, one can travel by intellect any distance in space, time and thought, whilst sitting in one place. Thus it is that, when one sits in meditation, withdraws all the senses and turns them inward in total absorption, one can perceive all that there is to see, feel, touch, smell, hear, and travel without having to move from his place.

Dimension of 'feel':

When one can feel the distant exploding star as one's self; the distant stars or the distant void as one's self; the cosmos expanded beyond conception as one's self; then one is indeed in a highly advanced dimension of 'feel'. The 'feel' of the entire span of the cosmos is the dimension of 'feel'. The awareness or the feel of internal body, each cell, its evolution, its lustre, its movement, its individual awareness, all would come in this dimension.

Similar are the dimensions of sight, of touch, smell, hearing, and speech or communication.

Highly advanced yogis can hear, see, smell, know, be heard, be seen, distances and times away.

These are the dimensions of an advanced yogi.

The orbit of evolution:

Depending upon the stage of evolution of a man's mind, he will be in a particular orbit of evolution, and accordingly will be his span and mastery of the various dimensions, the sharpness of perceptions, and the power of transmission in these dimensions. A great seer will be a past-master, travelling with ease, perceiving and transmitting accurate beeps in any of these dimensions, instantly, backward and forward, simultaneously.

Theoretically at least, the span of the orbit of each dimension could, for a yogi, reach infinity, total purity, and ultimately the Lord. But as the human body offers its own inherent limitations and constraints, it remains a topic of speculation as to whether any yogi, any saint or seer, in the history of man, has ever achieved such an infinitude of consciousness and all the shaktis (powers) attributed to the Lord in their divine fullness. But such is the greatness of divine attributes that even a modicum of progress along this path of purity will bestow huge dividends in the life of man, improving his intelligence, wisdom, perceptions, creativity or expression, and his glory!

The orbit of consciousness:

When one is in the purest orbit of consciousness, one has merged with the Lord.

In this consciousness are contained all the other dimensions. Your span in these dimensions depends upon which orbit of consciousness you are in. This is the matrix of all dimensions. The wider the orbit of consciousness, the wider the orbit of other dimensions and the greater the mastery over oneself.

When you remove the dimensions of space and time, all the universe shrinks to less than a point and finally becomes non-existent.

The same way, when you remove the orbit of consciousness from man, he ceases to be man.

Finally, all dimensions merge into one entirety corresponding to the orbit of consciousness. Depending upon which layer of consciousness you are in at that time, all the dimensions of that span, named and unnamed, simultaneously and instantly manifest before you. To a master, the switch into different orbits of consciousness can be instant and faultless. To the Lord, all the past and the future are compressed into the present. So He sees and comprehends all the past and the future all the time. They are within Him, of Him. Past, future and all the other dimensions are within Him, as He is all-pervading and eternal . . . beginningless and endless.

Finally, a grain in a sack of rice contains all the properties of the entire rice in that sack. Similarly, the tiniest component of this great principle, the Infinite and its infinite consciousness, is an exact replica of the whole. It contains all. It contains all the aspects of the Infinite and all the knowledge of the Infinite; so it contains all the spans of all the dimensions.

Thus all the knowledge and all the spans of all the dimensions are within a human being. There is no need for man or the consciousness in man to 'travel' as 'all' is there within each tiny component of the human being. All that is required is a heightening of his consciousness so that the consciousness becomes aware of its own entire span, or the entire span of each of the dimensions. By heightening to the extent possible the individual awareness to the universal awareness, we can tune in to the Knowledge of the Supreme.

When the consciousness of man becomes pure and penetrating, he becomes divine.

7

Experiences 1

Friday, January 13, 1984:

I was Krishna in the morning. Again I was told about this rare mastery over both the states simultaneously, unlike many others who tend to lose their body-consciousness. I was once more told about the book that will be written by me. Repeatedly, I was blessed. I found myself doing profound obeisance (namaskars).

Again there was union with Krishna. The whole day I was aware of a tremendous cosmic force acting upon me. I felt the movements of the universe within me. The winds of the cosmos were raging within me, and, I was in deep meditation in both my sleeping and wakeful stages. Though I would be in a state of deep meditation, I would be always aware of everything. Thus when I was awake, a part of me was asleep; and in meditation, a part of me fully awake. Every cell of mine was infused with bliss and ecstasy. The inner voice talked to me all the time, explaining and expounding on various matters.

In the evening, I was again Lakshmi, the goddess of wealth, and saw the house filled with her grace and 'aishvarya'.

In my deep sleep, I saw vividly the picture of a man with his insides lit up beautifully. This man had no flesh on his body, and the entire network of 'nadis' (subtle nerves) was lit up with a bluish, softly glowing light. The nerve centres were pulsating gently, emitting rays. Behind the head of this figure, there was a thick, massive, vibrant golden lotus. The petals of this lotus circled the head like a luminous halo, giving the figure a majestic appearance. The lotus was as though of gold, each petal thick like a succulent cactus leaf, with a depression in the centre, a pointed tip, and extending about a foot and a half from the head. Though there was no flesh on his body, and naturally no features, I felt this being to be exceedingly handsome and spectacular. I knew then as to how a halo or a sahasrara chakra (the thousand-petalled mystic lotus) looked like.

Slowly, I started getting glimpses of the 'nirvikalpa'—of going beyond thought and beyond my identity. I had heard from the Sadguru that this would be a frightening stage, so every time that I felt myself getting into the 'nirvikalpa' state, I would force myself to snap out of it. Even in my deep sleep, I had a premonition of getting into the 'nirvikalpa'; an inner fright of the unknown, as if a part of mine knew what it was and was afraid, and the other part was watching this part getting frightened. Earlier, I had slipped into 'nirvikalpa' state unknowingly. Now a pre-cognition of the event about to take place was bringing forth this fear.

Only on assurance from Raja that he would look after me did I relax and allow myself into this state. Here there was a complete break of identity from oneself. A total demolition of even the identity of having merged with the Lord, of being the Lord. No thought, hence no identity. There is only an awareness of just being, no other awareness, not even of knowledge—simply nothing. Just existence, and a feeling of well-being. It involved a total snapping of the ties of the known and entering alone in a mysterious world of solitude and the unknown. Entering into this total loss of identity and total solitude was most intimidating.

I got up with a start and called out to Raja. I was not prepared to go back to sleep, lest I slip back into that unknown. Raja advised me to totally relax and remember the Sadguru, and, thinking of the Lord, enjoy the peregrinations through the subtle realms.

I went back to sleep. As I slept on, I felt the galactic movements of the universe within me: It was a heavenly sensation. The planets, the countless suns, the myriad stars were within me. All the space and time within me. I was larger than the universe. I was encompassing it. The universe was me! The revolutions and orbits through space and time were taking place within me. I was the movement. The movements were smooth and rhythmic, without collisions. Each body moving beautifully in its allotted orbit at a pre-planned speed, and a pre-set timing. One guiding the other, being led by the other, happy in the presence of the other; snug at being a part of the whole, all at total peace, governing in part the whole, following an unquestioned universal pattern, a movement, a rhythm. It gave me a magnificent feel. The entire movement was one grand movement. A part was an indivisible, un-isolated movement of the whole.

And then I was myself a galaxy. A huge galaxy comprising of untold numbers of stars spreading out to infinity, revolving in a grand pattern, following the cosmic rhythm. For some time, I enjoyed this galactic movement. The entire expanse revolved as one whole, the seen and the unseen, smooth and unhurried, permitting no individuality yet allowing each to hold its own.

Suddenly, this formidable galaxy with all its vastness wanted to disappear in nothingness! It wanted to be sucked into non-existence. Petrified at this impending doom, I tried to wake up. The feeling was something akin to knowing in a dream some sinister being was approaching to choke you! Here a sublime experience gave way to a nightmare. I wanted to be myself and snap out of being the galaxy. I saw a vast, bear-like, fearful shadow looming ahead, advancing menacingly towards me, the galaxy, intent upon engulfing me. With a Herculean effort, I snapped myself out of sleep. Feeling terribly let down by Raja who was nicely snoring away, I shivered all by myself, my heart pounding away, in the horrifying darkness of our bedroom.

The jerk must have woken up Raja, and he sat up reassuring me. Much later, it was revealed to me how an experience that started out on a sublime note could change and end up being a nightmare.

As I have already mentioned earlier, one part of me was watching the other part getting frightened. Now the part that was getting frightened was my individuality, and the part that was watching is the eternal witness—the universal. As the individuality is demolished, it merges into the Infinite. This demolition of individuality leads to the 'nirvikalpa' state. This is the demolition of the final covering of mind. The mind or the individuality gets frightened of the demolition or the final negation or total extinction. The witness only watches the subjugation of mind, and then the state of 'nirvikalpa' sets in, in which is experienced the Infinite in all its glory, the final veil covering the mind having been finally lifted.

As I was experiencing the sucking in of myself in the form of a galaxy, my inherently timid nature prevented me from entering into this adventurous plane of subtle consciousness and prevailed upon my negated or suspended mind to awake from this experience. But as I was in deep sleep, my waking mind not yet fully in command, the subtle mind gave way to the dreaming mind, and a sublime experience got transformed into a nightmare. I should have relaxed, said Raja, and allowed myself into the realms of subtle consciousness, and followed through on what happens to a galaxy when it disappears. Thanks, I told him, he could explore such horrors for himself.

8

'Sadguru' and the Trinity

If I am non-existent, have no will, no mind, no emotion, how am I aware that this universe is my manifestation, and, how do I enjoy it?

I am always in a state of deep, unwavering meditation. Concentrating on nothingness. Endless and beginningless. I am non-existent, I have no will, no mind, no emotions, but I have an awareness. An awareness within me, self-born like me, born of me, ever-present, all-pervading and all-permeating. This awareness within has an element of the revelatory, of the educative, of being the Guru. As it is ever-present, unchanging and eternal, it is called the Sadguru (Sat+Guru). It is within me, born of me, and yet it is my Guru, my revealer and my educator. This principle pervades everywhere, inseparable from me, not independent of me, indistinguishable from me, down the line to each object, to each man. Within each object and within each man, there is this awareness, my awareness that pervades the universe, in each according to its or his inherent nature.

In man, this my awareness prevails predominantly. It is his Guru within him, teaching him and revealing to him. As the purity of man increases, he becomes aware of this inner Guru, the Sadguru, and thus realizes me. Till he perceives this Sadguru residing within him, he frantically pursues other Gurus externally. Guru will lead this man back to his own inner Sadguru, and he will realize himself, his Sadguru, and me. This self-revealing force in the universe is the Sadguru 'tattva', the principle of the eternal true guide. This cosmic Guru is the essence of my awareness, and, through this cosmic awareness, I see, perceive and know my manifestation.

This cosmic awareness that is self-revealing, guides the living and the non-living. It lends them an awareness, to a lesser or greater degree, each according to its inherent nature. Man too is guided by this awareness and is made aware of everything by this awareness of mine. The external Guru will lead him only up to a point, till the man is ready and prepared. Then it is this cosmic awareness—the inner Sadguru—that will reveal the truth to him. It becomes his true guide and he realizes that the Sadguru 'tattva' he was seeking outside was all the while within him . . . it is himself ... it is me.

In animals, this Sadguru 'tattva' is in the form of their instinct, racial memory, intuition. Instinctively they simply know. In plant kingdom, each plant knows naturally—through me—when to bloom, when to shed leaves, how to survive, and multiply. I form their basic nature. Because of me, they are. Because of the Sadguru principle, they know, they have guidance.

To inanimate things, I lend them their inherent quality. I lend heat to the rays of light and wetness to water. The Sadguru 'tattva' makes them obey the laws of nature. It controls their inner core. It makes them follow a pattern. Each cell, each particle, each component of the fabric of this universe knows and obeys a grand pattern. It is the Sadguru 'tattva' within each that guides them, controls them, and reveals to them.

It having been revealed by my Sadguru 'tattva' that only through my manifestation can I know or enjoy myself, like an artist can know and enjoy himself only through his art—Brahma, the Creative aspect of the Trinity, also born out of me, omnipresent and omniscient like me—created the cosmos for me. Constant, continuous creation has to be balanced with constant, continuous dissolution. The destroyer of this creation is Shiva, that aspect of mine whence springs the dissolution, omnipresent and omniscient like me. Enjoying the marvel of this stupendous creation, ever in a state of bliss, is Vishnu, my third aspect, of sustenance and enjoyment.

These four, the Sadguru 'tattva', Brahma, Shiva and Vishnu, are born of me, are my manifestation, my different aspects. They are my 'indriyas', organs, and I work through them. They are inseparable from me, they are me.

The Sadguru 'tattva' is guiding every component and creature of the universe.

Brahma, ever-creating, gives me my form—my manifestation, my bursting forth. He gives me a body. This cosmos, his creation, is my body. Shiva impels the re-absorption of my body unto myself—the great withdrawal to facilitate the ever-renewing of the universe. The manifest again becoming the un-manifest. This cosmic dissolution creates energy and movement. Vishnu sustains this flinging out—this flamboyance. He preserves it, enjoys it, and spreads enjoyment.

This is my pattern, my rhythm. This pattern forms the essence of my creation.

Brahma, the cause, is reached through knowledge. Shiva can be reached through yoga, and through formulae and penances, and consequently is more easily reached. Vishnu is reached through bliss and contentment; 'bhakti' (devotion) and 'vairagya' (renunciation) that come 'sahaja', that is, voluntarily, casually, or naturally, play a leading role in it. As voluntary 'vairagya' and total devotion are elusive, so also to please Vishnu is not easy. To enjoy the 'aishvarya' that is given to one, to be content with it, and to be in 'bhakti' all the time, leads one to Vishnu. It is so easy and yet so elusive.

Finding the inner Sadguru is finding oneself, or self-realization, or God-realization, as self and God are one.

I can be reached through any of these or through total surrender to the formless that is me.

The deities, the seers, the saints and prophets and yogis are spreading the message of the Lord: that the Lord is One. The Lord has no form, all form is His. He is all-pervading, all-powerful, ever-present, the creator. He can be reached through purity, humbleness, contentment, patience and generosity. The Lord is love, bliss and happiness. He reveals Himself in His creation. He can be found within oneself. You and God are one and continuous.

9

Five Divine Qualities

The Lord is Sat-Chit-Ananda and Dnyana and Shakti.

Sat:

Sat—Existence. The Truth. 'Being'. This is the true knowledge of the Lord. Sat is the only eternal, unchanging Truth. He alone as Sat is the Reality. Existence is self-subsisting, self-supporting, the sole principle, the true existence of the material world.

The soul makes man live. It is man's essence. Sat makes the universe live. Sat is its essence.

Sat lends its existence to everything. It is pure, immaculate, imperishable, invulnerable, invincible. An all-pervading force, forming the life breath, the soul, of the changing cosmos. It is a throbbing Reality, unencumbered with any form, emotions, or involvement.

Sat is the nature of the Lord. Sat is the Lord, born of Him. inseparable from Him . . . the font of life, the source of all energy, of creation, of matter. The only truth; the rest is relative, changing, evolving, subject to errors, and to the changing perceptions of the inadequate senses of man. Formless, self-born and self-supporting, existing by itself, undecaying.

This Sat, this Reality, is the real man, the essence of man; not his body, not his mind, not his intellect and knowledge, which are always changing. A spark of divinity in him. A spark of continuity that joins him to the rest of existence and to the Lord.

Sat is pure Existence. It is because of this Sat, this Existence, that the universe is, man is, the existence of anything is.

Chit:

Chit is the Awareness. The one awareness that permeates throughout the cosmos, both micro and macro, continuous, uniform, harmonious, unchanging, everpresent. The awareness of the Lord, through which, without sense organs, without form, without mind, He can know His entire manifestation, without missing anything, without overlapping, without confusion, all at once. Aware of each feeling, each thought that is generated in the universe. Awareness that makes the Lord aware of Existence and Bliss; omnipresent, omnipotent, omniscient.

Awareness that permeates in every cell, every being, and makes it aware of its own existence and its bliss or emotion. It is the true awareness of man. It is the real man; his real being.

Chit is the awareness of all that is, all that is not, all that was, all that will be, endless and eternal. Awareness of Sat and Ananda. Awareness is knowing with experience and understanding. This awareness is dormant in mineral. It is stirring in plants. It is awake in animals. It is divine in man.

It is because of this Awareness that man or any being is aware.

Ananda:

Ananda that is Bliss: The Lord is always in a state of bliss. Bliss in the form of nectar. The bliss immortal—Ananda. The natural state of the Lord.

The true nature of man is to remain in bliss.

The Lord in the glorious state of pure existence, of just being without thought, without emotion and without involvement is in a state of deep meditation, samadhi. Being in a state of deep samadhi, He is yet fully aware of existence, of bliss, of the universe, its thoughts and emotions, its creation and destruction, its evolution. He can see, hear, feel, smell, taste, and know perfectly His entire creation as He is suffused in it.

In the uninvolved, thoughtless and sheer existence, is bliss, permanence, immortality, and freedom. The Lord is steeped in this bliss and enjoying this bliss. The Lord is in ecstasy! Love wells out of this ecstasy, and creation out of this love.

Man too is steeped in Ananda, only he taints it with his emotions, and thereby draws upon himself misery.

Dnyana:

Dnyana or Knowledge. The natural outcome of this state of samadhi is dnyana or pure knowledge. Self-known, self-witnessed. The continuous, ever-present, unchanging, true knowledge, un-biased by emotions, ego or the inadequacies and limitations as are faced by man.

The revealed and the unrevealed knowledge. The entire fund of knowledge that is present in the universe, forever, is inseparable from the Lord. The knowledge is the Lord. The all-powerful and the unfathomable intelligent awareness of the Lord, is the knowledge of the Lord permeating with him, uniformly and harmoniously.

Man too is endowed with this knowledge, though he covers it with his prejudice, ego and bias.

Shakti:

Shakti or Power. The divine, cosmic power, encompassing all other powers. It is the power of the Lord, inseparable from Him, pervading throughout.

Man too is endowed with this power. It lies dormant in him.

So the Lord exists as Sat, Chit, Ananda, Dnyana and Shakti. He pervades the cosmos with equality and uniformity. This is the essential nature of the Lord.

This is the essential nature of man, too. This stark and sublime nature of man has to be rediscovered. His divinity has to be recovered.

10

The 'Nirvikalpa' State 1

Saturday, January 14, 1984:

The whole day, the cosmic winds were blowing through me. I was transported into higher realms. The death anniversary of my father-in-law was near, and I was told to pay my respects to all our ancestors.

More confident now about the 'nirvikalpa' state, I allowed myself to go into it during the rest of the day. I relaxed and let go and saw the state of 'nirvikalpa' approaching. Even in deep sleep, there was an awareness that alerted me to its approach. There was a steady demolition of identity, and, as the mind was relaxed, the stage of 'nirvikalpa' set in quickly. Here there was no sense of identity, not even of form. None whatsoever except a feeling of just 'being'—only existence and a steady sense of peace and tranquillity, unsurpassed by the fulfilment of any other desire. It was divine and imparted a deep bliss unmatched in its profundity and its feel of permanence.

The crossover to this state, though it takes only a few split seconds, was initially a bit disturbing, but once I learnt to relax and enjoy, I slipped into it without effort or trouble. Coming out of it was no problem. This state is beyond words and beyond knowledge. There is no mind, so there is no knowledge or thought. There is only an experience of mind stilled to such an extent that there is only an awareness of peace.

Only when I came out of this state, that is, came back to the world of words and thought and memory, did I know I had been in the 'nirvikalpa'. In this state, I realized, one lived in 'that moment', in 'the present'. There was no memory, past, future, words, or knowledge. Pure existence. This state can perhaps be compared vaguely to the state of a newborn babe. It can feel the movements, it can feel its existence, it can feel peace, a sense of well-being, but it knows no words to be distinctly aware of such things and to identify them. The difference, of course, being that the newborn babe has not yet reached the world of thought, memory or knowledge.

In 'nirvikalpa', having passed through this world, a person is in a state of negated mind, words, thought and knowledge. The awareness here is heightened and it is an intelligent cognizance, whereas, in a babe, it is vague and undeveloped yet. It is intelligent cognizance and knowing, but wordless. The yogi, having subdued his mind which forms a matrix for words, thought, knowledge and memory, has in fact gone beyond this world and has surrendered his identity or 'ahamkara'—he has merged with the formless, the fathomless, the wordless, the infinite. As the attributes of this infinite are 'Sat-Chit-Ananda', there is after this state a spurt of knowledge along with bliss and pure consciousness, the source of which is divine, in words one can understand, in which previous knowledge, reason or intellect plays no part.

I found that there was an alternating pattern of the actual 'nirvikalpa' state, and an awareness of 'nirvikalpa', of almost equal duration even in deep sleep. Slipping from one state into the other was now proceeding fairly smoothly, and by now the fright had also gone. The only thing was that, every time I got into the 'nirvikalpa', Tejaswi would get up and break the link. But as the duration of the 'nirvikalpa' was tiny, I don't think I missed much except the continuity of it. After the 'nirvikalpa', there would be the dawning of some divine knowledge which came in a flash. In one such flash, I was told that the golden lotus, the sahasrara chakra, of Tejaswi was about to open up. In another flash, I was told that she would be a partner of mine in this golden quest, and my experiences would be experienced by her simultaneously, only, as she was tiny and beyond comprehending these things, knowledge would not be imparted to her now. But, in due course, she would understand everything of her own accord. This made me understand why she was disturbed every time I had some spiritual experience. Eventually, she stopped getting up even when I had some experience.

Perhaps, along with me, she too had learnt to relax and enjoy these subtle wanderings.

The entire night I was one with the 'vishwarupa', the universal spirit!

11

The Divine Communication

How do Man and the Lord communicate?

The Lord is in a state of nothingness; simultaneously, He is in the state of being omnipresent, omniscient, omnipotent and being 'all'. He knows, understands, perceives and enjoys His entire manifestation through His grand cosmic awareness.

As the Lord is nothing but purity of the highest order and is of the nature of tenderness, compassion and understanding, He does nothing but enjoy and remain in a state of bliss. He is also present in every cell and every being as Sat-Chit-Ananda, Dnyana and Shakti.

The subtle mind of man—his subtle awareness—receives, perceives and decodes this, His presence. The gross mind of man then interprets this presence according to the purity of his mind, his individual evolution in his spiritual ascent, his convenience and his self-interest. Accordingly, he suffers or enjoys. All this is understood by the Lord as He and His awareness permeate every cell and particle.

As the creation is the Lord and the two cannot be separated from one another, the Lord knows and feels His creation intuitively, infinitely more so than as a man knows his body.

As the Lord is immaculate, pure and perfect, He is devoid of different planes of awareness. He is also free of prejudices, biases, emotions and thought, and is thus impartial. As He is eternally in a state of meditation, He is an unparticipating, just, uninvolved and passive onlooker, an eternal witness. With His inconceivable, unfathomable and homogeneous super-consciousness, He simply knows all. He does not require an elaborate system of receiving, decoding and interpreting data.

Absolute Truth is the Lord's presence everywhere, in every cell and being. It is unchanging, eternal, undecaying. It is perfect and immaculate and needs no evolution. It is self-sustaining and needs nothing for its own existence, but lends life and nature to everything. It is this vibrant, dynamic yet unassuming Truth that makes man aware.

It is of the constant nature of bliss, awareness, power and compassion.

It is stark, free of thought, so free of vacillations and emotions.

This, its presence, is the Reality—the Absolute Truth.

This presence has no form. It puts forth form. By itself, it cannot be cut, mutilated or destroyed. Nor can it be made to change. It is unaffected by wind or water, fire or heat. It cannot be seen, heard, touched or tasted. But it can be 'felt'. It can be experienced. It can be merged into.

Because of stark purity, pure knowledge, lack of emotions and prejudices, unfathomable equanimity and faultless perceptions, and an absolute feeling of oneness without a second, the Lord remains in a state of supreme enjoyment, uninvolvement, eternal composure and fulfilment.

But man is an altogether different proposition. He is influenced by his emotions, ego, prejudices, and his faulty, inadequate knowledge. His awareness not having reached the super state, it is layered in different planes such as his conscience and his mind. He thus requires, in his evolution, an elaborate system of receiving, decoding and interpreting data.

Under these conditions, the continuous stream of beeps or messages or knowledge of all aspects of the Lord that passes through man is either ignored by the gross mind of man or is faultily interpreted. The Truth now becomes relative.

Due to his changing mind, and the threatening feel of fragmentation and competition, and the lack of the divine qualities of the Lord, man is subject to marred enjoyment, faulty interpretations and undesirable actions. Man's deep involvement in life is exposed to misery and dissatisfaction, varying in degree according to his own purity which in turn depends upon his progress towards self-realization.

This is man's manifestation. This could be called man's creation of a universe of his own.

If the totality of the Lord and His universe is the Lord's manifestation, the totality of man and his achievements, which include his attitude to and in life, his reactions and his deeds, is man's manifestation.

Just as the Lord is Sat-Chit-Ananda and Dnyana, so also is man Sat-Chit-Ananda and Dnyana, but of a varying degree according to his perception and capacity which in turn are dependent upon the degree of his inner purity.

The Lord perceives man. Let man too perceive the Lord! The Lord has a perfect manifestation. Let man too perfect his!

Awareness is the principle through which the Lord experiences His manifestation. The entire universe is, as it were, its own sensory organ, and from each component of it, the universe receives its experiential impulse. So through each component of the universe the Lord lives His experience. Because of His purity and true knowledge, the impulses received by Him are direct, honest and 'as is'.

At man's level, this awareness can be said to be his mind. It works at two levels. One is the inner subtle mind, honest, pure, and 'one with the Lord', and, it tells man, no matter in how small a voice, the truth 'as is'. It guides him, warns him and generally acts as his conscience.

The other is the lower mind or the gross mind which, according to each individual's purity, progress and environment, circumstances, his strength of character, etc., interprets the above voice of conscience into convenient, faulty and changing conceptions, and acts mainly according to his self-interest.

He may listen to this inner voice and wisely keep it alive and active, or ignore it and bury it deep as it suits his whims and moods.

This gross mind of man is open to evolution. From the lowest rung of ignorance, it can develop into a beaming flash of intelligence. From the gross, enwrapped in ego, emotions, misery and faulty judgement, it can evolve into a subtle, sublime, all-knowing, compassionate and eternally blissful state.

This mind, composed of thought, discrimination, intelligence, acquired knowledge, memory and ego, is an individual segment of the whole, universal, unregimented and homogeneous awareness of the Lord.

The Lord and His inseparable awareness permeate everywhere, including in man as his soul and mind. The soul is the Absolute Truth—the essence of existence, pure, stark and formless. Mind is its awareness.

Because of this soul or existence, there is awareness; as the soul departs, awareness departs. Ananda or bliss represents the state of enjoyment and contentment the Lord is in, eternally, a self-contained, self-absorbed fullness; a desireless and want-less, self-sustaining, uninvolved, detached, ego-free and emotion-free state that results in equilibrium, stillness and a nectarine bliss.

This is the eternal state of meditation, effortless, spontaneous and continuous. This is the true nature of the Lord, inseparable from Him and His awareness.

As an indulgent, compassionate, tender father, the Lord caresses his erring children. The children, in their self-centered and self-absorbed behaviour and deeds, ignore this compassion and tenderness and fall a prey to illusory, fleeting joys, and the wheel of Karma binds them to misery and bondage.

Ananda is inseparable from the Lord as it is His essential nature. Along with Him, it permeates every cell of the universe including man. In man, it gets segmented into emotions, ego, thought, prejudices and biases. Emotions like wrath, love, hatred, jealousy, sentimentality, miserliness colour his thought and judgement in varying degree and bar that divine Ananda from flooding his being. This bliss or Ananda gets tarnished, dulled and buried deep, surfacing only occasionally with difficulty. Emotions, thought and ego together cover the Ananda; and along with it, gets covered the awareness of Truth and Knowledge.

It is upto man to peel off these sheaths of emotions and ego, of prejudices and conditioning, of assumptions and inferences, of impressions and ideas of varied imagery that he has enwrapped himself in, and allow the brilliant Truth to shine forth and heighten his awareness of true knowledge and eternal bliss as he progresses towards the path of evolution. Or stifle the truth and draw upon himself untold suffering and agony.

12

Meditation 1

You seek the Lord through meditation. In meditation, you try to raise yourself to the state of the Lord; that is, the state of thoughtlessness and mindlessness, a state of purity. By acquiring this state through constant practice, you slowly merge in the state of the Lord and become one with Him. At once, you become a partaker of this state of pure existence, of His awareness, His Knowledge and His power. You transcend your limited existence, awareness and knowledge, and reach a state of super-consciousness and super-knowledge which is limitless, pure, true and immaculate.

As you still your mind and allow your self to be revealed, you slowly experience or comprehend that what is without—the entire cosmos—is truly within. Knowledge comes to you of its own, bliss comes to you, power and freedom come to you, and your awareness heightens to become supra-awareness. You experience with stark clarity the oneness of the Lord and his creation, oneness of the Lord and man. A supreme oneness pervading everywhere.

For a perfect yogi, or one who has transcended himself and reached the realm of the Lord, all the arts must come naturally, just as all knowledge comes to him of its own. Such a yogi must and will become highly versatile.

Ananda, as also exists in their very absence, peacefully, in non-existence, non-awareness, non-bliss.

13

The Inner Voice 1

Sunday, January 15, 1984:

The whole day, I had a dialogue or rather a monologue with the inner voice, a voice independent of my mind, intellect or feelings. My own mind, which was a rapt and mostly silent listener, took in every word of the prompt answers intently, only raising a slight doubt occasionally. Clearly, this inner voice appeared to have been illumined by the rays of the divine and to have glimpsed the brilliance of the Infinite. It had authority in it and a deep concern. Very obviously, it wanted to guide me and steer my thoughts; but it did this in a detached and aloof manner.

It was also clear to me that it was my own voice but transformed into something divinely extraordinary. This voice was aware of its origin and its own identity. It knew very well what it had set out to do: Its sole task at the moment was to reveal to me my true origin, my true identity, and my duty. It had to educate me, in gentle steps, that there was an Overlord who permeated the cosmos as a subtle infinite consciousness which formed the matrix for the Sat-Chit-Ananda, and for all the energies and the powers pervading the universe. This infinite consciousness or the Lord permeated all the manifest world including all the living beings and, in its highest form, in man.

It was this Lord within us that was to be sought out by the negation of mind, or subduing of ahamkara or ego within us, by completely surrendering to the Lord. Once this Lord is revealed, one quickly learns that the individual is an indivisible part of this whole; that the Lord without is the same as the Lord within us;

that all the universe, the space and the time that stretch beyond our conception, lie within us; and as we are born of the Infinite, we can merge back into the same Infinite and partake of that ethereal and divine Sat-Chit-Ananda and enrich our lives with its totality in due course.

The inner voice was cautiously educating me step by step, unfolding to me the profundities, revealing to me my progress. Now again, it proclaimed to me in no uncertain terms not to doubt it, as if it guessed that I had not yet grasped the full extent of the value of these revelations. It explained why only glimpses were enough for me; it said that my basic task was to continue being a housewife. With a stronger dose, I might fail to cope with my wifely chores, and abandoning my duty, wish to merge uncontrollably with the Infinite. Being in control of oneself, performing the allotted duties, carrying on in life unchanged and yet meditating upon the Lord, is a state of the highest order. These glimpses, it said, were only to reveal to me and to remind me of my true identity—that I was not apart from this Lord, and having now once glimpsed this Ultimate, the attributes of the Lord would be my nature henceforth.

Just as the brilliance, the heat and the light are the manifestations of the Sun, my children and their achievements would be my manifestation. They will shine in the world and bring fame and honour to the family and to me. Another manifestation of mine will be my writings. To write a book on the Lord, explaining in very simple language the glory of the Lord that is man. Explaining, in words that every individual will understand, that the Lord resides so humbly in every heart waiting only to be recognized.

Later on, I realized that this inner voice was my own mind. Having been cleansed of the ego and emotion and having now become pure, crystal-clear and radiant, it was now my newfound guide. Eventually, even this voice was negated as Knowledge came direct. In fact, the Knowledge was there already, now it only shone forth.

This inner voice should not be encouraged, as it can mislead one in the day-to-day happenings. It can also lead one back to ego and the gross mind. It likes to prattle on and bestow favours and boons. It should be respected rather as a showerer of blessings than as a foreteller of events. It tends to exaggerate and use hyperbole. All that it prattles need not come true. The validity of this voice depends upon the purity of an individual mind. Finally it gets dissolved though it can be invoked at any time, which is dangerous as it often tells you what you want to hear. In such a case of even unconscious wishfulness, the voice is tainted and ruled by the wants of the gross mind. Only in a state of total purity is this voice reliable, honest and educative.

Luckily for me, the inner voice got dissolved in no time.

14

Meditation II

In the afternoon, in deep meditation, I saw from a distance, but quite clearly, a couple, lost to the world, enjoying the divine pleasure of each other's bodies and the quiet ecstasy of deep love. Nature lent the necessary quiet and seclusion. I saw the couple on the sands of a remote silent beach as does a distant witness; yet I shared with them every emotion, ecstasy, calm, the love and yearning that they felt. It was as though I partook of every physical movement each one made. I was the seer and I was also what I saw. There was no sun, but there was no darkness either. Their bodies were healthy and had a quiet glow on them. They moved as if in somnolence. There was no passion, no hurry, no greed, no lust, but there was a knowledge of love and contentment.

The bodies moved as if in slow motion, gracefully, and I felt and experienced all the grace and smooth flow of the movement, and the thrill of the union. It was the same movement one experiences in the yogic 'kriya'—the automatic bodily movements that take place as one advances in meditation. The body moved of its own accord, knowing each move in advance, yet the individual mind did not play any part in it; the smooth flow of the movement itself giving pleasure and ecstasy; gliding into dif-ferent contortions, spreading peace and contentment through the body. With perfect ease, the bodies shaped themselves into seemingly impossible postures, locking, interlocking, ballet-like, assuming yogic sexual 'asanas'. It was one continuous move-ment, enjoying one posture after another.

It was purity, divinity and love of godly nature where the mortal passions of human flesh could not reach. The delicacy, grace and loveliness of the experience of enjoying and imparting pleasure to each other in such an ideal and holy way, I was told by the inner voice, was the yogic way of enjoying marital bliss by the ancient rishis. This was the basis of Kamasutra. All the knowledge of such postures and their pleasure revealed in the Kamasutra was received intuitively by the rishis in their highest state of meditation. Born of the divine where love and yoga prevailed over lust and passion, it spread divine intoxication.

I was told that this was an essential part of an all-rounded bliss, engaged in by the gods and their heavenly consorts.

This is the thought behind some of the sculptures of our ancient temples. They were immortalizing this pure union and pure love from which cascaded forth the rapturous embraces outlined in stone. These brought to the fore the ecstasy and fulfilment that man is eternally seeking through both the body and mind. The body is an integral part of his being and is allotted certain functions. By negating the carnal desires like lust, greed, passion, without repressing its divine functions, a magical state of wondrous love can be achieved. In total purity, love is sheer ecstasy. It is bliss. It is divine.

15

'Vishwarupa'— The Universal Form II

When I tried to wake myself up, I felt as if I was drugged. Yet it was a wonderful feeling. I was gliding in and out of this state, but all the time I was aware of a force radiating from me, a brilliance around me. The powerful force was, as it were, also moving within me and I felt that perhaps I might be crushed by it.

Raja and I had to attend a puja in the evening, so I had to get up. I felt I had power enough to destroy the world. I could also heal the whole wide world. There was joy around me and inside me. This world, I knew, was born out of me and was sustained by me. I stood there surveying the world. It looked so insignificant, so light and unreal. Why was man so attached to this world, I wondered, why did he sorrow for it so much? Why did he not see the grand unity instead? Why did he not open his eyes wide and see the love and grandeur spread across? I wished I could physically open the people's eyes and make them see the magnificence that overlaid the rocks and fissures. All their ignorance would vanish and each would stand there in the full knowledge that the world sparked forth from him, just as I was myself now aware that the world sparked forth from me.

I moved. The ten arms of mine moved with me. The power of ten arms intoxicated me. I knew I could move faster than lightning and crush the world and the evil that disturbed it. I could move faster than thought as I was everywhere. If I was everywhere, all the space was within me. I was here before birth and I would still remain after death, and, I stood there contemplating on all the time that was thus within me. Along with power and love, supreme knowledge radiated out of me. I looked at the world, the weapons in my ten arms readied for its destruction.

But no, the mood turned benign. To spread peace and love. I stood there basking in this love. I was goddess Bhavani in Her glory!

As usual my two states continued side by side. I remembered the engagement for later in the evening and forced my attention on getting ready. The mood of Bhavani ebbed, but left its aura behind. I was once again a housewife now, going about my duty as a friend to attend a puja. My movements as I proceeded were slow. My eyes were ruby red and my head tilted down. I was reminded of the image of goddess Durga as she stood during the puja celebrations to receive the homage of the worshippers.

I was in a mood to wear red. As I dressed in a red saree, I felt the peace of the eternities. I saw clearly I was Brahman, without change and without difference. Everything was the Brahman.

All phenomena were part of the same Brahman. The Brahman that was outside me was within me, not fragmented from it nor independent of it.

The same principle flowed through everything and every being. The individual and the universal were in essence one and the same. The Lord in man is the Atma. This was the Reality of the nature of Bliss and Knowledge. I saw clearly I was the Lord. Free, sustaining the universe, but not bound by it. Light, above space, time and causality. I felt Karma and Causality slipping away from me. I was above the universe. I knew this was the original nature of man till it got tarnished by his ego, thought, and ignorance. No pleasure of the world could have matched this mood. Thoughts got suspended. Mind was totally subdued. No ego. It was a state of complete dissolution where there could be no distinction between body, mind and the Lord. I felt the spell of illusion, Maya, was broken, and I saw a complete unity and harmony in nature. Bliss and Knowledge poured out of me. I was at peace with the world.

At night, I experienced within me the existence and non-existence and the emergence and convergence of the universe. I felt that I was non-existent, but not dead in the usual sense of the word and then that I came into existence as I was breathed out by some entity. As I was flung out, I formed into a luminous point having all the potential of the universe, as a seed has the potential of a mighty tree. This luminous point quickly expanded and fragmented into a myriad luminous points which in turn expanded and spread with lightning speed, widening and spreading into stars and planets speeding away from each other and from that entity. But the more I sped and the more I spread out, I still remained close to that entity. In fact, there was no distinction between Him and me. We were one principle occupying one space and form. There was no duality. Both were one.

In hardly any time, I was the spreading universe with more potential universes within me. Stars spangling, moving, forming patterns, becoming one giant universe, spreading out through infinities. Each star was me, each universe was me. I was the whole moving as one. I could feel and see each star, each atom, each sway and each rhythm. I was the awesomely massive universe, spreading everywhere, swinging through the never-ending cosmos, moving with a quiet rhythm, enjoying the beauty and the movements of the stupendous spangled spectacle.

Slowly, I began contracting and converging in size. The infinite vastness that was me was now converging towards the original point at which I had been flung out of the entity, being drawn back by its inhaling breath. I became smaller, individually and universally, but retained the pattern of the pervasive rhythm. Suddenly, I was sucked in and 'became' non-existent. But I was not 'dead'. I was non-existent only in form. I had my awareness about me. I knew my pattern and I knew my time. As suddenly, I was flung out again. Far and wide. The process repeated itself in a soothing rhythm.

Slowly I became aware that this inhaling and exhaling action was not of some other entity but my own. The universes came from and went back into my own self. The universes were me as much as my nose was me and my breathing was me. I realized with a start that existence and its manifestation in the form of universe were flung out of me and disappeared back into me.

Along with this appearance and disappearance were the birth and death of time and space. Time and space were all within me.

If I am spread everywhere and present at all time, can time and space be apart from me?

So this was the divine scheme of continuous creation and destruction that was revealed to me. It dawned on me that our breathing and the rhythm of the cosmos are related; that they pulsed to the same rhythm; that 'pranayama', the science of breath, brings under control both the breath and the forces of nature. Mastery over breathing would ensure mastery over cosmos. 'Pranayama' is a conscious link between man and divinity.

It was clear now that the cosmic soul or the Infinite and its expression—the universe or nature—are one yet different. The cosmic soul or the cosmic father is the Purusha from Whom and into Whom later merged back Nature, the Prakriti, the cosmic mother.

The cosmic soul or Purusha, remained eternal, all-pervading, unchanging, unparticipating, unmoving, ever in a state of meditation, thoughtless, mindless and ego-less.

The power of this Being, His glory, blossomed into creation which in turn merged back into this Being, unaltering Him, un-affecting Him. Emergence of creation did not reduce Him; re-absorption of creation did not add to him. His presence, His existence alone, was enough for this grand cycle of creation and destruction of the universe.

Prakriti was the divine mother giving birth to everything, nurturing it, evolving it and then dissolving it to give new birth. All was one continuous stream. One, yet multiple. Reversible, yet separate, and still one.

Born of the Purusha, not different from Him, inseparable from Him, equal in all respects is Prakriti. Eternal, changeless in the rhythm of birth, evolution and dissolution, all-pervading. Highly organized.

Purusha and Prakriti, His potency, His virility. Purusha and His spontaneous creation; His power, force, glory, manifestation. His energy and consort—Prakriti! Purusha the subtle, the invisible, blooming out into Prakriti, the creation: much the same way as the invisible, subtle water vapour precipitates into clouds, water, rain and ice. And then again back into the subtlety of the water vapour.

Purusha and Prakriti—the Lord and His creation. Purusha gives birth to Prakriti, sustains Her and remains independent of Her. Yet not so independent! He cannot help bringing Her forth, no more than the sun can help radiating light and heat. Light and heat and the sun are the same yet different. Purusha and Prakriti are the same yet different. Two aspects of the same Parama-Purusha or the Uttama Purusha, Who is beyond the Prakriti and the Purusha and Whose power and soul the Prakriti and Purusha represent.

This sameness yet independence of the two was clearly indicated by two experiences: On the 13th, the experience was from the aspect of the Cosmic Being wherein the soul and the stars and galaxies were one and the same, yet the feeling was retained that the Being was one apart, not bound by the creation, yet intimate enough not to be separate from it.

Here I was the Cosmic Being, feeling the stars and galaxies within me, knowing them as my own self alone, and sustaining them. The two were the same and yet the Cosmic Being was not bound by it.

On the 15th, the aspect shown to me was of myself as the universe being born and being dissolved. Again this manifestation could feel oneness with the Cosmic Being, knew that it was sustained by the Cosmic Being, and that its source was the Being.

16

True Meditation and 'Sahaja' Samadhi

True Meditation:

All the experiences in life and in meditation are revelations and knowing. Even in the 'nirvikalpa' state, one only experiences and learns. True meditation is to be in 'nirvikalpa' state, completely thoughtless, experiencing only existence and bliss. In this state, one is truly one with the Lord; or, having negated the segmenting mind, one in fact becomes the Lord. There is only a vibrant and intelligent awareness of pure existence and a sublime, un-excelled bliss in this state.

There is a feeling of deep stillness and permanence. As this stage is beyond words, the awareness is not in words or thought but is by sheer intuitive knowledge. All the four aspects of the Lord, existence (Sat), awareness (Chit), bliss (Ananda), and knowledge (Dnyana) are enwrapped in one inseparable state.

This state can be maintained whether one is in meditation or in an awake state in the midst of work and life.

This stage is beyond the various gods and beyond duality, when mind and worship, thought and duality, are submerged and what emerges is stark Reality, that is, non-duality and sublime oneness and a homogeneous continuity and unity in myriad diversity.

Life and living are not apart from the Lord. So, the Lord or this state of 'nirvikalpa' samadhi can be, when mastery is achieved, experienced whilst walking, talking or doing any other chore.

This is then called 'sahaja' samadhi or a state of spontaneous, natural meditation—with no conscious effort, no conscious wishing or willing to it.

There are no thoughts even while carrying on with the normal life. Work is done on the right impulse or by intuition. Dynamic motivation springs from a deep inner silence. There is no identity; nor any emotions, attachments or desires to mar the inner peace, the calm and the constant equipoise or the quiet bliss that pervades the soul.

All action and movements are spontaneous now. Witnessing is done with no reaction to events or happenings, no desire for change lurks anywhere, everything and every event seems natural and as it was meant to be. Mind is steeped in the present; the past is not there; the future is not there. There is no desire or involvement, but there is no neglect of duty or action. Efficiency in action comes automatically.

The 'nirvikalpa' mind or a thoughtless mind leads the body to the state of samadhi as the body and mind are in fact one continuous stream or one continuum only. That is why, in 'sahaja' samadhi, because of the thoughtless or pure mind, the body gets into a state of samadhi even in the midst of full activity of daily life. Now there is no need for a conscious effort at meditation, as the body and mind are, of their own, in a constant state of samadhi or meditation.

This state can be reached either by subduing the mind by a conscious effort at meditation in the beginning, or by emptying the mind gradually of ego, emotions, desires, thoughts, and getting slowly in a state of bodily samadhi. Either state leads to the other state.

Ordinary samadhi or a sensation of oblivion during an effort at meditation is an interim state. This can lead to consciousness during samadhi. However, here the body would be at rest.

But in 'sahaja' samadhi, a being can be in a state of samadhi, with no effort at meditation, without curtailing any activity, with full or heightened awareness, without another person even coming to know about it.

17

Inspiration and Creativity

Brahma and Saraswati:

The god Brahma is the cause, the creator of the universe, a universe of, perfection, of the utmost beauty, and eternal—with a cosmic rhythm of blossoming-out action, animation, pause, and re-absorption. He is that aspect of the Lord that effulges out into creation. He is born of the Lord, he is the Lord and as such is himself eternal and all-pervading. As he has sprung from the Lord, so has the creation sprung from him, of its own, inspite of himself, the source being the Lord; the source of purity and eternity. The creation thus ballooning from purity and eternity is itself pure, beautiful, divine and eternal.

Brahma could not have created an universe of such magnitude, perfection and resplendence without himself being pure knowledge. Eternal, unbroken, unending, undecaying knowledge. Divine knowledge that had come from within him, in spite of him and from the same source as him—that is the Lord! This supreme knowledge cannot be separated from Him. Creation without such perfect knowledge would be incomplete and limited.

If Brahma is the creator or the cause, Knowledge within him is his consort—the goddess of learning, Saraswati. Brahma and Saraswati cannot be separated one from the other. Knowledge and creation go hand in hand. Saraswati is also that aspect of the Lord that showers knowledge on man. Knowledge that differentiates man from beast. Knowledge that lends divinity to man and to his deeds.

Brahma within us:

When we are in true meditation, experiencing only the existence and bliss, with total negation of our ego and individuality, we become one with the Lord. The god Brahma within us 'awakens'. Slowly, we become the Supreme Knowledge itself. The Sadguru-tattva within us awakens, and makes us aware of who we are and what is to be our manifestation. The universe is the manifestation of the Lord; deeds are the manifestation of man.

Because of the awakened Sadguru-tattva within him, man is aware now that he is Knowledge, and words flow out of him. He can feel them, see them, and comprehend them. He knows he is them; he is the cause from whence they spring, in spite of him. They flow from somewhere deep within him, slowly, clearly, in a language he can follow, and express himself in. Should he be a poet, then fully-formed beautiful verses come out of him; if he be a musician, music flows from him; if he be a scientist, theories and formulae occur to him. According to the vocation or the field of interest of the man, knowledge in that particular form will spring out. He does not will such knowledge; it wells out of him, without his conceptualizing it, and perhaps even without seeking it. This is divine knowledge coming directly from the supreme source, the Absolute Truth.

Then, no matter in what state you are, whether in 'nirvikalpa' or in deep meditation, or in day-to-day living, a certain amount of concentration will bring forth this outflow of divine knowledge, or a masterful revelation, or a spectacular idea, or an understanding.

All this is through inspiration, with no participation by man's intellect. It is not the doing of the man, as at this point of time, he is lost to himself and is in a mood of total self-absorption. His own thinking and reasoning are submerged. Unknowingly, he has gone into a no-thought realm. The thought that emerges is not a man-thought; it comes with a bang, as a revelation, no doubt according to the evolutionary stage of that particular man. This is a divine thought, marking the purity and concentration at that time. Each man will get such ideas in his field.

These are the moments of the unfoldment of creativity in us. It is Brahma stirring within us. According to the purity of the man and his individual evolutionary stage, the ideas he gets will be extraordinary or plain.

Each man, because of the divine in him, enshrines within him Brahma, Shiva, Vishnu, and their divine consorts, Saraswati, Shakti and Lakshmi. He also holds within himself the Sadguru-tattva. It is upto us to invoke them.

The Vedas and the scriptures have streamed out thus. They have all flowed out of Brahma enwrapped in sublime knowledge. They have come out in fully formed verses, in unexcelled perfection, and carrying eternal verities. The rishis or the great seers of the past were the instruments for this divine flow of words. These scriptures have to be treasured, cherished, respected and worshipped. They contain the highest truth and the luminous supreme knowledge.

The rishis of the past, being of the highest order, the highest knowledge, came welling out of them. But any one can awaken the god Brahma within him, and experience, understand and enjoy the same knowledge himself as is written in the Vedas and Upanishads, in his own time. And as his purity increases, he can understand the scriptures in all their profundity, and he will himself be expounding the truth. When the purity becomes absolute, there are no two interpretations or versions of the truth. Such differentiation comes in only when diverse persons, being in different states of purity and concentration, start interpreting knowledge that has welled out of the perfect ones. The knowledge itself is one, divine, unchanging, eternal and universal.

18

'Avatar' and Me

Monday, January 16, 1984:

The two states, of being the Lord and simultaneously being an ordinary housewife, still ran parallel.

After the morning chores, I relaxed on the bed. As the attention shifted from one subject to the other, knowledge pertaining to that particular subject dawned. Attention was now focused on India, and, I was told by the inner voice that the golden lotus of India was now opening up. The long-awaited days of her 'aishvarya' and fame were about to start. She will be a country of great prestige and great name. My hand lifted of its own from my lap, and the fingers formed into a 'mudra', in a gesture of a lotus opening up in a pond, as if, with my 'mudra', the golden lotus of the Indian land was itself blossoming out.

The inner voice then went on to tell me the difference between an 'avatar' and me. Though the veil of Maya had been lifted from me and I perceived myself as the Lord, yet I was not an avatar, it said. Far from it. What I now perceived was the truth that the original nature of man is in no way different to the nature of the Lord, which sin or evil cannot touch, where Karma cannot reach, and where only love and beauty abound. Yet I was not an incarnation. Far from it. An 'avatar', I was told, came with a mighty mission in life. A mission of crushing evil. An 'avatar' was mostly martial by nature, and bearing arms. He would have his self-awareness developed to a gigantic scale and his cosmic awareness would be also equally great.

I was born to enjoy myself and bask in the glory of the Lord. Enjoy 'aishvarya', which meant wealth of happiness, contentment, and comforts. I had no mighty mission in life and certainly not anything of a martial nature. My mission was only the spreading of the word of the Lord, in a language as simple as the Lord is; in a manner and style as plain as the Lord is.

I was again told that my true self had been revealed to me, as I had lived the ideal life as described in the Bhagavad Gita by Lord Krishna. Continuing to lead my life as I have led all these years, and writing down what was being revealed to me was meditation enough for me. There was no need for a special, conscious meditation for me, as life had itself become my meditation.

19

Shiva and Shakti

The Lord, steadfast in his state of meditation, realized, through His Sadguru-tattva, that He can know Himself only through His manifestation. The god Brahma, the creator within Him, set to work and created this universe. Instantly, Shiva, born of the Lord, set himself on the path of probing and unravelling the mystery of this creation. As the Lord and this creation are endless, Shiva is said to be still on the path of discovery.

Through dynamic concentration and yoga, which is the sublime unity of co-ordinated faculties in anyone, Shiva codifies this mystery. Through mantras and tantras, he lays down religious treatises of formulae, calculations, rites of worship, astrology and other explications of the mysteries of this creation. Through this yoga, which is a purposeful direction of concentration, knowledge and devotion, Shiva manifests in action.

Through yoga, he is one-pointedly in unity with the Lord and with His deeds. He is in eternal unity with creation, maintaining continuation of life through destruction. Destruction leading to creation; death of one moment leading to the birth of the next moment; death of the old giving rise to the new.

Shiva is unity. Unity of the male and the female. Purusha and Prakriti. Shiva is 'linga'. Shiva is yoga. Shiva is continuity. Unity is continuity. Shiva is life.

Out of this yoga and unity emerges action—energy. This aspect of Shiva that results in movement, in energy, is Shakti. Born out of him and inseparable from him, springing from the same divine source. His consort, the goddess Shakti or Parvati. The energy of movement or action and deeds. The primal energy, the primal force, pulsating through the creation. The dynamism of the universe. The living force of creation.

20

Layers of the Mind

Tuesday, January 17, 1984:

I felt one with Tejaswi. For a short spell, I was Tejaswi. She and I had become one. She was sleeping soundly in her cot. I myself was sound asleep in my bed. In that split second, I saw Tejaswi sleeping in her cot but it was me there. I was her soul. I was asleep myself, but one part of me was fully conscious, and it was conscious that it was Tejaswi.

The next moment, I was simultaneously both myself and Tejaswi. I was one but I had two bodies. I had the two individual consciousnesses of both Deepa and Tejaswi, yet there was a common consciousness that was aware of the other two. And yet all were one and they were me. Though I was sleeping, I saw the two bodies clearly in their respective beds. I felt that, had we been awake, I would have known the thought processes of the two of us together.

Suddenly, from the self-revealing, universal consciousness, I, the individual self, knew that this was what is meant by being an 'antardnyani', or all-knowing. The soul of everyone is the one continuous universal soul; all souls are one in essence. So, still retaining one's own identity, one could be everyone or anyone at the same time, just as the Infinite is, and know and feel exactly as the others do, all at the same time. In fact, be them.

In a crystalline state, the individual becomes one with the universal, with no demarcations and fragmentations, and feels the oneness in all.

I was fully awake by now, though it took me some time to recover from this baffling experience. I understood now why a spiritual master knows almost everything and can penetrate every heart. He is everyone. That is how he can send telepathic messages far away, and work other wonders. His awareness merges with the universal awareness and becomes one gigantic whole.

I must have been drawn into another oblivion. For, out of the silence of the night, I heard a clear voice: 'This is my awareness, but I am other than that!'

Another oblivion, and I saw myself now as 'Knowledge'. I was fully conscious of being knowledge. It was a physical feeling. A certainty. It is difficult to describe how one can feel to have become knowledge. All these various states are difficult to describe. But there they are! I had lost my identity and was in the 'nirvikalpa' state, where I was experiencing the knowledge aspect of the Lord

I was the supreme knowledge, all-permeating and ever-present. Words in the form of flowers flowed out of me, like water from a fountain. Knowledge spewed out of me, like luminous sparks from a giant firecracker star-burst, and spread out everywhere.

I had become Knowledge, yet I was also the font of knowledge.

Another part of me, which was also equally conscious, said in a clear voice—'Knowledge is me, but I am other than the Knowledge! Knowledge is only one aspect of mine. I am beyond Knowledge. Knowledge is contained in me.'

There are many layers to the mind. One layer was witnessing, one was sleeping, yet another had gone into the 'nirvikalpa', and yet another was educating me. The individual negates himself, gets into the 'nirvikalpa', negates the informing voice, and finally merges into the witness. Then he only witnesses and enjoys and simply knows. Not in words, but in a transcendental way which only an inner experience can make clear.

Sometimes, man is conscious of all the states, as in 'turyavastha'; sometimes of two, three or one. This mind keeps flitting from one state to the other. During such 'experiencing', this flitting is in quick succession, so that experiencing and education can be side by side. Sometimes, there can be a gap between the two. With mastery being gained over this process, witnessing or experiencing can be simultaneous with knowing or perceiving. Here this mental layer is established in the higher recesses of the mind and does not have to flit around. There is no end to perceiving and knowing.

21

One with the Universal

Such a state should become the natural state of a waking mind, even though it is involved in full activity.

A mind which witnesses, perceives and knows simultaneously, without having to flit across the various states, is a 'turyateeth' mind, that is beyond the 'turyavastha'.

The faithful voice that used to educate me was dying down now. It did not address me any more. Its function was over. Knowledge came directly to me now. I just knew or heard or saw.

Wednesday, January 18, 1984:

I was no longer frightened of getting into the 'nirvikalpa' state. The fright of the unknown that I had, even in deep sleep, whilst getting into the 'nirvikalpa', had been overcome. Freed from the compulsion to cling on to things known, and having lost my identity totally, I had learnt to become one with the oneness of the universe. Once the initial apprehension was overcome, and the demolition of my identity was over, I could explore unhindered the unending frontiers of the newly-discovered identity of the Universal Self.

So it happened with me now. Completely relaxed in my sleep, I experienced universality in various forms.

I was air now, invisible but spread everywhere. I was high up, as also low down, moving in one body, sometimes briskly as a breeze, sometimes hardly so as still air. I was boundless and light, yet I had a consciousness. I could see everything, feel the smooth flow, enjoy my wide sweep. There was an awareness that seemed to know all.

Then I was the clouds. A huge body of white clouds spread

everywhere, unending, high up, moving in a smooth-flowing, soothing mass. I felt my lightness and my vastness. From my great height, I saw the green ground below, and I was aware of the blue sky above. As I moved, I saw clearly the receding waters, the trees, the mountains, the entire landscape. Here too, I had an awareness of knowing and of enjoying.

I saw some banana trees on my way. Now I was myself the banana fruit. I was now everything. I was the clouds, I was the air, the fruit, the trees; I was the earth, the vast expanses; I was all, down to the smallest atom. It was only myself everywhere in its individuality and in its universality. I felt each individual nature as my own; I felt their movements, their individual awareness, but I felt all this was myself and it was all one. This was the cosmic vision and the cosmic mind or cosmic awareness. I was all.

To be one, to be multiple; to be everyone, to be everything. To be cosmic, yet be each individual and each tiniest particle, all together. One principle permeating every cell. Intelligent, cognizant and all-knowing. I was this consciousness.

Simultaneous with this cosmic awareness is the individual awareness inherent in each individual object, say, in a banana, an ocean-tide, a wave and so on. All together, yet without any mix-up.

Because of my being the eternal witness witnessing every event, and because of having my supra-consciousness, I would simultaneously feel the limitedly-developed consciousness of each of the objects separately. I would feel the inertness of the stone, of a banana, of a cloud, and yet, because of the cosmic awareness alongside, I would experience the bliss, the knowledge, the peace, the calm, the cosmic movement, too. None of the individual consciousnesses interfere with one another, nor do they overlap each other.

Each individual entity is a part of a bigger group, expanding its consciousness likewise. For example, a tiny cell is part of a tissue, a tissue part of a muscle, a muscle part of an organ, and thus it goes on, each cell or group instinctively knowing what to do. However, each cell and each group retains its separate identity.

This self-knowledge permeating every cell and each group, living or non-living, is due to the cosmic 'Sadguru-tattva' suffusing it. The whole cosmos is totally organized. If there is any seeming disorder, it is part of a bigger order, and, it is seen that it has been put there in an orderly way. There is no panic; no haste, no inquiry. Each little group, each cell, knows its function, its time. It is all due to the inner controller—me—and my 'Sadguru-tattva' suffused therein. But the particle is not aware of me.

I felt all this. I was all this. A molecule of water is part of a wave; the wave is part of the tide, which in turn, is part of a current experiencing the dirt, the heat, the movement, the lightness, the heaviness. I felt all, individually and together. I was all.

The various depths of the sea, different light effects at different depths, the movement of a fish, of each moving bit: I experienced it, I saw it, I was it. I was everywhere and I was full of joy.

The immobility of the mountains, their vastness; the flight of a bird, the movement of air, of clouds; the heat of the sun, its light, and its scorching quality; the wetness of snow: I was all. I felt all. All at the same time, and much more.

I was the matter. I was the energy. I was the consciousness. I was the macrocosm. I was the microcosm. I was all. Individually and cosmically. I had truly become cosmic.

In the universal awareness, I experienced oneness. Knowledge, peace, and a feeling of non-interference with anything. In the individual awareness, I experienced the limited awareness of the inherent nature of that object. Both at the same time. And, I was also experiencing the individual awareness of all the objects all at once, along with universal awareness. Yet there was no confusion. It seemed a perfectly natural state to be in, nothing extraordinary; becalming, effortless, spontaneous and eternal.

With the limitations of the senses, it is difficult to fathom such a state or such a vision, and that too on a cosmic scale. But in a state beyond the senses, it seems a most natural and spontaneous state. The only state to be in.

Having experienced the microcosm and the macrocosm, I experienced the rhythm of knowledge and awareness. I was the knowledge of everyone and everything, and then I was the awareness of everyone and everything. And in that knowledge of oneness and the knowledge of Knowledge, I knew my education was over. I had realized I was That. I was That universal self, from which springs the universe with all its energies and its evolution: from which arises the knowledge, the awareness, the bliss, the existence—All. I had been That always; only, I had needed this to be revealed to me. I needed not to make a great effort to realize this supreme truth. I was That. I was the goal, and I was the traveller; I was the Lord, as also I was the worshipper. I also knew that, for me, life itself is yoga, and living itself, the Gita. I had a task before me—to write a modern Gita with a clear message to every heart that it too is That!

I had experienced personally what was Sat-Chit-Ananda, Knowledge and Power. And now suddenly again, I was the centre, and the universe, far-flung. I was nothing but a minuscule non-existent point. Like the ballooning parachute drawn in by pulling on its strings, the outer rims of this universe started converging towards me. The entire universe began contracting and drawing in towards me. Finally, as the stars and galaxies came closer, they entered into me and disappeared within me. A time came when the entire universe was within me, and I myself nothing but less than a mathematical point. Then even this point began contracting inward till the universe and I both disappeared.

In this great convergence disappeared all space, all matter and energy, all form and shape and time, all existence, all consciousness and all bliss. Nothing was left. Nothing!

But in this in-drawing, when even the consciousness withdrew and disappeared, I found that there was no discomfort, no choking death.

But there was nothing. Not even plain consciousness. A total extinction. A void, a darkness, a total non-existence. Sat-Chit-Ananda were not there.

It was as if a light had been snuffed off. Like one sleeping like a log, dead to the world.

Then, ever so slowly, one by one, all the galaxies came out and rolled across the void to fill it up in its original dimensions of form and shape, and expand to its fullest on the omnipresent, endless scale. Again, light had slowly emerged. Bewitching galaxies whirled and spread. Then again the in-drawing began.

The rhythm continued on its own with no participation or involvement of the Lord. It just took place. It is this potential, His nature, His presence, that perpetuates this grand pattern, His grand pattern.

If consciousness is not there, who experiences this extinction? Who experiences this void? Who experiences a sound sleep?

Who is this great entity who nurtured life through this great extinction, ever so gently, leading it delicately to the threshold of a new birth? Who is it not to have experienced any discomfort, is at ease, at rest, in repose, through this great extinction? Who survives at peace, fully potent, experiencing uttermost calm, serenity and equipoise?

And, with a shock amounting to a cosmic awe, I realized the tremendous personality of this Being. He exists as Sat-Chit-Ananda, as also exists in their very absence, peacefully, in non-existence, non-awareness, non-bliss.

Totally withdrawn, subtle and self-absorbed. Totally free of matter, energy, time, form, though these are His very being. Totally free of any manifestation .

A mere presence. A force. A divinity. The Lord.

The Lord is 'beyond' Sat-Chit-Ananda, space, time, form, knowledge, the various gods. But 'beyond' does not signify their exclusion; it only means their acceptance; encompassing, containing them, being their very font. But He is larger than any, separately or combined. All these are grounded in Him. But He is free of them. Independent and unaffected. He knows of them, as also knows not about them. It does not bother Him. These get flung out of Him and get re-absorbed in Him. He remains unchanged. The consciousness and form get absorbed. Not He. The joy, the bliss and the knowledge get absorbed. He remains calm, poised and in equipoise.

This is the Lord, the rest is all His nature and form.

He is complete, without their aid. He is beyond both. He contains both. He is the 'Parama-Purusha Purushottama'.

This process went on, synchronized with my slow breathing. I, as the point, was everywhere, flung across the cosmos. There was no particular centre.

Every point was the centre. I and the process of effulgence and re-absorption and my manifestation, were one. Thus, the universes came out from and disappeared into me who was spread out throughout the cosmos.

Thus the appearance of matter and energy in the form of the universe, and its disappearance, occur eternally throughout the cosmos. Thus are the Sthiti, Laya, Pralaya; birth, pause, and death. Again, pause. So it goes on, the eternal 'happening'.

22

The 'Nirvikalpa' State II

Man realizes or experiences the Lord in 'nirvikalpa' samadhi. In this samadhi, there is no individual self-awareness nor any other awareness of any particular entity. The individual becomes the Lord, and experiences and lives the Lord.

In the 'nirvikalpa' of 'Sat' or Existence, the individual transcends his mind and quickly slips into a state of naked 'existence'. Vibrant, pulsating, throbbing existence. Pure, immaculate and sheer. This existence is pure energy. Alive and charged. Dynamic! This pure existence is eternal, undecaying, not needing to evolve, ancient yet ever-fresh and intact, self-born, self-subsisting, self-contained.

He is now experiencing the dynamism and the throbbing pulse of life. He is experiencing himself. His true inner, divine Self that makes him move, think, and live.

Though he experiences the dynamism, the energy, the throb, he also experiences simultaneously a rare stillness, an indescribable calm and an unexcelled peace containing complete satiation, fullness and contentment. In this fullness is rooted everything that there is. It is such fullness and satiation that it leaves no room for further desires, wants, or longings. This satiation and contentment induce the self to be self-absorbed. This self-absorption gives it stillness, self-sustenance, permanence, and equanimity.

This pure 'existence' is inseparable from cosmic awareness and bliss.

If he can maintain this stream of experience of Self, he slowly becomes aware of the universe as the manifestation of his stark existence. Still remaining in this state, he starts experiencing everything that exists in the universe, without the help of any sense organs. Suddenly, he acquires, as it were, as many heads as are in the universe and experiences all the individual components that make up the grand universe.

Inseparable from this comes bliss, ecstasy. Ecstasy that tingles every pore and the very core of his being. Steeped in this bliss and fullness, the individual is now none other than Maha-Vishnu himself, reposing on his own cosmic energy in an ocean of nectar.

In this state of 'Sat', there is neither light nor darkness; there is only a luminous glow. There is a feel of an ocean, and a feel of being neither in the air nor in water. The ocean has no waves, yet it is alive and full of life. There is no one there, yet no loneliness. There is nothing there, yet a feel of full creation. There is one-pointedness yet the feel of full expanse. The gaze seems final there, and unblinking, yet it is all-seeing. There is no knowledge, no thoughts, no words, no language, yet the feel of intelligence, of knowing all. There is a complete humility, yet the feel of total power, total supremacy. Thus the mighty contradictions of nature merge into that outburst of glory, the unfathomable Creation.

This 'existence' is the soul of mankind, man's 'Atma', in its purest form, and is continuous with the soul of the universe. Formless, limitless, un-exhausting, unsleeping and eternal.

The goal of an individual should be to maintain this stream of samadhi in both sleep and wakefulness, without consciously sitting for meditation, thereby being constantly tuned into the state of the Lord.

Before this state, in all experiences and revelations, there is guidance, there is education. There is the identity of the Lord, as also of the mortal; there is a duality; and a perceiver who is made aware of his evolution, of his ascent into the 'Parabrahma'; there is a journeying through the universe. There is the perceiver and the perceived, no matter how subtle the awareness or how far in time and space he goes.

In 'nirvikalpa', he is That. He is not apart from the Principle. He is the Principle, the source, the seed, the womb, the font of creation, the creation itself. There is no perceiver or feeler. Even in the deepest of sleep, if one is made aware of being in the 'nirvikalpa' state, that state is other than 'nirvikalpa' state. One is not aware of being in 'nirvikalpa' state, because the individual who has gone into 'nirvikalpa' is exposed to pure existence, and as such, he experiences only Existence.

He now experiences aspects of the Lord.

The Lord does not need to go into 'nirvikalpa' state, as His natural state itself is pure existence.

The individual becomes aware of having been in 'nirvikalpa' only after coming out of it, when he is back into his individual awareness. No matter how deep the sleep, the 'nirvikalpa' state is beyond that. In this, the awareness is very sharp and intelligent, and there is only experiencing and witnessing. There is a feeling of freedom and non-involvement from the manifestation.

The gross mind goes to sleep and experiences manifestation of the mind, such as, dreams. The transcended mind goes into 'nirvikalpa' and experiences the Lord.

In this state, there is no debate whether the creation is part of the Lord, or a thing apart from him: it is real, or an illusion! There is only the act of experiencing, knowing, witnessing, as one witnesses or experiences one's body. There is a feeling of freedom and a feeling of non-involvement from the manifestation, which does not reduce the magnitude of knowing or experiencing the manifestation.

It is man who is busy trying to establish whether creation and the Lord are one or not. In the meantime, the Lord, in whom are contained all the grand contradictions, for example, existent yet non-existent, still yet dynamic, meditative yet active, self-absorbed yet vibrant, nothingness yet all, formless yet having all forms, elusive yet present everywhere, etc., thereby maintaining a supreme balance and equilibrium, absorbs yet another contra-diction of being the same with His creation, yet being free and apart from it.

23

Vishnu and Lakshmi

When the Lord, through his 'Sadguru-tattva', realized that He can know Himself fully only through His own manifestation, (like an artist knows himself through his paintings), the Brahma in him, born out of Him and inseparable from Him, created this glorious world.

The Shiva, in Him, born out of Him and inseparable from Him, through yoga and meditation got down to probe and solve the mysteries of this ever-mysterious creation, and what emerged was a wondrous feeling of marvel and bliss.

The aspect of the Lord that eternally sips this ambrosia is Vishnu. He is in an eternal state of bliss reposing on an ocean of nectar, snug in His knowledge and power. He is the preserver of this blissful state of the Lord. He is eternally in repose and calm, steeped in the basic and soothing 'sthiratha', steadfastness. He preserves this 'sthiratha' or this sovereign internal peace and equipoise, ever rendering a sublime coherence to the stupendous creation.

Vishnu is thus the preserver of the noble creation.

From this majestic bliss springs splendour—'aishvarya'—Goddess Lakshmi. Inseparable from bliss, and the consort of Vishnu. Splendour, 'aishvarya', not just of money and gems but the sublime wealth of knowledge, of bliss, wealth of grandeur, of beauty, of contentment, of generosity and compassion. And also wealth of gems and gold! Wealth of every aspect, exaltation and purity, peace and happiness! Peace born of beauty, peace born of comforts, peace born of knowledge, and peace born of grandeur and purity. This is the Vishnu–Lakshmi aspect of the Lord, which

He spreads and distributes in full measure throughout His creation.

The Vishnu in us:

When we see the beauty in nature, the innocence in children, sweet gestures of fellow-beings, we sense a rare peace descending on us. It makes us feel exalted. It makes us see glimpses of divinity around us. This exalted mood of peace in turn takes us to rare heights of generosity, kindness, love, for however fleeting a moment. These noble emotions in man, generally suppressed by none other than himself, blossom forth at such times, and he enjoys spreading these very emotions and getting more peace in return. This is the Vishnu–Lakshmi aspect in us. Inseparable from us, although suppressed. Peace and equanimity bring forth these suppressed emotions.

Similarly, wealth of true knowledge, wealth of true comforts, wealth of gold, when come of its own, when not hankered for, when not accumulated by employing base means, will bring peace or bliss, which will bring splendour, 'aishvarya', into our lives. 'Aishvarya' is the pure enjoyment, not just of wealth. The extent of accumulation of these things does not matter, but the happiness derived from what one has matters. Contentment matters. It is this 'aishvarya' or happiness or contentment that one strives for, and misses due to the misconception that wealth of money alone will bring happiness. Man runs after base accumulation, employing any unfair means and justifying them, having no time to enjoy simple beauty and the true wealth scattered around either in nature or in spontaneous gestures, and then, discouraged, he runs helter-skelter in total confusion and despair.

Wealth is not a deterrent to self-realization or to true happiness, if enjoyed with a feeling of 'vairagya', detachment. If no base means have been used to accumulate it, and if base motive has not been the spur for it, the accumulation of wealth need not be shunned. To enjoy wealth with a feeling of 'vairagya' is to be always aware that wealth is not permanent, as also that, by itself, it is not the giver of true happiness and eternal peace. Wealth has been bestowed on us by the Lord's generosity! No misuse of this wealth is to be indulged in. In fact, it is to be used with magnanimity, kindness and generosity, and a firm control of mind, in that a sudden disappearance of this wealth should not bring grief and a feeling of calamity.

24

The 'Nirvikalpa' State III

Thursday, January 19, 1984:

Just as during the day I exist in two streams, so at night I lie asleep in two parallel streams nowadays. One part of me would be sound asleep the moment I lie down. Another part of me is wide awake, fully conscious of my surroundings, watching quite clearly what goes on in the room as if my eyes are open.

In this samadhi-like state last night, I opened up Tejaswi's 'Brahma-Kamala', that is, the majestic thousand-petalled lotus. It was done without any prior intent or volition on my part. I got up from a deep slumber and, retaining the flow of the other stream unbroken, that is, remaining still in the samadhi-like state, went and gently rubbed the top of her head where the 'sahasrara chakra' is located, and a force flowed out of my hand and I knew that she is a partner of mine in this spiritual voyage. Whatever experiences I undergo, she does too, only she will not understand anything now till her time comes when, all at once, she will know all.

I had been writing a day-to-day account of my experiences and now I wondered how I would cope up with putting on paper all that was happening, as, on one hand I did not get adequate time, and on the other, knowledge and experiences were daily being received by me in massive doses. How could I remember it all? Immediately, I was made aware that nothing pertaining to this knowledge would be forgotten as I was now conjoined to the source of supreme knowledge, which is self-revealing, permanent and inexhaustible. When this happens, memory in the ordinary sense of the word is irrelevant, as knowledge comes direct as and when needed. And, at once, I felt my brain being wiped clean from inside. Not that the brain disappeared in the material form, but its function as the storehouse for the memory of the knowledge of the Supreme Self was over, as the Infinite Consciousness had now taken over.

This referred to the Supreme Knowledge only, and not to the acquired knowledge that would require study and memory. My memory otherwise had not failed.

Friday, January 20, 1984:

In the dead of night, in my deep sleep, I knew clearly that my education in the Gita was over.

The whole night, there was an alternating pattern of getting into 'nirvikalpa', and then coming out of it. In this state, there was no identifying with anything, not with the universe, not with any gods, not even with the Supreme Lord. There was only an awareness of pure existence, 'Sat'. There was no knowledge, yet no ignorance. No thoughts, only an awareness of peace, permanence, and perfection. A state immaculate. A state of being sheer energy—primal and pulsating. A state of pure awareness. But the lack of any identity did not smack of imbecility, impotence, blankness or dullness. It exuded perfection, fullness, dynamism and intelligence. It contained everything there is.

There was no need for identification, as this state went beyond any state that would feel such a need. This was Existence, 'Sat', pure and divine. From this stark existence sprang up awareness, bliss, knowledge, power and energy. This was the true being, the naked self, the mark of 'Brahman', the one coherent stream running through the otherwise changing world. It was That. That was the Infinite. That was me.

During this time, my body was in a state of subtle vibration, 'spanda', and the 'chakras' at the temples, the brow, the nose, head and the neck, in fact, everywhere, fully activated, were throbbing hard.

This pattern of getting into the 'true state', and coming out of it, settled down into a smooth rhythm, and soon I found that it was in tune with my deep breathing.

In fact, my breathing got regulated to my experience. Breathing pattern changes with the spiritual experience: slowing down, and even stopping, as one goes into deep samadhi, all depending upon the type of samadhi. Often, I found I was not breathing at all, or if breathing, the breathing was subtle enough to be almost non-existent.

25

Mind as Obstruction

Late in the night, Raja posed a question, 'My business is not improving. I am fed up of struggling against heavy odds. Tell me, what is the cause of this bad phase?' I concentrated for a minute, but got no answer. I continued to concentrate, but still no answer. I probed further, but my mind was blank. No indication of any message. After a good long lapse, suddenly the inner voice spoke, and that Raja too heard. It was my voice, but it was speaking on its own without any volition on my part. One part of me was sleeping, and another part of me was responding to Raja's query. It said, 'There is a solid obstruction in the path that does not allow me passage to probe or to act. This obstruction is not like ordinary matter; that I would have hacked away. This is of a different nature. Un-hackable. Like a computer, I have to be fed with the proper data. The data is not coming forth because of the block.'

Again, there was a long pause; then it said, 'The obstruction was obstinate, but I have managed to bore a hole in it. It was hard going, as the obstruction was severe, but a beginning has been made. Now, slowly it will crumble. It will take a long time. The unpierceable obstruction was an obstinate opinion that held that you should not get the business. But now, slowly things will change. Matter can be hacked off, but the obstruction was the 'mind' of someone who held a firm opinion. The most impenetrable obstruction is always of the mind. That is why I cannot work when the mind is closed. Mind is most difficult to change or hack. Mind itself is always the greatest obstruction.'

Raja agreed that it was prejudice on the part of someone that had kept his business at bay.

This in its own way explains how, in spite of Infinite Consciousness permeating in all individuals, they fail to see the Infinite Truth. They cover their consciousness with their emotions, thoughts, prejudices and intellect, and draw upon themselves a thick veil of ignorance that keeps them in eternal darkness about the Supreme. This further explains how, in spite of the Lord Himself residing in each individual, the individual behaves so basely, and why he is such a sorry victim of his own emotions. His mind, made up of ego, intellect and emotions, is the most obstinate and wilful barrier to the Infinite working upon him or making Its presence felt in him.

So, thought keeps man from Divinity, and the individual from the universal! And, as his emotions, intellect and ego are variables, varying with time and his mood, these are not the Absolute Truth which is unchanging. Only the Almighty is the Absolute Truth!

26

Duality and Non-Duality

In the beginning, there is the Lord and his devotee. This devotee prays to the Lord, and yearns to merge with Him. This is duality, when he thinks he and the Lord are separate, and he identifies with his body, and begs the Lord to reveal Himself.

As self-realization dawns, the body-consciousness is broken, the veil of ignorance is lifted, and, he realizes that he and the Lord are not separate or different, and that he himself is the Lord. This is the state of non-duality, when he perceives the oneness of the Lord permeating and pervading everywhere.

This state of non-duality is rarely permanent; and soon, body-consciousness and awareness of separate existence or individual identity or duality creep back, although the knowledge of non-duality remains. As the yearning of the devotee to merge with the Lord (now with redoubled force, having experienced the supreme bliss, and having the certainty about the possibility of non-duality), continues, consciously and unconsciously, he reverts to the state of non-duality again and again. He slowly masters the art of retaining the awareness of his body and this world simultaneously with knowing and being one with the Lord. By mastery and control, he can retain both the states at one and the same time, enjoying both the states equally and in full measure. This is rare but can be done.

With greater mastery over himself, and with more and more revelations of the Lord, the devotee can live simultaneously as (a) fully the Lord—as one experiences the Lord, as being oneself the Lord; and (b) as the most humble servant of the Lord, in awe of the Lord, and with a tremendous feeling of humility, believing in doing the Lord's bidding and being an instrument of Him. In short, he remains a total man, doing his chores, discharging his duties and obligations, with a prayer, in contentment and sincerity, bringing divinity into life, steeping every action of his with divinity, and letting this divinity be a boon in his life.

This state of leading a 'double' life, of duality and non-duality, without neglecting his duties, obligations or chores, remembering the Lord all the time, leads him into the higher realms of bliss and glory. Although man and the Lord are one, as long as man has body and mind, he is subject to relative levels of purity, and there is always a chance of slipping out of this state of divinity through the emergence of his ego. Humbleness and prayer, along with pure awareness, knowledge and bliss, will allow him the best of the worlds.

Total merger with the Lord, losing the identity of body and mind for a long time, would make him functionless in the world.

Total mastery over both the states of duality and non-duality will make man achieve glorious heights in whatever he does. With the awareness of divine knowledge, and having the divine touch, anything he attempts will be haloed with brilliance.

Awareness of body will make him remember that the Lord is above everything, and there will always be in him which will again reflect divinity.

This dual state gives unified control over reason and emotion.

Action is important in life. It is the culmination of knowledge. Its crowning glory. Abdication of action is neither intended nor is it natural. Nature too is ever engaged in action.

Movement and action form the basis of nature As also of man. Nature does not envisage inaction for man, hence inaction is unnatural in him. Wrongly understood meaning of renunciation or misrepresentation of action could lead man to inaction. Abstaining from action need not keep his mind from base thoughts either.

Guided by knowledge and pure thought, action surges ahead towards perfection and divinity, and will in turn lead to creativity and radiance. Knowledge and action complement each other. One enhances the power and the splendour of the other.

Divinity does not advocate renouncing either life or action, but in fact it asks for suffusing life itself with divinity. Action does not stall the progress towards divinity either. Action not prompted by emotions, prejudices, ego, personal feelings, or with an eye on its rewards, but motivated by reality 'as is', springing from purity, is non-action. Such non-action, or pure mind, reflects divinity. In this purity, the doer, the doing and the done, become one. There is no longer any difference between them.

In the ideal state, man is ever in meditation, or ever in 'nirvikalpa', whilst he is still performing all his daily functions. He is in deep meditation in his sleep, fully aware of his surroundings and his own state. He is also in a state of meditation during the day, while busy working through his routine. So, when the world sleeps, a yogi is awake, fully conscious and aware in his sleep; and when the world is busy and active, the yogi is reposing snugly in the equipoise of Reality.

In this 'nirvikalpa' state, there is no concentration, even on a mantra or God. The mind is totally free of any thought or focal point. It is in a state of total negation, relaxation and freedom, as opposed to concentration or one-pointedness. This does not make man inactive. If a person is, say, eating, he is simply eating, thoughtlessly. Not in a moronic manner or in any way un-coordinated, but dynamically aware and alert, fully intelligent and cognizant. No nagging doubt, worry, hope or emotion, will taint this mood. Any activity, however important, can be carried on by such a mind. Gradually, the sphere of consciousness widens. Out of this silent mind effulges intuitive knowledge and right impulses at the right time, an impetus to work, telepathy and other 'extraordinary' faculties.

As he is ever in 'nirvikalpa' state, words, knowledge and divinity, flow out of him at every step. His life, his thoughts, his deeds, all become one. He is totally merged with the Lord, still retaining his own identity. This state is rare and difficult, but can be achieved.

This retaining of individuality or this segmented awareness is a great protection. Unlike the Lord, man, with his limited faculties, no matter how advanced, cannot remain in universal awareness all the time, seeing all, feeling all, being all, etc. His mind will be blown out. Only the Lord, with His unlimited power and faculty, can always remain in such a state. There will be chaos if all the pain, misery and hurt of the world are shared and felt by all. Even for the great seers, who can see, feel, and know all, if required, this is a protective aid in that they can see, feel or know, only that which is required, by focusing their attention on a particular field. The rest should not become a burden on them. Also, this way, they can witness and experience without getting affected.

The Lord has perfect segmented awareness, as also faultless universal awareness. He is aware of what each being thinks, talks, knows, tastes, hears and smells, individually and collectively, as also has a universal panoramic view and feel and knowledge of the entire expanse, all the time, always. He is truly the eternal witness. Because of His superb command of Himself, He can manage to be uninvolved and free of his creation, and remain unaffected.

Just as the Lord is Sat-Chit-Ananda, and his manifestation or the universe is, as it were, His body, man too is a compound of Sat-Chit-Ananda in varying proportions, and his body and his deeds are his manifestation. The state of Sat-Chit-Ananda of the Lord is eternal; and his manifestation too is eternal, although having a rhythm of creation and self-absorption. Man's Sat-Chit-Ananda are varied depending on his purity, and his manifestation of deeds, moods, understanding, etc., which are continually changing in countless variety and degree.

But this dual state helps him get steady in his purity of thought and action, and enables his manifestation to culminate into divine brilliance.

27

'Ananda'—Bliss

Saturday, January 21, 1984:

Tonight there was an alternating pattern of bliss and sleep, synchronized with the rhythm of my breathing. This bliss is not describable. All I can say is that I was conscious of ethereal bliss pouring from every pore of mine. Every pore, every cell, every atom of my being was set a-dancing with this bliss. All the joys and all the pleasures of our worldly life pale into nothingness before this bliss, this 'ananda', this feeling of supreme well-being. This 'ananda' is charged, dynamic, containing the entirety, the universe, the manifest, and the unmanifest. Yet this 'ananda' is total peace, absolute equilibrium and sheer equipoise, relaxing every cell, every pore, demolishing totally the individual identity, and suffusing every cell with the divine nectar.

Then again, there would be a spell of sound sleep, followed by another spell of bliss. Through both these states, I was aware that this pattern coincided with my slow breathing. Along with this breathing, repeatedly I lost my individual identity and became 'bliss', and then again regained it in sound sleep. This was the 'ananda' the scriptures talk about and glorify in paeans of magnificent poetry. All the praise and the glory woven around this 'ananda' are inadequate, as it is all that, and much more. It is the nature of the Lord Himself. Indescribable and all-pervading, suffusing the cosmos. This is bliss. I am bliss. This is the original nature of man too.

Sunday, January 22, 1984:

I generally refer to getting experiences in the night. This is because the whole day I am busy with house-work and, as such, have no time to relax and experience such profound revelations. At night, after I have gone to bed, I would be relaxed, and the time would be mine, and the experience would follow.

Alternately, I would be aware of deep sleep and the 'nirvikalpa' of mere existence, resting on a sea of nectar that is itself in a state of quiescent yet vibrant resonance—'spandan', where neither light nor darkness penetrate.

Breathing too followed a different pattern. The inhaling, the holding of breath, and the exhaling. With the drawing in of breath, a sort of ambrosia was drawn in. Then it seemed that breathing was of no consequence. One could very well do without breathing. It was comfort par excellence, without breathing at all. The world was poised on that pause in the breath, it seemed. The breathing-out suffused the world with life, it seemed. This was the real 'pranayama', the control of breath and the life-force.

Monday, January 23, 1984:

The whole day, the feeling of being the Lord was very pronounced. I went about my jobs, fully conscious of the power of the worlds within me, and the knowledge of the universes within me. I was conscious of who I was. I was elated and exuberant. I felt an aura of bliss around me. I was the Lord in His full glory. All my 'chakras' were vibrating. My eyes were half-closed. They were like rubies, pools of compassion. I moved in a world where sin and evil had no existence. All was beauty, innocence and perfection. A world of eternal peace, bliss, and completeness.

As I proceeded with my work, I observed an elder person of our family dealing in an unjust manner with someone much younger to her. The unfairness and the untruth of it all was appalling. Such behaviour enraged me. I bristled, and along with me, the power in me bristled. I felt the weapons in my arms trembling. A bad thought was about to form in my mind, when a voice intoned, 'Compose yourself! Bear in mind, control of the self is the first prerequisite. Always remember that restraint is the most powerful weapon. The Lord is non-interfering. He watches on, only as a witness. He allows every soul free-wheeling options, to be rewarded or punished by its own actions. The Law of Karma misses nothing. Let the law of 'Karma' (the Law of the deeds) handle such situations. It knows how to reward or punish justly. It allows nature to take its own course. You remain in bliss. Remember, you are not an 'avatar'. Certainly, you can help as a fellow human being. But be just and discriminating. Do not get involved and let emotions reign supreme!'

My rage immediately subsided. I saw the wisdom of this message. How much can one interfere, to what extent? Is one competent to know who is at fault? Does one have a sufficiency of facts to mete out the right judgement? Is each action independent of the previous one? Mediating without emotion, to see that nobody got hurt, was the only thing to do. Uninvolved and without rage.

In deep sleep, a clear message came through: 'Nirvikalpa' or pure existence is true meditation. In this state of meditation, the individual is totally merged in the divine, and freely partakes of the divine knowledge and the divine bliss. Eternal bliss permeates him and true knowledge flows out of him.

Tuesday, January 24, 1984:

As I was coming out of my afternoon nap, I became conscious that, in my sleep, I had been directing my breath upwards, towards the brain, instead of to the lungs and, then, as usual, exhaling through the nostrils. It was a soothing process and I felt no suffocation despite not breathing normally. I tried to maintain my half-awake state and observed the breathing process. The breathing was going on smoothly, deeply, with no effort or discomfort. I could not help becoming fully awake. Though I tried to continue with the stream of upward breathing, I soon got tired and gave it up.

The secret is to maintain the state of half-consciousness or half-wakefulness. In this state, the difficult processes get revealed and get done on their own. One state reveals, and gets things done; the other state observes and learns.

Wednesday, January 25, 1984:

The whole day, I had the feeling of being the Lord. The mood was exuberant. As I sat in the 'auto-ricksha' to get Tejaswi home from school, I laughed to myself and wondered if the 'rickshawala' could even guess that the Lord Himself was his passenger today! I chuckled to think as to what would be his reaction if I were to tell him so!

Tremendous energy exuded from me. Sometimes, it was unbearable. The sensation was pleasant, nevertheless.

In this state of being the Lord, there was a clear consciousness, an absolute certainty about being one with the universe. No doubt assailed me that I am the Lord; the Lord of the universe! I felt I am the master, arranging everything happening in the universe. I am supreme! All is me. I am everything, all-pervading, all-engulfing. Knowledge and bliss are me. With all this, there was the deepest equanimity in me, an undisturbed peace, and a rare stillness. Time and space had lost their meaning. It was endlessness, without a beginning and an end. I felt eternal. As much as I felt supreme, I felt humble, non-existent, without any identity whatsoever. Only compassion flowed out of me. There was beauty and innocence all around. There was a deep understanding of each one's behaviour, secure in the knowledge that each acted thus in his innocence. Beauty and innocence underlay each man and object.

There was no joy either. There was only eternal calm. A feeling of completeness, a feeling of complete satisfaction, where want or desire would be meaningless. A feeling that everything was in me, and that all that was without would be absorbed by me. This was Reality.

This state would continue for many days.

Thursday, January 26, 1984:

A queer weakness was slowly creeping over me. It was not the weakness one experiences after fever or an illness. It was more a lethargy and somnolence. A reluctance to thought and to movement. A desire just to lie down and to relax. Relax every pore. A desire to hold still the time. But this weakness had pleasure in it. A pleasure difficult to match. A pleasure that was intoxicating, a feeling of completion, a feeling of negation of want. I wished I could remain in this weakness ever.

It no longer mattered whether things were done or not done. Just to remain in this weakness was enough. Misplaced things, undone chores lost their meaning, their power of nagging. Doing nothing, staring blankly, thinking nothing, was heaven itself. My movements became slow, eyes heavy, and the head felt like having a support all the time. But the chores had to be done. They were getting done somehow.

However, I could snap out of this state of pleasurable weakness instantly, whenever it was required, merely by a flick of thought. But quite often, this flick of thought would be elusive, and the will to summon it would not come forth.

I was 'bliss' at night. Just as in my 'nirvikalpa', I would sometimes be aware of mere existence, sometimes be conscious of sharp awareness, similarly, now I was conscious of being bliss itself, not just enjoying bliss. Bliss was me, I was bliss. Again and again, I would be bliss, but every time I became bliss, Tejaswi, who was not too well, would get up and disturb my 'nirvikalpa' state. Yet I had a feeling of bliss and peace the whole night, even in deep sleep.

Friday, January 27, 1984:

At night again, I was in a state of bliss. I was bliss itself. I was the bliss, the eternal and unchanging 'ananda' of the Almighty, pervading every atom of the universe with Him, inseparable from Him. As bliss, I entered my sleeping daughter, Akshata. I was in her now as the Supreme Bliss, capable of transporting her to the heavens. But she was oblivious of me. I tried to make her experience the state of the ultimate one can get into. But she was insensitive to me. I had failed to penetrate the wall of her individuality.

Next morning, I entered two other children who were busy playing. I was bliss, and I was in them, pervading them, playing with them, jumping with them. I tried to make them be aware of me. Get them into a state of bliss. Make them see what heavens await them. But they too were oblivious of me. They went on playing, as if nothing else mattered in the world but their play. I had failed to pierce the barriers of individuality of even innocent children who were awake and in command of themselves.

I knew now that, though bliss is all around us and in us, unless the individual's awareness is heightened, he fails to perceive it and thereby experience the ambrosia that lies within everyone's grasp. Even the Infinite fails to awaken the individual, unless the individual himself seeks out ambrosia.

Along with the creeping lethargy and weakness, slowly there developed now a strange bodyache and a dull headache. It was not an ache really, but in the absence of a better description, the word 'ache' will suffice, as will the word 'weakness'. The body felt heavy, and the movements were reluctant. Again, it was not a real heaviness, only an illusion of heaviness. Also, I could snap out of it at will. But again the will was lacking most of the time. When I did snap out of it, I would feel absolutely normal and healthy. However, this lack of lethargy would also last only as long as it was absolutely necessary for me to do my chores, and then the lethargy would instantly creep back.

This lethargy made me feel drowsy. I was now always in a half-asleep, half-awake state, till such time as I would consciously break this current and snap out of it. This current had another aspect to it. It generated energy. I felt a tremendous force of energy in me. Sometimes it appeared to enter me from outside; at times, I appeared to be exuding it; often I thought that it was contained within me. It left my body in a state of mild tremors. The tremors could not be seen, but only felt. This energy was different from that felt by a sportsman all geared up for action. This energy, as I said, gave an illusion of lethargy, weakness, tiredness and drowsiness. Yet this energy or this current seemed to be divine. It made me feel satiated and wanting nothing. This state was perfection.

It was a state of immaculate peace and quietude. In spite of the drowsiness, this state was sentient and percipient. The current varied in its intensity.

Saturday, January 28, 1984:

The current was very powerful today. The energy, tremendous. Headache, bodyache and weakness, excessively pronounced. It was like a continuous current of electricity passing through me.

Sunday, January 29, 1984:

Mr. Nemlekar, our dear friend, visited us. Just by a touch, he reduced my headache and bodyache. He laughed, and said that it was the cosmic force, the 'chaitanya shakti', that I was experiencing. He said that my body would slowly get used to it, to the point where I would not even notice it.

Tuesday, January 31, 1984:

Tejaswi was still not well; she had vomiting and a bad cough. She was restless at night. She had synchronized her getting up with my getting into the 'nirvikalpa' state. So, no new knowledge came forth, no experiences. Only some vague feeling that something was being done and learnt in my deep sleep.

Wednesday, February 1, 1984:

Tejaswi was worse tonight. In spite of medication, she could not sleep. I decided to see if I could cure her. I concentrated and put my hand on her forehead, and with my third finger, gently pressed the centre of her forehead. Slowly, she quietened down. All became quiet. Tejaswi seemed to have had relief. She appeared to have fallen asleep. But, before I could breathe easy, she was beset with such a spasm of cough and vomiting that I was petrified. She could not breathe. She turned red, and I thought her intestines would come out with the coughing spasm. I vowed that I would never experiment again. I would let things happen on their own. I dared not tell Raja of my experiment. He would have scolded me for playing with the forces before gaining mastery over them. I thought that a doctor would have to be summoned at that ungodly hour. Suddenly, however, Tejaswi appeared to be improving. She definitely looked relieved and at peace. Her eyes looked calm and composed. Soon, she fell asleep. In fact, she slept through the entire next morning and afternoon, waking up occasionally only to vomit out phlegm. When she finally got up at about 5 p.m. the next day, she had no fever, no vomiting, and the rumbling sound in the chest had stopped. She looked around, threw a beatific smile at me, and ran off to play. She seemed cured of her illness.

Thursday, February 2, 1984:

At night, Tejaswi was restless again. I got up in my half-awakened state, and pressed her forehead with my finger. She was reassured and fell into a sound sleep. This time I had done this action without a thought or a conscious motive.

I had a tremendous yearning for Lord Krishna. After a minute or two, I experienced a sublime intoxication, and then felt one with Him. Energy currents, somewhat like electric currents, flowed through my body with great force.

The whole night, I knew I was in a state of deep meditation. I was aware that I was taking long flights into the unknown. I was conscious that some knowledge was being given to me, but I was too lulled to decipher it. Vaguely I knew that there were some 'rishis' and some voice guiding me, educating me. But, in the morning, I remembered little of what they said or did.

Friday, February 3, 1984:

In the morning, I heard that my mother-in-law was suffering from a severe headache. She felt as if someone was hammering at the inside of her head. It was unbearable. A thought came to me, that I could give her relief. I went to her room. She was lying down on her bed. I felt too self-conscious to say anything or do anything. I just sat next to her. Both of us remained silent, each engrossed in some private thought. Suddenly, she got up and said she wanted to visit the bathroom. When she came out, she was talking as if nothing was wrong with her. She had forgotten her headache!

But along with this incident came the admonishing not to make use of this power purposefully. Intentionally doing such things, with a motive, will only generate ego and create a flaw, and stall further progress, besides making the attempt perhaps an unsuccessful one. Such gestures or impulses must come spontaneously and without an ulterior motive; only then would the ego not develop, and the gesture is sure of fulfilment. Desist from such temptation, I was told.

At night, a clear flash came to me, 'Knowledge is me. But I am other than the Knowledge!'

Saturday, February 4, 1984:

A clear message at night: 'I am other than the bliss! Through bliss, you know and understand me, but I am other than the bliss. Bliss is only my state. The bliss you experience in the 'nirvikalpa' is my state. But I am other than this bliss. Only by merging in this state of my bliss can you know and understand me. This is the Infinite Consciousness.

'I have a consciousness—the divine consciousness—which is infinite. This infinite consciousness forms a matrix to contain all my aspects, This matrix contains all the existence, all the awareness, all the bliss and all the knowledge.

'All the existence is me. The born and the unborn. The macrocosm and the microcosm. The universal and the minuscule. All is me.

'All the awareness is me. The vast universal awareness, as also the tiniest individual awareness. All bliss is me. All knowledge is me. Power and kindness spring forth from me. This matrix, like me, is non-existent in form and thus cannot be destroyed. It pervades with me into the all-reaching, far-reaching cosmos, just as it permeates with me into the micro-micro being. Like me, and inseparable from me, this too is eternal, beyond time, beyond cause, without beginning, without end! Devoid of joy, devoid of grief! But still, this is my consciousness. I am other than that! All this springs from me, but I am other than that.

'At your level, whatever is, I am that. At my level, what is, whatever is, is me. But I am other than that.'

Sunday, February 5, 1984:

By now, there was some mastery over the body. There were no aches due to the play of energy, but sleep had taken their place.

Deep sleep would overtake me at any time of the day whenever there was a slight lull in the household work, or if I ever so slightly relaxed, physically or mentally. Sleep from which I would find it difficult to come out. I used to feel drugged as though, of all the layers of sleep, I had sunk to the lowest one. Often in this deep sleep, I would be conscious of being awake. I would be fully conscious of the depth of the sleep, as also of being awake, and of enjoying bliss, all at the same time. Sometimes, I would be conscious of being in deep meditation in this state, sometimes be oblivious of everything, sometimes have meetings with vaguely visible 'rishis', and have equally vague conversations with them. In whatever state of consciousness I would be, it would be pleasurable. But the transition of getting out of sleep into full ordinary wakefulness was discomforting. It was always accompanied by a slight bodyache, headache, ache at the temples, the brow, and the pupils of the eyes. Also, I had to come up through different layers of sleep. The feeling was somewhat akin to the one after an attack of 'flu', only of a lesser intensity.

This feeling of discomfort at the waking stage still persists, though the intensity is less. There is never a feeling of freshness after sleep. It seems that it is one continuous state of simultaneous sleep and wakefulness, where the processes of getting into sleep or coming out of it are mere intrusions.

28

The Lord and His Creation

How does the Lord enjoy His Creation?

The Lord has no form, and so no organs. The Lord is in a state of eternal bliss, and has no mind. Then how does He know or enjoy His own creation?

The Lord has no organs, but the entire universe is His organ of sense or one continuous network of awareness. Through each particle and cell, through each creature and individual, He enjoys His creation. As when you are very happy, small mishaps fail to bother you, and you are in a mood of generosity even towards your adversaries, so is the Lord, who is endlessly in such a state of bliss, not perturbed by the mishaps suffered by creatures of His creation, and is ever in a forgiving mood and continues to remain in a state that brings only enjoyment to Him, no matter what He perceives in His creation.

As all the creatures are His, are born of Him, their joy, sorrow, and sin are His, but His state of eternal bliss does not allow Him to be perturbed by this. This is the 'sthiratha' or sublime stillness of the Lord.

The Lord is all-pervasive and all-permeating. Imagine an invisible cobweb, mighty of dimension, running through the entire universe. Through this cobweb, which connects every particle to Him, the Lord receives impulses. So He sees, hears, knows, smells, feels everything in the universe. He even guides them through this network, but often this guidance is ignored. Through this network only, each particle is connected to the divine Sat-Chit-Ananda. If only that particle could realize this!

As the entire body of the individual knows what he smells, hears, tastes, feels and sees, so does that all-pervading, all-permeating, ever-present supreme Being. This is why He is called 'antaryamin' or the Inner-Being. A true yogi can also become, to a great extent, all-knowing.

Why is the Lord called heartless?

As the Lord seems to be unmoved by the ills and mishaps befalling His creatures, and seems not to hear their cries and prayers, He is sometimes called heartless. The Lord is truly beyond emotions. He is an eternal witness, in a state of true meditation, and is ever still and calm. So He appears to be heartless. He has set rules for His creation, and created gods and prophets to govern it. He is free to remain in bliss and self-absorption.

He is beyond interfering. He allows perfect justice to rule His creation. He allows the superb Law of Karma or the law of deeds to take effect unhampered. As ye sow, so shall ye reap.

This sowing and reaping is spread over a cycle of births. He distributes His calm and stillness, and sends His guidance, should anyone care to receive them. But people want miracles. Miracles are an interference, and the Lord does not interfere. Assured that the Law shall be obeyed, He remains rock-like in eternal bliss. And out of this bliss flows kindness. Kindness and generosity to one and all, in equal proportion. That is why He is also called all-kindness and all-love. To the sinners and the virtuous alike, the same kindness is bestowed.

Only, we do not understand His rule. His laws are unfathomable to us, so we feel He is heartless. But there is a grand design and an intricate pattern, to which even the gods and prophets bow. Laws are obeyed, and rules followed, and nature continues on its course.

Events will take place in accordance with the laws, inspite of prayers. The intensity of the effects of an event might be reduced by prayers. If an anticipated event does not take place after prayers, may be the event was not to take place anyway. All one should pray for is to get the strength to bear the calamity. Then the grief will surely be reduced to more tolerable levels.

29

On Miracles

A miracle implies interfering with nature. Anyone on the path of self-realization finds that he slowly acquires certain powers by which he can perform small miracles. But these are to be shunned. Even the Lord does not interfere with nature. Why should man? These powers are trivial, base temptations offered to the yogi to see if he falls a prey to them. These should be shunned as their exercise can lead to their misuse. There is nothing great or extraordinary in the acquiring of these powers. There are regular formulae or 'mantras' or certain penances prescribed, and by invoking various deities, even a non-yogi can acquire these powers. But then, that individual should be prepared to accept the repercussions, usually detrimental to him for it is a rare yogi who will not eventually end up using these powers for selfish reasons, with an impure heart and with base motives. An occasional miracle performed with sincerity, only to restore faith in the Lord, or one that will not interfere with nature, is allowed, but only when done with a pure heart and in innocence.

For a yogi advancing in purity, as also prophets and true messengers of the Lord, miracles happen on their own. They do not will it nor do they exert at it; just their presence or their remembrance or their touch manifests in miracles, just as the entire miraculous creation manifests from the Lord, effortlessly and without willing it.

Just as the sun remains impervious to all our pleas and cries, and is an abundantly miraculous manifestation of heat and light, equally, every minute of the day, for everyone, irrespective of their hearts and deeds, the Lord too sends his constant guidance, blessings and love for all to share.

Imagine the plight of the world if, like men, the sun were to be moved by his own emotions and moods, and the flattery and supplications of others. Then he would will his manifestation according to his moods and emotions, like a man. He then becomes a being with the limitations of a man, with impurities of the heart, and his manifestation will also fluctuate in power and brilliance. He ceases to be a celestial being having eternal energy, brilliance, splendour and power, worthy of our worship.

Often men and monarchs in the pantheon of Indian mythology have acquired these supernatural powers by chanting 'mantras' and following certain penances. Many have acquired powers comparable to those of the gods. Some have turned these to the good of humanity and become saints, and the rest have misused them and become demons and 'rakshasas'.

When saints are said to perform miracles, the miracles 'get' performed. Not because of the volition of the saints, or their desires, but because, having transcended mind, that is, having gone beyond want, desire, volition, ego, emotion, etc., they become pure consciousness and instruments of the Lord. Miracles are not detrimental to these saints nor do they bring to them ego, arrogance, and other impurities of the mind. As instruments of the Lord, the supernatural things get done around them, for the beneficiaries of these miracles were anyway destined to get succour. Such miracles are not an interference with nature. These were preordained to happen, one way or the other. Saints only become the catalysts.

30

Total Permeability, Equilibrium and Bliss

Monday, February 6, 1984:

This half-asleep, half-awake condition persists day and night. It has a feel of permanence. A quality of stillness, of a deathless calm, in which the world exists and does not exist; in which I am *in* the humankind, yet not *of* it; in which, amid a world of material and forms, I am a special island of isolation where the material seems an illusion. In this, matter is permeable; walls of the cells of every material are permeable, in fact, nebulous. Where are the walls then? I exist in a form subtler than the subtlest component the world is made up of. I am in all of it, inside it, outside it. Then, where are the forms and structures? They are there, as long as the attention is focused on them. They withdraw as soon as the attention is withdrawn from them.

This sense of total permeability is one continuous stream pervading the cosmos, where barriers and walls and hence structures are only a concept, as is a plan of a building in the mind of an architect. He knows each detail of it, he can live in it, expand it, or break it. It is as real as he chooses to make it. The plan is not unreal, the concept is not unreal, but the building is, the structures are. The confusion arises in mistaking this plan, this concept, for reality. The confusion arises in deciding that a building is actually there, and constructing a locale around it. Misery can be avoided by knowing that the building is not real. When this stream flows, barriers break, walls dissolve, and reality stands apart in its proper perspective.

One finds in this stream that structures and forms are binding, limiting, confining—and the reality, free. Free of size, of time, of cause, of birth and death, hence, of joy and grief. A new name arises for this reality that is free of all such binds. It comes to be known as the 'Reality'. The Absolute Reality, the Absolute Truth—The Infinite. The Reality appears stark, stripped of all encumbering layers. It appears crystal-clear. It appears to be everywhere, uniform, radiating, and slowly it dawns on one that Reality is in you, it is you!

But man is oblivious of this continuity, this entirety. He thinks that he lives an isolated, individual, segmented, fragmented life, independent of all. This is his great ignorance, the failure to see the continuity, the oneness, his slot in the grand pattern that exists as one!

In this half-awake, half-asleep condition of mine, when the focus was on work, the equilibrium would tilt towards full wakefulness. But a slight relaxation in the focus on work would lead to a quick dip towards drowsiness. In fact, relaxation brought on this drowsiness. In the wakeful state, the world *is*, the work *is*, the individual *is*.

In the drowsy state, the world receded and, along with it receded the individual me and my private world. Then there was only the Reality and, along with this Reality, there was total bliss and the true knowledge, tranquillity and a feeling of permanence.

I began to live in two worlds simultaneously. One, a world of work and form, the other, a world of Reality and tranquillity. By a mere flick of attention, I could choose to switch my worlds. But slowly I learnt to live in both the worlds simultaneously. To fuse the two worlds. To live with equal focus on both. To work in the world of form with the tranquillity and calmness of the other world.

Tuesday, February 7, 1984:

This was a current of bliss. This current set the body in a state of fine vibrations, so fine, they could only be felt. Even at its highest intensity, no other person could have discerned this state of vibration. Each cell, each component forming the cell, seemed to be in vibration, thereby causing my entire being to be in a state of the ultimate in relaxation. My entire body, to its tiniest component, deep down to the bones, had been made bereft of any tension or any will. There was no mind of my own now. I just existed—in a state of bliss, enjoying the bliss and the total relaxation. My body would be limp, seem heavy, movements deliberate and slow, if any. Thoughts ceased, mind negated. Though fully cognizant of the world, the world ceased to exist. Now there was only existence, cognizance and bliss. Bliss of the ultimate nature!

But there was no joy. The needle of the scales seemed to have got lodged at 'O'. It would neither move towards joy nor towards grief. But there was peace, tranquillity; the peace of the hermitage, of a forest 'ashram'. Peace of such depths that any pleasures of the world paled before it. The world and time stood still in this peace.

31

The Compulsion to Write

Wednesday, February 8, 1984:

There is a growing compulsion to write. Language, though generally adequate and at times even rich, cannot do justice even in a small measure to the enchantment of the super-consciousness and the boundless glory of the Lord, especially when one finds oneself sustaining the universe, when one finds oneself being the source of life, the source of the universe, the font of all power and knowledge. And yet, there is an urge to point out to the world the simplicity and the grandeur of this supra-Being, the sustainer of the world.

I have put pen to the paper, only when the words have come on their own, with no participation on my part in anticipation, and no engaging of the intellect or knowledge. I have not read any of the scriptures, nor have I delved into any of such high-flown topics. Whatever knowledge came naturally and spontaneously, I noted down in two notebooks—in one, I wrote down a day-to-day account of my experiences, and in the other, the knowledge that flowed out. Later I combined the two notebooks.

During the periods when I identified myself with the Lord, I felt that there was an unlimited library of knowledge within me, all knowledge was me, and the words flowed out with no preconception of what to write. There would be an urge to write, and I would go to my desk and lift my pen. Whatever thoughts spilled out, I took them down. Knowledge came from some unfathomable and eternal source in a steady and smooth flow which made memory truly redundant. This applies to Absolute

Knowledge that spurts out during the 'true mood'. This is apart from the worldly knowledge that requires studying and a good memory.

At times I have written when I was in the thick of the current, and totally identified with the Lord. At such times, I have written as the Lord, and when relatively out of it, as a devotee.

Though the urge to write was very strong, the body would be very weak, racking and limp, as if drugged, and each move of the body would be a big chore. But the urge to write would be irresistible, even though I had a tremendous pressure in the head, and I would be unable to hold my head erect, and I would long to go back to a deep sleep.

This is a true and honest narration—I have taken down the words as they came. Certain repetitions are purposely included, as they came with the flow and aptly stress particular points.

Thursday, February 9, 1984:

Feeling very drowsy. Even in sleep, getting a drugged feeling. My body was feeling very light, almost weightless, and yet the movements were deliberate and involved an effort.

Even in deep sleep, I wanted to get into 'kriya'. On the one hand, there was the deep, drugged sleep, and, on the other, a persistent urge to get into 'kriya'. I resorted to mental 'kriya'. Whatever the body movements would have been in a 'kriya' movement, I carried them out in my mind, without moving the body. The movements were concentrated around the neck and head. In the mental 'kriya', I got the same relief and pleasure as I would get in the actual body movements. Appeased, I went to sleep.

During the day, I could get into 'kriya' anytime.

Friday, February 10, 1984:

In deep sleep, I had another experience. I saw in colour, in vista-vision, a gorgeous seascape with golden, cool sands, all bathed in brilliant moonlight. In this molten gold, lay a young couple, deep in love, involved in yogic or ballet-like movements, enjoying love without physical intercourse, only in thought, happy in each other's company. The love they shared for each other was ecstatic and supernal. They had immersed themselves in an ocean of nectar, of fullness, of completion and bliss. There was no need of an intercourse here. They were in a realm that lay beyond matter and body, where bliss and ecstasy effulged.

I had lost my body identity. I was just an onlooker, but not separate from them. I was not on the beach, but I could feel the cool sands and the pouring moonlight. The bliss I was getting was the bliss they were deriving.

I understood in a flash the meaning of 'divine love', and that an intercourse is only at the level of the body and matter where physical union is a must; but that there is a supreme love that transcends the physical love and reaches transcendental heights giving eternal satiation and fullness. There is no nectar other than this bliss, that leaves one ever wantless and desireless. It was beautiful.

I also understood perfectly the eternal witness, the grand cosmic awareness, all-pervasive, ever awake, eternally present, how it experiences all the experience of all the micro and the macro entities of this universe.

32

'Avidya'–Ignorance

Is this world, our life, a myth or a non-reality or a dream?:
If we take the Lord to be true, His manifestation should also be true. If the Lord is real, His manifestation should also be real. So are all of us and our dreams.

Just as we live out our emotions and episodes in dreams, and till such time as a dream lasts, it is a reality, and we allow the dream to take its course, trying to come out of it only if it turns into a nightmare, so is the case with our lives. Just as, only after we awake and gauge our past, present and future life, do we find the dream was not our true life but was a minuscule experience of our mind (real all the same), apart from our true life and with only a momentary repercussion on it, so also, at a very highly developed stage when we can perceive the past, the present and future lives, do we realize that this life is also like a dream, a tiny episode in a long cycle of lives, leaving only a momentary repercussion on it. Till then, this life is a reality, to be endured, just as the dream was a reality and had to be gone through.

What is not a reality is the assumption that it is our true life, and that we are actually taking part in it. Even in a dream, man thinks he is taking part in it, even though actually he is sleeping. The real he was a seer there, and is only a seer even in life. The real he or the 'atma' is watching this bigger dream of the outer life. The illusory he takes part in the dream and is now performing in life. He has to realize that he is apart from the real him, or that the true self is apart from this life also; that actually it is a part of the Lord and not as restricted or confined as he understands it to be. The totality of himself as understood by him is different to the true self that he is.

What is not a reality is the assumption that we are apart or different or bifurcated from the Lord. This is called ignorance or 'avidya' or darkness.

What is not a reality is that the Lord has a form, or that this universe alone is the Lord, or any one aspect of Him as we see or understand it, is the Lord.

Why restrict Him in shape and form, and why confine Him in the binds of a religion? He is beyond all that.

What is not a reality is the assumption that the world of our life is as it appears to us, subject to changes according to our moods and emotions.

What is reality is that this world is the Lord's manifestation, only one aspect of Him, and that we are all part of Him and can become Him. Then the reality is transformed into Reality.

Why must one strive towards Self-realization?

Self-realization only means realizing that the soul or 'atma' of a man is of the same eternal all-pervading principle as the Lord's. The 'atma' of man and the Lord are the same. The 'atma' of man and his body are a replica of the Lord and His universe, undoubtedly in a very small measure, but a replica all the same.

A replica that is a co-partner, a co-sharer, of the eternal truth, Sat-Chit-Ananda. Not only that but the 'Sadguru-tattva' and other principles represented by Brahma, Vishnu and Shiva, which are born of the Lord, are all within us, and can be awakened to the extent that we choose to: 'Sadguru-tattva' or the intellect, Brahma or the creator, Vishnu or the preserver of bliss, Shiva or the curiosity to solve the mysteries of nature.

But just as the Lord knows that He is the creation, yet He is apart, He is the universe, and yet non-existent, He is all-pervading, endless and eternal, yet nothing, so can we be detached in our outlook towards our body, mind and our lives, and live in humbleness, taking all to be our own and our equal.

Just as the Lord knows that He has all the powers, and yet is above moods and emotions, so can we desist from base and ugly emotions. Just as the will of the Lord is directed towards preserving His state of meditation, thereby existing in a state of bliss, we too can direct our intellect towards achieving sublime results.

The Lord knows that all the sins and ills of the world are of His making, just as the good and the sublime are. He showers only kindness, blessing, and love. We too can contemplate and realize that our agitation, grief and discomfort in life are of our own making, and spread peace and happiness around.

In short, the intellect sharpens up. Wisdom, the ability to perceive things correctly and to be able to react to situations appropriately, also develops. Bliss or peace, for which all strive and struggle, will enfold us, and we will be blessed persons. Our deeds and achievements will reflect divinity, and, our lives will assume a brilliance of their own.

Whether true realization dawns or not, or till it dawns, the peace that always eludes us can be brought within our reach by a simple change in our attitude to life. And this peace alone will lead to the eternal peace. Because, all knowledge, achievements and their awareness are of no value without this peace. This peace and the eternal peace are the same; that much we can comprehend and strive for.

33

Samadhi and the Mind

Saturday, February 11, 1984:

Not easy to get out of sleep nowadays, as some deep, unfathomable process seems to be going on. Also, the current keeps on passing through the body.

Sunday, February 12, 1984:

Lethargy is less, as also bodyache.

Monday, February 13, 1984:

In my deep sleep, I saw thoughts flitting across like fireflies. Thoughts would spring up, flit across, and die down like the sparks from a roaring fire disappearing in mid-air.

These thoughts could be kept at bay and a no-thought condition could be maintained. That much mastery I had. This control can be cultivated.

Thus was revealed that thoughts originate in the expanse of the mind, outside the purview of the self. They can be kept at bay, and self-composure maintained. Also, the thoughts flitting across can be scanned, entertained or rejected.

Hitherto, I used to slip into 'nirvikalpa' samadhi rapidly. Occasionally, I would get a premonition of its approach. Tonight, I witnessed the process of getting into the 'nirvikalpa' state, as though I was my own observer. I saw my body identity being slowly demolished. I saw myself then slipping into a deep, deep oblivion, and like the flame of the wick, being snuffed out. The entity getting into 'nirvikalpa' disappeared; only the witness remained who was watching this other being getting into 'nirvikalpa'. So there was one part of me watching the other part receding and then suddenly vanishing. Now only the witness remained in solitary glory, brilliant, glowing, pulsating, enjoying the state of Bliss.

Suddenly a message flashed: 'This is the witness the Gita speaks of. The eternal, ever-wakeful Witness, pure, stark: 'alive'. This is the real you. This witness has to be emphasized, magnified, developed, till He alone presides in your life, till all actions and thoughts are rooted in this, till He alone shines, becoming the guiding beacon of your life.'

I now understood the real meaning of the Gita.

I continued to be in 'nirvikalpa'. Tejaswi woke up and cried out. I sat up, patted her, covered her up again, and waited till she went back to sleep. Throughout, I remained in the 'nirvikalpa'. The stream of the 'nirvikalpa' state had not been broken.

Tejaswi got up again and again. As many times, I sat up, made her sleep, and yet remained in this state of glory. I was now conscious of my surroundings, of Tejaswi, of her getting up, my being awake, watching everything, doing what was needed, and yet I was pulsating with divine life. I was in that divine ecstasy, my body was in a state of the most subtle vibration, and I was the sheer witness Lord Krishna speaks of in the Gita.

It is the individual who gets into samadhi and finally into the 'nirvikalpa' state. The individual or the mind has to go through these various stages. Once the 'nirvikalpa' sets in, and the mind or the individual is no more, the shining, universal self remains, uncovered and unveiled now in solitary splendour and grandeur.

Initially, I would get into this samadhi only for a few moments at a time. That too, in my sleep. But these few moments were enough for my education.

Great spiritual masters may remain in this state for a longer period, all depending upon the intensity of their state.

This state need not be only in the state of purposeful meditation. It can be shining forth in the midst of all activity, in the wake of living and waking, in the very act of going through life and with full awareness of one's surroundings, as also of this Great Self. This can be a permanent state.

Types of Samadhi:

'Savikalpa' samadhi: Concentrating on a particular deity or on a 'mantra' stills the mind and stops it from wandering. This leads to pure samadhi—the individual is there, that is, the individual mind is there but at rest. It is centred on the deity or the 'mantra'. The object of concentration slowly dulls and becomes smaller and smaller till it disappears. Now there might be total oblivion, void or nothingness, and the body will be still. Now there is nothing to concentrate upon, and the mind suddenly relaxes. This transcended mind that has negated the seed or the 'beeja' of concentration reaches the state where, remaining in a relaxed samadhi, it regains the awareness of its surroundings.

'Nirvikalpa' samadhi: Here, the body is in samadhi, and is still and motionless; and the mind has totally lost its individual identity, and is experiencing various aspects of the Lord. This is his education through intimate experiencing. The mind is free and un-centred.

'Nirvikalpa' mind: He transcends the above state when his education is over for the time being, and reaches a state of 'nirvikalpa' mind, when his body and individual identities are both there, as also his cosmic identity. There is contradiction here, in that the moment the cosmic identity is found, no identity is left. Yet the identity is retained in a very, very subtle way.

Now the mind is always dynamically thoughtless or in a state of samadhi, even when the body is in full activity, carrying on any chore of normal living. This is the 'nirvikalpa' state of the mind.

'Sahaja' samadhi : There is duality as well as non-duality. There is a fine equilibrium between body-samadhi and the mind, between the ordinary and the divine. This is 'sahaja' samadhi where, without being functionless, without being immobile, the being enjoys constantly all the benefits of a high samadhi. No conscious effort is required to be in this samadhi. The being is in this state as he has reached and got established in this state.

'Nirvikalpa' and 'sahaja' samadhi are identical. Here the body is in action as well as in samadhi. 'Nirvikalpa' is the mind; samadhi is of the body. Each leading one to the other.

The merger of one state into the other, the transcendence of the mind, the gradual changes of body and mind, could be a quick or a slow process. An individual can get stuck in a particular state for a shorter or a longer period, all depending upon the progress in the purity of his being.

Of course, this is also the time when the mind can·slip back into the gross mind and get back ego, emotion, etc., and fall a prey to temptations.

An individual may also find himself skipping some of these stages, and surging forward rapidly in this path of self-discovery.

Tuesday, February 14, 1984:

We met an astrologer. On an impulse, Raja showed him my horoscope and asked him to tell what I might be going through at present. The astrologer pondered over my horoscope for a long time, made some calculations, and though Raja had not mentioned anything about my experiences to him, the astrologer said that my horoscope was highly extraordinary, and that from January 5 to 20 in 1984 there had been such a conjunction of stars as to very obviously lead me through spiritual experiences of a very high order, going on to true enlightenment. He said that I must have been in 'turyavastha' (the 'fourth state') and my body must have been rocking and dancing to an unknown tune and rhythm. When we hinted that something of the sort did happen, he said that the state of 'turyavastha' would be repeated very strongly in March 1986, and eventually it would become permanent. He said that my horoscope clearly indicated 'soubhagya' (well-being), contentment, 'mangalya' (auspiciousness) and happiness; that all my wishes as a housewife and as a mother would be fulfilled. He also said that this state must have occurred to me every six years since my birth, but that I had somehow missed catching it, whereas this time I could not miss it as it had been pretty strong.

The inner current was very powerful today and there was heat in the current.

Wednesday, February 15, 1984:

'Kriya' still continuing. Lion still roaring. Drowsiness too continuing. Experience of 'nirvikalpa' still continues, and I realize how true was what I had written earlier about 'nirvikalpa', that it can become stabilized in the midst of action.

With mastery, awareness too sharpens in this state. I also realized that this state is not a void, a vacuum, 'shunyata', but it is a complete whole, perfect, encompassing all, and that this is the beginning of a new life. By acquiring mastery, one slowly becomes progressively a bigger part of the whole; the periphery widens; cosmic awareness, true knowledge, awareness of bliss all sharpen, and one becomes a partaker of a bigger share of Sat-Chit-Ananda.

34

Freedom and the Projected World

Thursday, February 16, 1984:

Mind blank and peaceful. No thoughts. Slight pain in the body. Sleep deep and drugged.

In my deep sleep, I became aware of a tingling sensation in my throat. This tingling sensation was galloping up and down the throat in a rhythmic manner. It was very pleasant, with a light touch. It then increased in speed and intensity, like a tiny fan rapidly moving up and down, creating pleasurable vibrations.

As suddenly as it had started, it stopped.

Friday, February 17, 1984:

Same experience in the throat, but for a longer period and of a stronger intensity.

Saturday, February 18, 1984:

I saw clearly that the world I lived in now had no grief in it. I saw with a stunning clarity that man drew upon himself sorrow where there was none. That there was no sorrow was so clear that I wondered why others could not see it as I could. This clarity was strewn everywhere, for everyone to see. Yet man built a world for himself, riddled with emotion, thought and attachment, and super-imposed it on this untainted world and brought misery upon himself.

I wondered why people were so concerned, so bothered, were even frantic. Did it really matter?

According to their thoughts and emotions, they were trying to project a world for themselves and for others, and again, according to their thoughts and emotions, they were scanning other worlds, projected in turn for their benefit. Was that reality? Could they not see reality? Reality, free of encumbrances, free of misery, agony, sorrow? Reality that meant complete freedom, liberation?

Freedom from thought. Freedom from emotions, freedom from expectations, from attachments, from projections, from disappointments and disillusions. Freedom from sorrow and grief.

Sunday, February 19, 1984:

I could not get over the fact that people could not see what I saw, could not feel what I felt, when reality was so abundantly and obviously splashed across. The world and its sorrows seemed so frivolous, so trivial, so inconsequential. The principle that governed me, governed them. Yet they could not see, just as I had not seen it all these years. The principle monitoring my vision was the same one monitoring theirs, yet it required a heightening of awareness to pick up the extremely sensitive and subtle impulses of reality. Everyone finally rises to this heightened awareness. Providence allows ample time for this heightening, to the extent of it being without limit. Each one is allowed to take his own time, follow his own path, till this glory becomes his.

Freedom or liberation or 'nirvana' is not a place to reach, a destination. It is only a state where there is freedom from thought, and thereby from emotions. This leads to freedom from sorrow and agony. Liberation from sorrow and agony immediately drops one onto the lap of 'ananda' or bliss.

'Ananda', true knowledge, awareness of pure existence, all are one homogeneous whole. Experience of one immediately and automatically leads man to the others. This bliss, this knowledge and this awareness are eternal, not momentary.

35

Experiences II

Monday, February 20, 1984:

Visited the Sadguru: He told me to continually identify myself with the Infinite Force and to experiment with it for my personal evolution and enhancement, but never for improving our business or with the ostensible motive of helping others. With time, I will slowly develop telepathy, intuition, etc, but I should never take undue advantage of it or exploit this force, only develop it in a casual manner. Do not take myself too seriously. He also said never to guide others with the aid of these faculties nor try to steer my own life with them, as such faculties will mislead me often as also develop my ego, 'ahamkara'. Do it for fun. You cannot change destiny, so do not let them be your guiding forces. At least, not yet.

When I started identifying with this Infinite Force, the inner current became very powerful.

Tuesday, February 21, 1984:

At night, I was a ball of light rapidly spinning around Shri Anandamayee Ma, a great living saint, who appeared to be seated by my side. She was dressed all in white. After whizzing around her a few times, the ball of light that was me entered Anandamayee Ma and merged into her.

After some time, I found myself again circling her, in a similar brisk manner. But now I had no form. In my non-existent form, I entered her.

The third time around Anandamayee Ma, still in a sitting

posture, and then I was her. We two were one. A ball of fire, this time it was neither me nor not me, orbited several times around the seated dual personality, and entered us.

Then a non-existent ball orbited around us, and entered us.

The first time, there was a distinct duality. I as the sphere revolving round Ma was aware of only myself, my movement, and I saw Ma as a separate identity. After merging with her or the Infinite that she is, I could feel the movements of the other fire-ball also. I could feel it enter me. There was no thought or question as to whether or not this fire-ball was me. It was a pure witness observing a sphere orbiting, and experiencing the movement, and seeing it disappear in me. There was no identification, no emotion, no surprise, no thought of oneness or of duality witnessing this. All seemed perfectly natural and as it ought to be.

After merging, there was first a total blanking out. Then a sudden cosmic awareness, with Ma as me, and the other sphere as myself and yet distinct from me.

Wednesday, February 22, 1984:

The energy that usually pours into me is always formless and colourless. Tonight, it was distinctly like the pouring down of rays of shining moonlight, and I felt an aura of glow in and around my body. Even the internal cells glowed luminously. It was beautiful.

Thursday February 23, 1984:

Saw the dark of the night crowded out by the faces of many children arrayed before me. Faces of varying degrees of beauty, from different families, from different countries, of different financial strata. Each one looked happy and beautiful. They were all smiling. And, I saw vividly a uniform, homogeneous current of innocence, of purity, of chastity, of cleanness, of delicacy and sinlessness, a resurgence of love, passing through each one of them. This current slowly became so powerful that it obscured any differences in their beauty and other features, and cast them into an identical mould of bliss and innocence, so much so that I could not differentiate one face from the other. Not even Tejaswi's, who was also in the vision.

What is true of the child is true of the grown-ups. All have the same homogeneous undercurrent of innocence and purity. In essence, they all are one, undifferentiated, whole.

Friday, February 24, 1984:

The vibratory movement in the throat was very powerful. It went up and down the throat. Now at the front and now at the back of the gullet. Now all over. Now as if a big butterfly was fluttering and touching the different nodes of the vocal chords, as if it was gyrating on the keys of a piano. Swirling, racing and tip-toeing.

I saw at once how the entire throat is like a harmonium with different sets of octaves. To emit different notes, we have to press on different keys and bring different parts of the throat into play.

We need only to know which part of our throat is to be brought into play, to get a clear mastery over each note of the octaves in our singing.

I experimented, and found myself singing without much difficulty in a range that I could never before have managed. In a moment, I had improved my range.

During my afternoon siesta, I found my breath being directed upwards towards the brain, instead of towards the lungs. I was half-awake now, and observed this process. It was very comfortable, and I found it brought with it an immense feeling of equilibrium.

Slowly I woke up, but I tried to maintain the upward flow of breathing. This was a rare instance of my doing something of my own volition, and I found I could manage it. I breathed thus for quite some time without any feeling of suffocation.

The moment there was some distraction, and the state of half-awake, half-asleep meditation was broken, this stream of upward breathing discontinued.

Later on, in the evening, I often reverted to this unusual form of breathing, and I found that I could, on my own, restart this process. The state of half-awake, half-asleep meditation was continuing.

Thereafter, once this stream of meditation was broken, it was not possible for me to once again induce it on my own efforts.

36

The No-Mind

Saturday, February 25, 1984:

There was a great pressure in the head.

In the state I am in nowadays, I feel no joy, no grief. When I search for the mind, there is no mind. There is a great emptiness. But this emptiness is not melancholic or desolate; it is peaceful, intelligent, and brings a feeling of tranquillity and a sense of permanence. I feel cleansed and free. The state of no-grief, no-joy, removed all burdens away. It made me feel light and uncluttered. The needle stayed put at the zero of the balance. Absence of joy did not mean misery. It only meant un-budging supreme equanimity, calmness, stillness, and deep silence. All expressions of joy are fleeting, and are capable of swinging back to a point which can bring sorrow. This peace, contentment, and fullness, which wiped out want or dissatisfaction, was permanent and blissful, and brought one to a state where nothing mattered, as each moment was perfect and complete in itself.

Sunday, February 26, 1984:

I also observed that there was no past and no future. I was living in the present. This disallowed any thought formation; and peace pervaded throughout. Conversely, as there was no thought there was no past or future. The past is also a thought, a memory, or acquired knowledge. The future is again a thought, a hope, an expectation. In the absence of this past or future, there was the supreme serenity of the present. Thoughtless. Incapable of misery, of want or hope. With no hope or want of future to clutter up the mind, nor any agonizing memory of the past, there was a supernal calm.

I was mostly an onlooker now, witnessing the present, and observing things as they are, without associating them with either hope for the future or rage against the past.

My actions were also now based on these observations. This does not mean that I was vegetating. I was active, running a household, looking after a family, and whatever else this involved. Right thoughts came spontaneously at the right time; they were neither distracted nor tainted by my own unnecessary or emotional, and thereby biased, thinking. These right thoughts made me take right actions whilst a stream of calmness, stillness, a clarity of mind was maintained of its own.

Monday, February 27, 1984:

I pondered today whether there was any marked change in me after these experiences. I concluded that there was one change. Yet there was hardly any change. Even from childhood I had this inner peace, this composure, this feeling of nearness to God. Earlier, there was duality and I used to get visions and dreams of God. Now, I had experiences of a state of non-duality, a feeling of 'I am everywhere; all is me, all reside in me; I am the eternal witness; wherever, whatever happens, I am a witness to it.'

But once a particular period of non-duality is over, I revert to the same familiar composure and inner peace. The same inner world of self-absorption. Earlier, I was not conscious of this peace. My attention was not focused on it. Now it is. I am constantly aware of this calm, this equanimity, which is the essential nature of the self. Being self-conscious is also an integral part of the self. The self, being self-absorbed, is always conscious of the bliss, the peace, this ambrosia. It is deriving this from itself. Its mere existence is offering it.

It is deriving this bliss from itself as also from the expanse of the universe which is also It. It is deriving this bliss from the minutest particle which is also It. And the Self is conscious of this pleasure, this bliss, this peace.

But, as before, I live in the present. The experiences and the consciousness of 'I am' are quickly forgotten, and all that remains, when not experiencing this state, is this awareness of peace and a feeling of goodwill.

Tuesday, February 28, 1984:

When I say there is no mind, I mean thereby that there is an absence of thought, and thus of joy and misery. The mind does not get negated. Mind has to remain to perceive, experience, and to live intelligently. What is meant by negation of mind is that the apparent turbidity of mind, its entangling cobwebs, its clutter, its distinct wanton restlessness, its unsettling wants and desires are removed. Mind becomes so clean, so still and unwanting that it appears to have effaced itself. But, in reality, it has become cleansed and purified of the extraneous activities that are familiar to man, and is now in harness, stilled, and made extremely subtle. It exists, though now its existence is rooted in its own purity.

37

Living in the Present

Wednesday, February 29, 1984:

Today is 'Shivaratri', the night of Lord Shiva. Went to take the 'darshan' of Swami Shri Paridnyanashram, our community guru.

At night, I had the 'darshan' of Shri Anandamayee Ma. The vision repeated itself thrice.

First, I saw her sitting, in white, gazing steadily at me. Immediately, I went into a difficult 'kriya', which frightened me, and I got up.

After some time, I saw Ma again, surrounded by her devotees and me. They all wanted 'japa-diksha' (initiation), from her. Ma was writing down 'japa-mantra', and giving it to everyone. All departed after receiving it. Now only I was left with her. She had only one piece of paper left. She wrote down something on it, and, though I had not asked for it, she gave it to me.

Peace and calm of an unusual type descended on me and enveloped me. But along with this, the muscles of my eye-balls seemed to acquire a life of their own, and started vibrating and zigzagging in the sockets. Again, disturbed, I got up.

I tried to go back to sleep. I saw Ma again gazing at me. Whilst gazing back at her, I fell into a deep samadhi. I was sleeping, and yet I was in meditation; I was also aware of my surroundings, and that all my 'chakras' were throbbing, and that I was immersed in vibration, energy and bliss.

Thursday, March 1, 1984:

It was on this day twenty-five years back that our previous community guru, Swami Shri Anandashram, had initiated our present guru Swami Paridnyanashram as his 'shishya', disciple.

There was celebration in the community 'math' at Khar to mark the anniversary. The celebrations were simple but moving. The lamps, the 'aratis', the 'puja', the tinkling bells, gave voice to the devotion our community felt towards the guru.

Friday, March 2, 1984:

On January 11, I had been told to offer my salutations to Raja's Sadguru; to our esteemed friend Mr. Nemlekar; to our community guru, Swami Paridnyanashram; and to our 'kuladevata' (ancestral deity), Shri Mangesh (Lord Shiva), in the temple in Goa; and to take their blessings.

To the Sadguru and to Mr. Nemlekar, I had gone personally and told of my experiences, and taken their blessings. Today, in the morning, Raja, our cousin Vasanti, and I went to the 'math' in the suburb of Khar to take blessings from our community guru. I told Swamiji briefly of my experiences and, listening attentively to me, he too said that what I am experiencing is the eternal 'sakshi'—the eternal witness—Lord Krishna talks of in the Gita. He said that this 'sakshi' has to be developed, and that life itself must be rooted in this 'sakshi'.

He said, 'Our blessings are always with you.'

Living in the present has become a way of life. This involves self-absorption, and results in an undercurrent of nectarine, mellifluous feeling of well-being. Time stops, thoughts stop, and wherever the gaze turns, there is a stamp of permanence and peace.

There is no burden of memory or knowledge. There is no bind of hope or anticipation. Thus, with no past as such, no future as such, the present is accepted in its totality, for itself. This total merger in the present, this lack of any expectation from the present, brings peace and stability grounded in the sublime 'ananda'.

'Living' cannot be ignored. Living brings with it grief, disappointment, rage, etc. These do not disappear. These cannot be wiped out. But, grounded firmly in the sublime 'ananda', the disappointments of life acquire a fleeting, a less consequential, a less intense, a more tolerable, a surmountable gravity. One's composure is maintained even through difficult phases in life. Even calamities are rendered less grievous.

This does not mean that the person becomes heartless or insensitive. It only means that, even amid tragedy and catastrophe, the rude shock is absorbed in a more serene way without losing one's bearings and without feeling that the world has come to an end. It also keeps one equanimous during prosperity and good fortune.

Total involvement in the present, or being totally absorbed in the present, is akin to samadhi. It shuns thought of past and future; the individual is now a pure witness of the present, involved in his work with purity and sincerity. The samadhi-like state is not marred by the lurking, alienating thought. Wisdom, clarity of thought, clear perception of reality and pure knowledge dawn automatically. Intellect sharpens, and solutions to problems arise of their own. Intuitive flashes occur.

Mindlessness does not mean carelessness or laziness or emptiness or dullness of mind. It only means a cleansed mind. Memory sharpens without becoming a hindrance or a drag. Right thoughts come at the right time. Right impulse to work comes. Future planning comes. Senses too become sharp. What does not come is the hope or the expectation of a reward for the toils. What does not come is the memory of the past grief or rage. So, in short, right thought, devoid of misery, comes. Devoid of expectations. When there is no disconcerting memory, nor any expectations of the future, life becomes erased of disappointments, of depressions, of melancholy. It becomes dynamic.

Mind is thought. Thought means emotions, hopes, memory. Erase the thought, erase the emotions, good or bad, erase hope and disappointments, erase the memory, and the mind will be stilled. It will be conjoined to some soothing, guiding, revealing source. Some eternal source that is effulgent, generous, radiating, and all-encompassing.

Such a negated mind will see objects or life with a dazzling clarity, as if for the first time, without the aid of memory or previously acquired knowledge.

38

The Dance of Shiva

Saturday, March 3, 1984:

I found myself circling the front courtyard at our community 'math' at Khar in deep sleep, as if I was doing 'pradakshina', (circumambulation), around our community guru. Suddenly, a thick beam of light came from the building of the 'math', and entered me. I wondered as to how this could happen when Swamiji was not there. He had left for Madras the previous morning. Immediately the answer came: So what if Swamiji is not there. 'Guru-parampara' is there. I then noticed that the beam entering me was actually coming from the photographs of the earlier Swamijis.

Thus was I made aware of the truth of 'Guru-parampara', the spiritual link-chain binding a guru to his disciple. The disciple in turn assumes the mantle of a guru, and passes his grace and his spiritual authority to the next qualified one, thus giving rise to a spiritual lineage, a heritage, which has a palpable continuing strength to it, and which is embodied in the living representative, thus clothing him with an enhanced aura of authority.

Sunday, March 4, 1984:

The vibrations and fluttering of the throat muscles were very powerful and, even in deep sleep, I could make out that some guttural sounds were arising without any volition on my part. The muscles of the upper regions of the throat were coming into play.

Monday, March 5, 1984:

The activity of the throat continued.

Later, when I was engrossed in the rhythm of my breathing, I became aware that the entire environment was engaged in a gigantic cosmic dance, a grand rhythm, whereby particles of matter were created and destroyed throughout the cosmos in a definite pattern. The vibrations of the body became pronounced. My 'chakras' began throbbing, and I saw the atoms of the elements vibrating all around me. The whole universe was vibrating with me. It was dancing. Thus, the house in front, the trees, the shrubs, the flowers, all were now a part of this rapidly pulsating, dancing, twinkling veil. A dancing veil within which subtle, golden birds were flitting around on golden flowers. People of shimmering gold walked past. It was altogether an amazing world of dance and gold.

It was the dance of cosmic energy, vibrant and humming. The soothing hum emerging out of this cosmic pulsation was reverberating gently all over. It was nectarine in its effect on me. This, I realized, was the sacred Aum. When the Unmanifest manifests, the process creates the primal sound Aum that contains everything, and becomes everything. I realized that this was the Energy Form of the universe before it was transformed into denser and denser material by 'Maya', a world which then could be experienced and enjoyed by the senses. This cosmic phenomenon, this all-pervasive beat and music and drama of creation, I saw, was the Dance of Shiva, the Lord of destruction, destroying, to create anew, destroying, for life to continue.

This dance made motion and change the essential features of the nature of things. As the matter became denser, the dancing specks became brighter and vibrated more vigorously. Because of differences in their subtlety and mode of vibration, each thing was distinct from the other, clear and recognizable, retaining its size, shape and texture. They were coming into existence and disappearing in a systematic and precisely individualistic way, that gave the whole environment its intricate, twinkling, pulsating, glowing nature of alternating light and dark. This was a world of pure energy. A throbbing, pulsating energy that seemed to be the mainstay of the cosmos.

I saw the basic unity of the universe and the mutual inter-relationship of all things. I saw the continuity that runs through all, and I realized that the goal for everyone should be to see this unity, this harmony, and feel the oneness of it all, to transcend the slippery notion of an isolated individual self and a fragmented existence, and to identify with the Ultimate Reality. This is the piercing of the veil of 'Maya'. This is the demolition of 'Avidya', spiritual ignorance. This is true knowledge.

39

The Stopping of the Breath 1

Tuesday, March 6, 1984:

Suddenly, I found that the feeling of drugged sleep had left me. Losing no opportunity, I began catching up with all the neglected work. I began spring-cleaning of the house.

Wednesday, March 7, 1984:

Bodyache had gone. Vibrations had gone. The drugged feeling had gone! There was a sudden burst of energy, and the mood to clean up the house continued for the second day.

Thursday, March 8, 1984:

Again, the muscles of the throat were very active. Sometimes, there would be gentle vibrations; sometimes, the muscles would struggle to bring out a sound.

And then, suddenly, I felt the muscles from all around the neck and the throat sticking to each other, pressing upon each other, and closing the throat passage. But there was no suffocation nor any discomfort. The muscular constriction continued, and then I became aware of a passage from the throat going right up into my brain. Halfway up this passage, some other muscles came into play and sealed off the cavity. My breathing stopped. The world came to a standstill, and an immense feel of equanimity and balance arose in me. I became aware of my life-force concentrated in the part of the cavity leading right up to the thousand-petalled mystic lotus in the head. This part had not sealed up. The concentration of energy or life-force here threw me into a state of deep samadhi. I did not lose my awareness of the surroundings, but I was not in this world either. I was traversing along the fine border between two worlds, the zone that separated the two worlds. Did I say separated? No, in fact, that zone linked the two worlds. Did I say I was not in this world? Nay, I was in both the worlds—the mundane and the ethereal, feasting upon the nectar the two worlds have to offer.

Friday, March 9, 1984:

Heard a voice come out of the throat, though no throat muscles moved.

Saturday, March 10, 1984:

I felt my gaze had turned inward. I was relaxing. Slowly, my eyes closed, and I felt that my eyes had suddenly somersaulted inward. Instead of my gaze being in front, it was inward, as if the lenses had focused onto the brain. The interior eye muscles were coming more into play. I got the impression that rays of light were coming from within me, hitting the lenses and merging back in me.

Tuesday, March 13, 1984:

I have begun to get an occasional pressure or heaviness in the head. The pressure falls off on its own after some time. Today, I found this pressure was coming in waves, rising and subsiding.

Thursday, March 15, 1984:

Tried to do some physical exercises after all these days. Immediately, my mind blanked out. I felt no thought could ever enter this dense mind. There was a complete blockage of thought, of even simple cognition, so much so that the brain refused to acknowledge the fact that I wanted to exercise, and even which move to make next. I felt this blankness pervade my whole being. I lay there a long time just staring, mindless, thoughtless, unmoving and unblinking.

Slowly, 'kriya' started. Head began nodding. Mind was totally withdrawn, though, slowly, awareness of peace and bliss came; there was no movement of body or mind. I gave up the idea of doing any exercises. Immediately, the blockage lifted, and I felt light and active. I got up and walked away.

The whole day there were extremely powerful vibrations.

I have mentioned earlier that I often felt drugged and terribly drowsy. Now, I became aware that whenever these spells of drowsiness approached, there was a gradual withdrawal of senses, the tongue became heavy, my speech got garbled, ending in drowsiness, and finally in sleep.

This was a state of samadhi where there was a withdrawal of senses, but not of awareness. I also found that it is the mind that makes the organs work. The sharper or more evolved the mind, the sharper or purer are the perceptions of the senses and organs. If the mind withdraws, the senses withdraw and so does the bodily activity. That is why, when the mind is indrawn, man cannot see, hear, feel or smell what is so evident around him.

In samadhi, body activity stops, as the mind gets stilled and poised. Now no activity of body or mind is there, till the mind transcends further and merges with the divine.

40

Merging in the Lord

Saturday, March 17, 1984:

Of late, I was finding myself drawn deeper into the merging with
the Lord. I was not doing conscious meditation, exercises, yoga,
or any form of worship. But I found that, in between my chores
or even during chores which did not require full concentration, I
would get lost in the contemplation of the Lord. There was no
'japa' or chanting going on in my mind, but to the exclusion of
thoughts, my mind would be tuned into some unnamed,
unclassified, nothingness. But by the peace, tranquillity, and the
feeling of love that descended upon me and the feeling of well-
being that pervaded me, I knew I was in communion with God.
I could not, by resolve, sit down to get into this mood, but,
gradually, without any effort or planning on my part, I would
get drawn into this heavenly mood, and derive immense pleasure
from it. There was such fullness and contentment in me at these
times that, apart from perhaps the chirping of the birds, I would
not notice anything else. Of course, all my chores I was continuing
to do, more out of habit, I guess, and by some inner guidance.
Nothing in the world seemed to matter any more. This peace
was so stabilizing that I found myself, at all times, staring away at
nothing at all. Even my body would not move. I would be
absolutely still and staring, breathing in the elixir of happiness
and bliss.

There was, in this state, such a feeling of fullness and completion
that there was no void of any unfulfilled want or need in any
form. Desire could not make an entry here. There was only a
wish here for permanence and continuity, and a feeling that

eternities of this state would not be out of place. The stillness of the mind would be so deep as would put to shame the stillness of the deep waters of the ocean. As much as thoughts and emotions caused agitation of the mind, an absence of these brought about only a peace and silence of the outer space.

Sometimes, I would get lost in the contemplation of Lord Krishna. I would derive nectar from that name. There was no passion in me at this time, no yearning, not even worship in my heart. But the thought of Him would be there in the background. I would be lost to this world, lost to myself. I would be wandering in some world beyond, where the mere thought of Him would steep me in ambrosia. My heart would be stilled, and I would be in deep repose in some unfathomable quietude. In this hush, I would be infused with a love divine, where nothing existed except that mood and this thought of Him. In this beatific mood, when it was a sacrilege to define this mood or even to take His name, I would lose my identity and merge with Him. This was bliss. This was ecstasy. All I would be aware of was a merger in Him and His eloquent smile that bespoke that He knew!

41

Cellular Awareness and Cellular Transformation

Monday, March 19, 1984:

I realized that there is a Truth beyond truth. That the two worlds are essentially one. There is no duality. But this Truth beyond truth had to be realized by seeking first the Knowledge of Reality. But this Reality had to be first identified by seeing the Lord as one's own tradition conceives of Him, in the way one's mind has been conditioned by one's religion and upbringing and by the individual understanding of what God is.

After transcending this individual notion of God above, one gets to the true knowledge of God or of the Ultimate Reality. Then there is a firm conviction that God is continuous with the concrete. Both are one and the same. There is no demarcation. The world is but an extension of the Lord.

Tuesday, March 20, 1984:

Whenever I sat thus in the realm of peace, a feeling akin to being in the 'nirvikalpa' samadhi descended on me, in my awakened state. The 'chakras' in the nose, forehead, both the temples and cheeks, would throb, and I would begin to stare fixedly, without bodily movements. With this, would come the state of no-thought, no-feelings, no-mind, and a peaceful though intelligent blankness, along with the feeling of my entire being concentrated at one point.

There was a tremendous but unexpressed feeling of 'bhakti', intense devotion, towards an unidentified or formless God, and a feeling of merger with God. Though I had previously experienced a merger with the Reality, again there was heightened awareness of these particular aspects during these experiences.

Wednesday, March 21, 1984:

When I sat down to write this morning, I found that my brain had stopped functioning. There was a sudden blocking of the brain. No thoughts, no words, no sentences were being formed. Normally, words and ideas came out in an easy and powerful flow. Ideas took shape without a conscious or laborious effort either by the mind, reason or intellect, and even without prior knowledge of the topic. At the root of all this writing has been an irresistible urge to write down my experiences, and the knowledge that is being revealed to me.

But, today, there was a sudden drying up of the flow. There was no memory, no episodes to recount, no ideas to impart. No thought was either entering my mind or leaving it.

The head seemed filled with a leaden mass, quite unlike during meditation or samadhi. The denseness and the weight of the brain began increasing, along with a pressure at the temples and in the head.

As this worsened, I left the desk and lay down on the bed. The head now felt like an oil-soaked lump of clay, impenetrable and seemingly still increasing in size. I had, as it were, suddenly lost a fine and sharp brain.

The pressure increased and my gaze turned inward. The effect was unlike in the past few weeks. It was neither sleepiness nor a drugged feeling nor the peculiar weakness I had been prone to recently. Nor was it meditation. This was a new process altogether. All I was aware of was the pressure and the clogging. With the increased pressure, the nerve centres at the nose, temples, cheeks, and the brow, were set in a state of vibration. A feeling akin to going into the 'nirvikalpa' state descended. The awareness of all the nerve centres of the body sharpened. All my muscles were in a state of gentle vibration now, somewhat like a column of air set in fine motion by a vibrating tuning-fork.

Gradually, I got the impression that my body, as also my head, was becoming lighter and expanding in size. A time came when my physical body was inadequate for this expansion. My subtle body slipped out of the gross body, and now, with no restrictions, expanded further. The air, the space, and me were one. On the one hand, I was the subtle body, which had merged with the universe and which was still diffusing further into the infinite, in the process losing its own identity; and, on the other, I was the gross body which also I could feel and which lay inert on the bed. I must have dozed off in that condition. I dreamt that the Sadguru and his wife were entering the house of our neighbour, whom they did not know. Instantly, I knew that, as my stoppered-up mind was denying them an entry, even in the dream, so they were planning to rest there, having come so far and not wanting to return home till I allowed them entry into my mind.

I woke up after about twenty minutes. The head still felt clogged. The lightness had gone, but the pressure persisted. All the nerve centres were still blazing away. Now I began feeling energy all through the body. The awareness of energy increased, and, I could feel each cell in my body infused with energy. Now, my awareness of the cells increased. I could feel the vibration of each cell of my body, no matter how deep in the interior it was. The actual process of vibration can best be illustrated by the working of the vortex that is brought into play in a kitchen mixer. All the outer mass is sucked in at the centre and suddenly seems to disappear, only to re-appear at the periphery in a reversing of the direction of the movement of the liquid or paste in the mixer. The process of disappearance into a centre and reappearance goes on continuously. I found that the process that goes on in each body cell was energizing it, revitalizing it. There was almost a palpable yearning in each cell for this process of vibrations converging to a point, being sucked into disappearance, into a non-existence, then reverse-vortexing back into the fullest expansion to form the entire periphery, and again getting pulled back into the centre. Again and again, the same movement.

I realized that this was the basis of all manifestation, this disappearing into a pin-point of non-existence, re-energizing, and once again emerging into the manifest. The cosmic cycle of the entire universe followed the same pattern. A constant destruction or disappearance and rebirth of particles of the universe. The bigger groups and the star systems too followed the same system.

The energized state of the body is a peculiar state; it is neither drowsiness nor tiredness, neither pain nor weakness, and yet the body is so limp, so incapable of moving. And yet there is immense potential in it, and an unborn will. Here there is capacity for the inertia to suddenly become dynamic, once the will returns. The body is limp and inactive, as it has totally withdrawn all its energy and directed it towards the generation of this psychic energy.

It took me a full hour to recover. Even then, there was a slight slurring of speech and thickness of tongue, and the normal sharpness of the brain took some more time to fully establish itself.

One can easily snap out of this experience. Some say it should be ignored, but the will to snap out of it is not there; besides, it is not an unpleasant sensation, apart from the fact that I had an overwhelming curiosity to observe and note the sequence.

Thursday, March 22, 1984:

There was a tremendous inflow of energy. Energy that would lead to somnolence and lassitude. This was in direct contrast to the burst of energy that usually results in activity and dynamism. That was because the basic energies were different. One was bio-energy generated by the body for the normal functioning of the body. The other was the cosmic energy, 'chaitanya-shakti', the living force of the cosmos. This is the unborn energy of the Lord. The born energy is the manifest, the universe, the creation.

The unborn or the unmanifest energy sustains the manifest. The 'chaitanya-shakti' forms the matrix of all other energies of the world, and it contains and transports all these energies. All other energies, like the solar energy, the electric, the gravitational, and so on, are restricted in their fields and spheres of action and effect. But this comic energy, in which exist all the other energies, is all-encompassing. It is an attribute of the Lord, inseparable from Him and pervades the cosmos. It is infinite consciousness. It is the essential motive force and the essence of all beings. It forms the matrix for all the attributes of the Lord. That is, the matrix for all energies, all the knowledge, all the awareness, all the bliss, power, force, etc. But just as, though the Lord is all-pervading and resides in each individual, few feel and glimpse Him, so also, this all-pervading energy energizes but a few.

Only those few begin to have the cells and atoms of their bodies transformed. The atoms and cells of such beings become charged with this infinite energy. As the entire body is made up of such cells and atoms and as all these are charged with this cosmic energy, the energy within the body and the infinite energy of the cosmos form one continuum, as if the body is not there, as if the body has dissolved. This energy now stops recognizing the body, as it has pierced through the constituents of the body and infused them with itself. The body becomes almost only 'chaitanya-shakti', just as, when the pot breaks, the air within and without becomes one.

So this being becomes one with most aspects of the Lord. Now he has access to the Absolute Knowledge, to true awareness, infinite bliss, powers, energies, forces, etc., which are nothing but different aspects of the Lord. Happenings, inexplicable perhaps to reason and intellect, take place around him or through him or are attributed to his agency, and are called supernatural.

As this being becomes more and more only 'chaitanya-shakti', and merges more and more with the Lord, he acquires more of these aspects. This is a slow process, as the basic constituents of the body have to change to enable it to accept such a tremendous transformation. The body cannot be exposed to such a stupendous charge all of a sudden, so this force itself gradually transforms the body of the person to be able to receive it.

This transformation consumes a lot of bio-energy of the person, hence the limp feeling and lassitude. All the bio-energies of the body are withdrawn, and directed towards this transformation or rebuilding. This results in sudden and acute drowsiness and a drugged feeling. The body becomes sensitive to fine vibrations, all the senses are withdrawn, including the will and the thinking ability. No movement of the body is possible now, not even of the tongue. Even to lift the head is a big chore. Any movement now requires a hundred times more effort, as the body seems very heavy now. Eyes shut tight and get pulled inward. The head cannot be kept up erect, and, no effort by the body or mind is tolerated. The body has to lie down, completely relaxed, with not even crossing of the legs; in short, be in 'shavasana', the posture in death, the posture of total relaxation. There is a dull ache to the body. It is the vibrations that give this effect. This inflow of energy can be either feeble, vigorous, or immensely powerful. In spite of initially feeling weighty, the body begins to feel so light, as though it is about to take off. This sensation is more at the arms and legs.

This energy transforms the 'jada' or the gross quality of the body into the subtle or 'sukshma' quality, to enable the being to live in a subtle plane of consciousness. As however, the body keeps on acquiring the 'jada' or the gross quality through the normal processes of life, such as eating, talking, mixing with people and so on, this is a continuous transformatory process, and only slowly does the 'jada' quality become less and less, to be replaced by 'sukshma' quality. As this process goes on, the person's body and mind react less and less violently to the 'chaitanya-shakti' till the transformation is almost complete, almost, because no human being can be completely transformed so long as he is in the bodily form. He can become similar to the Lord but not identical with the Lord. For example, unlike the Lord he cannot create, sustain, or destroy the universe.

42

Dreams, Visions and Experience

Friday, March 23, 1984:

Difference between dreams and an experience of Reality:

In a dream, you remain yourself, retaining your individual identity. So you yourself will be chased by a tiger, you will be jumping or flying or meeting someone. That is, you are the centre, and can relate people, places, and incidents in dreams to those in life.

In an experience of Reality, you transcend your personality, individuality and identity. You become a cosmic, universal self, watching events as an onlooker. Your identity is with the formless ultimate, or with a universal manifestation like a cloud or a mountain. You are that formless consciousness, and not an individual. There is no fright or joy as you are not participating individualistically; only witnessing.

The awareness is also cosmic and all-knowing.

Dreams are projections of the mind, or the experiences, aspirations or fears of the mind, as the individual mind has not purified or transcended itself. Spiritual experience is an education in Reality, as the mind has been cleansed or effaced, and there are no desires, fears, memories of the mind left for that moment.

An experience of Reality brings in a revelatory flash an understanding or comprehension of profound and eternal truths, and brings with it peace, calm and bliss, and also removes in a moment ignorance of ages, and brings in clear light.

A man who has his mind negated thus will not dream.

The difference between a vision and an experience of Reality:

In a vision, there is a duality, and you see some being or form other than you. Even in a vision of God, you see a form or forms of God in the way your mind has been conditioned about the concept of God. These are all relative and changing, and are projected much as the individual conceives of a particular person, place or thing or God. These are individualistic and influenced by your tradition, knowledge, mood and understanding. So these are projections of the mind, no matter how realistic and how convincing they seem.

But the experience of Reality is beyond form, even of God. The traditionally presented forms of God denote certain profundities which can be relative and changing from place to place, art to art, time to time. The Ultimate, however, is beyond change, beyond art, beyond time and form. It has only to be experienced by way of existence, awareness, or knowledge and bliss. This is beyond thought, so no varying emotions or varying conceptions can influence an experience of Reality.

An experience of Reality is universal. Anyone, any place, any time, will experience similar things, only the expression and understanding may vary. If there is variance in the description of an experience of Reality or there are conflicting opinions about its significance, it only indicates different states of spiritual advancement of the different persons.

And then, the Ultimate is so vast, so inconceivable, so unfathomable, endless, indescribable, inexpressible, that a variance in expression and understanding has to arise. And as the Ultimate is endless, all spiritual experiences of this type have to be true. Which one man would be so great as to perceive all of that unfathomable Being? Man, by the very nature of his limitations of perceptions, is bound to get and comprehend only a glimpse of the Almighty.

In an experience of Reality, there is no duality of either form or existence or bliss. You are *that*. You are yourself whatever you see or experience. There is none other than you, be it a cloud, a mountain or earth; simultaneously, you should be all. You, the seen, and even the act of seeing, should be one continuous whole.

Saturday, March 24, 1984:

Lately, I find that all of a sudden the 'chakras' at both the temples and on the bridge of the nose are set in a state of powerful vibration. This is different to the throbbing that takes place with a cold or headache. There is a pleasure in these vibrations, and, the whole body is thrown into a continuous tremor, soothing and immensely pleasurable. It reminds me of the stage beyond 'nirvikalpa' samadhi, wherein there is no awareness other than that of just 'being' and bliss. The awareness of dynamism of life, of the vibrant nature of pure life, the charged nature of sheer existence, is brought about by the throbbing of these 'chakras'.

Though I carry on with my work, these 'chakras' get suddenly 'switched on', as it were, and all through my activities, I get a backdrop of a light 'nirvikalpa' samadhi, spreading the same aura as in that state.

43

Death and Immortality

Sunday, March 25, 1984:

In a dream, the individual identity is retained. You are the same as the one participating in the dream. The persons, places, events and things can be recognized, as they have a bearing on your life. So memory also is retained in the dream. But the real life is forgotten, and the dream is a reality at that moment. The awareness of your everyday life is lost. You are not playing a role. You are living the dream. In a limited sense, there is no duality.

After the dream, awareness of the other world comes back, and now the memory of the experience of the dream is retained along with the realization that the experience of joy or sorrow or fright was only a dream. Again you dream, and the memory of your past dreams and your everyday life recedes, and the dream becomes a reality.

So over the days in life, there is one continuous thread of individual identity running through the intermittent awareness of dreams and everyday life.

In much the same way, a being, the inner being, 'jivatma', that is, an 'atma' still covered by an individual identity, undergoes the cycle of births. Each new birth is like a fresh dream. Like the thread of individual identity retained in life, a thread of identity is retained by this being in successive births. It is influenced by indelible impressions, 'samskaras', left on it by its experiences in various births, and by indelible racial memories of dramatic events. These 'samskaras' give this being an individualistic identity, which is retained through successive births with either addition or subtraction of new and old impressions.

Previous births are forgotten, just like, while dreaming, old dreams are forgotten.

The 'jivatma' is itself participating in living through the new birth, and again in a limited sense, there is no duality vis-a-vis the role that is played by it.

Then a stage comes which is beyond waking and dreaming states, when you find a third identity of yours that is not individualistic but universal and cosmic. This is your true identity, which is not influenced by your mind. This is the original and true nature of yours, pure, stark and glowing. Now you can be sure of cosmic awareness and permanent knowledge.

When slowly you get firmly established in this state, your new awareness and knowledge of your true identity will never leave you.

Just as a yogi knows even in a dream that he is dreaming and is fully aware of the dreaming and waking states simultaneously, now, you will be conscious of your individual and universal identities simultaneously and constantly. Even at the time of death, you will watch your body die, retaining your awareness and identity intact. You will slip into 'death' (by our vocabulary), and then get reborn, retaining your original identity and universal awareness. You will know the past, the future, the present, and you will be beyond birth and death. By you, I mean your awareness and your true identity, not your body which is now inconsequential and still subject to change and rebirth and death. You, as the consciousness, are immortal, ageless, and beyond birth and death. You are a continuity.

44

The Inner Force

Monday, March 26 to Wednesday, March 28, 1984:

Since the last few days, I am feeling extraordinarily free, as though some being that had held me in its grip for some time had suddenly released me. All the drugged spells, the energy-induced sleep, bodily weakness, continuous contemplation, blankness, spells of staring away, had all of a sudden disappeared. I felt totally a new person. I felt like singing, buoyant, energetic and full of ideas. The house had again assumed its due importance. Our servant had just left for her village, and I was wondering how I would be able to manage Tejaswi who is a ball of mischief, as also the housework, along with these spells of mental and physical lethargy. But with all these leaving me suddenly, I was now confident of managing everything. My brain too felt sharp and under my own command, as did my body. The thought of God, silence, meditation, altogether slipped out of my mind.

All the experiences of the last two months, as it were, had not taken place at all. There was no time now to relax, and even when there was a lull in the work, the spells would not creep back over me as they used to. Instead, I planned for other jobs, and, after many days, began directing my moves, actions and jobs. It was not as if things were somehow being done as in the past few weeks. Now, I was fully in charge of myself and doing things as I wished and planned.

As there was no lethargy, and no pressure or heaviness in the head, work was proceeding with ease and speed. Now in fact, there was a revulsion to reading anything pertaining to God or

to the thought of meditation or contemplation. It would bring
on an agitation in the mind, as would the chanting of the Lord's
name or any aspect of duality.

For several days, I felt free and liberated. I was back to being
the housewife of the olden days. I had completely forgotten
spirituality, and if occasionally something brought the thought
back, I would have nothing of it.

Thursday, March 29, 1984:

Again I got into the mood of contemplation; and it dawned on
me that conscious worship or contemplation on the Lord were
separating me from the Lord. Even contemplation of Him was a
barrier which kept me from Him. I was completely steeped in
Him, and thoughts, even on Him, caused duality and discomfort,
and ruffled the peace and tranquillity that had become inherent
in me by now.

The mood of contemplation had to come of its own.

Friday, March 30, 1984:

I was in a theatre watching a movie. Suddenly, after many days,
my head began nodding in 'kriya'. There was a gentle hum, and
the old familiar vibrations of the head from the neck upwards. I
wondered about it, as I had thought I was free from it all now.

When we came home, I found that the servant had come
home from her village at exactly the time my 'kriya' had started
in the theatre.

At night, I had a very strong spell, presumably making up for
the lost time! I realized that, now that the domestic help had
come home, the leave that had been granted to me was withdrawn,
and again my attention would be commandeered by this inner
force. Apparently, I was made to forget this aspect of mine, to
help me tide over the crisis of having no servant, and to make me
fully efficient and enthusiastic about work.

Again, it struck me how understanding and benevolent this
inner force is. It was not my will that had been giving me this
extra energy or this zeal for work, but this inner force acting on
its own, coming forth or withdrawing according to the free time

available to me. Whenever I had help from either the children or the servant, it would not spare me; but whenever I had to buckle down to my work, it would recede tactfully and graciously.

Monday, April 2, 1984:

This force is giving me more than adequate cooperation. It struck me that, even before a problem presents itself to me, the force supplies me with a premonition about it, and a solution. It acts with precision.

To the extent I need help, it spares me. However mild be the force, it relieved me of tiredness and enthused me with fresh energy to work, so that, in that short span of time before the spell would reappear, I would do double the amount of normal work. Thus, even with the amount of work remaining the same and the time available for it lessening, I managed to do most of my work with pleasure and ease. Only when the spell would come would I have to lie down and relax totally.

45

'Bhakti'—Devotion I

Thursday, April 5, 1984:

Slowly, in small degrees, a slight yearning for the Lord returned, along with my retreating into contemplation, staring in space, feeling peace and stillness, 'bhakti', and wanting to completely relax during these short spells. There would be, again, no movement of body or mind at this time, only occasional 'kriya' and, often, a shutting up of the brain.

Once I tried meditation. Immediately, I stood up without any volition on my part, and the body bent backwards and the head almost touched the floor at the back. A very comfortable position. I had an urge to double up and form a complete ring with my body, but the phone rang and I had to get up.

Friday, April 6, 1984:

Mr. Nemlekar visited us. He talked about Lord Krishna. Immediately, a strong yearning for Krishna returned in me. Whenever I found a little free time, I returned to the contemplation of Krishna. At such times, my head would become heavy and tilt down, eyes would shut tight, and there would be extreme drowsiness and a total withdrawal from the world.

Saturday, April 7, 1984:

I do not feel like writing. There is only an urge to just 'be'; to enjoy the spell of peace and tranquillity and the pleasant drowsiness.

Sunday, April 8, 1984:

When the spell came, I could work through it with a little difficulty, but I realized that I could control it to some extent.

Monday, April 9, 1984:

Even more mastery over the spell, possibly because the spell itself was mild. There was no total withdrawal of senses, no undue sleep. Writing also flowed beautifully. Work, spirituality and writing were maintained in equal measure, and I hoped that this balance would continue. A triumphant feeling for having pierced through this spell, this barrier. Reworked my daily notes.

Wednesday, April 11, 1984:

A clear message: 'Bhakti', devotion, is essential to enjoy the total bliss of Reality.

46

'Aum' the Primal Sound

Thursday, April 12, 1984:

A flash: When the unborn manifests itself, the conversion is to 'Aum', the primal sound, that contains everything. The most auspicious and the most profound syllable of all is 'Aum'. That one letter represents all that is. It represents the highest Reality. It contains all.

The unmanifest manifesting, the 'nothingness' blossoming into things, or the invisible becoming visible, the unborn getting born, creates a hum in the universe. This is the beginning of sound, containing all the notes.

The subtle, the unmanifest, the unborn, becoming gross, manifesting, coming into existence, creates a stir in the cosmos. A vibration, a reverberation. This vibration creates a sound, a hum, throughout the cosmos. This is 'Aum'.

What is coming into 'being'? The force of primal existence is finding an expression. Expression is creation.

This force of all-pervading Existence, the 'Shakti'—the 'Prakriti'—is coming into existence. All-pervading, inseparable from the Lord, not apart from the Lord, not different from the Lord.

The universe is being born. Suffused by Existence, Knowledge, Bliss. Suffused by His power and energy. Suffused by His vibration.

'Aum' represents the Reality. The formless assuming form. Forms assuming names. Names acquiring importance. A world of senses, a world of matter, a world of shapes and form.

'Aum' the auspicious, the worthy of worship, the primal sound, the primal letter, the beginning of representation!

'Aum' containing Brahma, Vishnu, Mahesh. 'Aum' containing Sat-Chit-Ananda! 'Aum' containing the body and the soul of the cosmos. 'Aum'!

47

'Bhakti'—Devotion 11

True 'Bhakti' is essential to enjoy the total bliss of Reality:

The one who has merged with Reality, automatically and spontaneously enjoys the bliss of Reality, as bliss is an essence of Reality. But even for one who has not yet reached this state of merger, true 'bhakti', true devotion, takes him a long way towards experiencing this bliss in daily living.

'Bhakti' is the ultimate, unconditional, and total love felt towards the Lord, a tremendous yearning, an unquestioned upsurge of devotion, pure worship, unwavering faith, and a sheer desire for merging felt towards the Lord or towards any deity of one's choice, the personal deity being ultimately a symbol of the Lord.

'Bhakti' helps nurture in the heart of the devotee a feeling of pure love towards everyone. There is an innocence here, a purity that cleanses him of all the debris and murk of a gross mind, and pushes him on, unknown to him, towards a spiritual evolution.

Steeped in the sweet intimacy of the chosen deity, the Lord is never away. There is ambrosia here in the divine company, and now every being and every object vibrates with a divine force. For him, the world and living itself are an expression of the beloved deity, to be gone through with worship in his heart. Every object and every being acquires a special meaning and a special status, as now the active presence of the deity is perceived everywhere.

The fervour of worship evokes in his heart a satiation, a rare contentment, that throws him in a deeper mood of devotion which makes him experience the throbbing force of divinity pervading everywhere.

This oneness allows him to experience the bliss of Reality, so what if he is not yet aware of the Reality? Total 'bhakti' and total concentration on his personal god will give him immense inner peace, inner sanctity and an outpouring of love.

This feeling of oneness will eventually lead him to the final merger with the Infinite.

To such a person, 'bhakti' in itself becomes fulfilment. There is no further goal. Without having to wait for the final merger, he enjoys the same nectar right now. Melting with love towards the divinity, he is losing his identity and merging in the Infinite. Here, 'bhakti' or this merger in the personal god, is the goal, and he reaches this quickly. The final merger or oneness is secondary, if at all, though this path too surely leads one there. Seekers on the path of yoga or of knowledge are also seeking this ambrosia, this ecstasy, of merger, but they are seeking it through a merger in the Reality. A personal god holds no appeal to them. They have to wait longer for this ambrosia, as it is harder to merge in the Reality.

This is the path of 'bhakti' or devotion. True 'bhakti' has to come of its own. It cannot be forced or put on.

A devotee, carrying on in the midst of problems of the world, enjoys the bliss of his devotion. He does not feel the need to renounce the world to attain the Reality. Plurality of the world or this duality does not bother him. To him, the world is not an illusion to be shunned, but a many-faceted expression of the Reality which is represented by his loved personal god. The natural and intimate relationship between a devotee and his deity is spontaneous and nectarine. It renders the devotee want-less and desireless, happy in only being absorbed in his deity. His unquestioning love renders his mind calm and soothed.

Though the Sadguru had asked me to identify myself with the Infinite force, I find this counsel keeps slipping from my mind. Whatever happens to me automatically or takes place spontaneously, I allow it to happen without any effort on my part to influence it. I have no identity now.

I am doing nothing to resist the current. I let go and observe where it leads me. I am not adding to it by my effort, nor do I resist it.

48

'Siddhis'—Powers

Friday, April 27, 1984:

There was an urge to turn inwards. I caught myself observing the process. It was almost instant. I had to only shift my focus. Without deliberation, a thought arose: I have been given the highest truth. Yet I have not got any 'siddhis', powers, from it. Anyone on the path of yoga, as he advances, is supposed to slowly acquire a number of 'siddhis'. I have not acquired even the elementary power of telepathy or intuition. Of what practical use then is the Knowledge of Brahman?

My hands began tapping my body all over and the reply came, 'You have been given everything that is worthwhile. The greatest boon in life is True Knowledge, peace, tranquillity of mind and contentment. You have been bestowed with these. "Siddhis" are a hindrance and a harbinger of unhappiness, ego, and temptation. They can reactivate the baser impulses of the mind. Yogis who acquire powers have to negate them before being shown the higher realities. They have to unlearn all they have learnt, before they "arrive". You have been offered everything on a silver platter with a golden spoon. Even this negation of powers has been done for you. You are already "there". You do not have to make any effort to arrive there.

'Your main role in life is to enjoy. To enjoy the greatest bliss and "maha Aishvarya" in the role of a housewife. Whatever had to be revealed to you to remind you of your true identity has been revealed. For this, a glimpse is enough. Later, when your duties in life are discharged, you will slowly be fully established in this state. At that stage, "siddhis" come automatically and spontaneously, without your striving for them, as they do to anyone in that state. Till then, shun any "siddhis" or even the desire for any.

'The powers acquired on the way have to be shunned. These "siddhis" are obtained by the power of certain "chakras". If the yogi is not careful, he might be held in thrall by the power of the "chakra", and might not reach the realm of the supra-consciousness. But "siddhis" accruing to a person after his being established in realization happen on their own, so there is no question of either shunning or entertaining them. They are in purified form. They serve a higher purpose, and as they are not influenced by emotions, ego or thought, the self-realized yogi only becomes an instrument of the divine for those seeking miracles, and the yogi is not affected by them.'

The 'siddhis' obtained during 'sadhana' are acquired due to the activation of certain 'chakras', certain very sensitive nerve centres in the body. This can happen despite the mind not having been fully purified. For further progress and purification of the mind, these have to be ignored, and effort focused on activating still higher 'chakras' till the 'sahasrara chakra' at the top of the head is reached. Any diversion will impede progress.

When the 'sahasrara chakra' is reached, and the individual is well lodged in the universal, these 'siddhis' arise direct from the supra-consciousness, the cosmic power, without his willing it, and not by the power of the bodily 'chakras'. The yogi then carries these powers and the knowledge of his heightened consciousness, even when he leaves his body and its 'chakras' behind. These are then available to him in whichever new body he might enter. In fact, he has them with him with or without a body.

The body 'chakras' can be activated and powers obtained without purification of the mind. However, the supra-state can be acquired only through complete purification of the mind. The yogi, with an impure mind and having these 'siddhis', is tempted to misuse these powers. He is also tempted to linger on in this state, or he might even slip down, immersed in these powers, and not reach the higher realms of spirituality.

Total self-control, which can be had only with a pure mind, is very essential on this path.

This question regarding the 'siddhis' had not been consciously posed by me as I had no desire or even any thought concerning the acquiring of any 'siddhis'. But perhaps the subtle consciousness had thus answered some tenuous tendril of a thought that might have been lurking in the deep recesses of my mind.

49

Enlightenment, 'Maya' and Myself

Saturday, April 28, 1984:

Whilst you are a 'sadhaka', a pilgrim in the quest, your philosophy should be that the highest Reality is 'not this, not this, not this'. Go on discarding everything as not true, a delusion, an illusion, till you discover the highest Reality. When this happens, you perceive automatically that all is only the Reality. Then everything is the Reality, yes, even this, even this, and even this!

Monday, May 7, 1984:

What I have understood by the word, 'enlightenment':

There are several words in common usage to denote this truly indescribable state, but once the meaning of it is grasped, other words will be found to be perhaps equally apt. Not having studied philosophy or any mystic literature or ancient scriptures, what I narrate here is purely an experientially intuitive understanding of a concept which is normally heralded by terms such as 'atma-sakshatkara' (self-realization), 'Brahma-dnyana' (knowledge of the Supreme), 'atma-dnyana' (knowledge of the Self), enlightenment or self-realization.

First of all, there is an unlimited substratum of life, all-pervading and all-permeating, and ever so subtle. This we call the 'Lord' or the 'Infinite'. He or It is beyond name, form, words, time, space, causality. He is self-existent, spontaneous, beyond birth and death, creation and destruction, and is ever-present. From this magnificent source, which is beyond our conception and comprehension, spring both the unborn and the born.

The unborn or the unmanifest is the primal force of the Infinite that sustains the born or the manifest. This primal force of the Infinite, containing all His attributes, changes into energy and thence into matter, giving rise to 'AUM' we worship so ardently. This 'AUM' is the cosmic hum of creation, the unborn transforming into the born. This cosmic energy, containing all the attributes of the Lord, setting itself into motion, creating sound and rhythm throughout the cosmos, breaks out into the primal elements of the universe, which combine and recombine to form various sub-atomic particles, atoms and molecules. Matter comes into being.

The universe is born. It is then sustained and evolved. A creation comes into being that we can see, feel and live in.

The creation is the Lord, but the Lord is not the creation. He is other than that; beyond his creation, unbound by it.

This creation is the 'Brahman', completely pervaded by the Infinite Consciousness of the Lord. The manifestation of the Infinite Consciousness of this 'Brahman' in the human body is the 'Atman'. The 'Atman' and the Infinite Consciousness—the Individual and the Ultimate Reality—are one. The Individual Consciousness and the Infinite Consciousness are one continuous stream!

The expanse of creation including man has, as its soul, the Infinite Consciousness. That is the Ultimate Reality. That is 'Atman', that is Man.

The Infinite Consciousness is the Lord. But the Lord is other than that. This is His consciousness.

Man fails to see the subtle conscious stream of Reality that runs through the entire creation, and confuses Reality with the more obvious, the creation. This restricted vision or this confusion, this stubborn misconcept, is 'Maya'. Not that forms and structures are unreal or false, but they are not 'Real'. By 'Real' is meant that which is formless, subtle, unchanging, eternal, not subject to evolution, not born, unending, self-subsisting, or the ultimate Reality. In its 'purest' form, the confusion is called 'Maya'.

At a much lower level, it is called 'Avidya' or spiritual ignorance. The Reality wrapped in this ignorance is the human mind or the 'Jivatma'. Pure or transcended mind is the 'Atma' in a body, which joins the 'Paramatma', the universal. The Reality is still and unmoving. It is the great potential. It is ever-unaffected.

However, the universe springing from this stillness is ever engaged in action and movement. It is sustained by this movement and action. Each component of the universe is dynamically connected to the rest, each thought, each action, each ripple, each event, affecting the whole. It sets off a chain reaction. This is 'Karma', which is the force sustaining life, its dynamism, and which propels the wheels of our destiny and which becomes the flow of our existence.

We have to pierce this veil of 'Maya' and understand experientially and clearly the totality, the oneness, the grand pattern of the 'Brahman', and act accordingly. Then, this binding 'Karma' is transcended. This is called 'Moksha', freedom.

The subtle play between the forces of nature and one's thought and action is now clearly seen. This is a very sensitive but unavoidable relationship, faultless and tenacious, in which cannot be transgressed the effects and repercussions of one's thought and deed. It is also clear that, however small, one is indeed a part of the all-pervasive whole. Un-isolated and unindependent. And that this pervasive stream, this entirety, containing the manifest and the un-manifest, the born and the unborn, is the Brahman. Including man.

Once this is grasped, there is Bliss divine and knowledge of Reality. A sublime unity and harmony.

There are many ways to attain this liberation: Yoga, meditation, devotion, knowledge, duty and action, and above all, love! Each as effective in its own way, according to the essential nature of the individual concerned.

The various gods and goddesses are but different aspects of the Infinite, representing His various forces or His different facets. To know this unity experientially is called 'enlightenment'. To seek this enlightenment should be the goal of an individual.

Tuesday, May 8, 1984:

What I have acquired or attained out of this:

I had always associated mystic or occult powers and miracles with people who were known to be enlightened. That they might not exhibit this power often was a measure of their greatness, and was due to their inherent dislike of interfering with nature. However, if experience of Reality is the only criterion of being enlightened, then by virtue of my experience, I could, in a small measure, claim to have attained enlightenment; because I observed that I had acquired no powers nor any exceptional skills of mystical importance. All I had to my credit were some experiences, of interest, no doubt, but greatly ineffective towards the performance of any miracles or display of occult powers.

All the same, these experiences, which are in a large measure spectacularly audio-visual, have given me a rare insight into what could be called a peep into the outer worlds. By experiencing oneness with the nature of Knowledge and Reality and awakening to the supra-knowledge that I am 'That', I have sipped a little of the ambrosia that is also called 'soma' or the elixir of life.

The world came alive differently when I now beheld it: It was as if a magical wand had been waved over the creation, endowing its beauty with a new grandeur. The world itself had not changed, nor its objects. But it was as if it had become transparent, unveiling its secrets in all their purity.

To experience a state of purity and to identify myself with the Infinite and its beautiful different aspects, to find myself beyond the universe, sustaining it yet not bound by it, reaching out everywhere yet remaining where I am, is something grand. It is a physical feeling, a distinct awareness, a stark reality, to find myself free from causality, from 'Karma', from bondage. A feeling of liberation has descended on me. And, what is more striking is that there is no marvel at it, no disbelief, and no questioning. No response, no reaction, no awe. It was only experiencing. It all seemed such a natural and normal state to be in, and I knew that this is the original nature of man and that he himself with his impure mind, his ignorance, his ego and indulgence, has carved out for himself a world full of misery.

There is an irresistible urge to share with others the experience of rediscovering myself. It is a mood so supernal and rare, and yet within the reach of man. Having experienced it for some time, it has left my life so much richer that, wanting to share it with others, I have tried to describe it even though I feel that it is an almost impossible task.

Piercing the veil of 'Maya' has filled my storehouse with glorious memories. Most wonderful of these is the feel of the expanse through the cosmos and to know the distant stars as part of me, to move in the fullness of 'Brahman' as one unlimited, gigantic entity, and yet to feel and know each tiny constituent of it, to feel the rhythm of the cosmic movement and to hear its cosmic beat, and to bring forth and then destroy, repeatedly, the divine creation in the very act of my breathing in and breathing out. This rhythm of creation revealed to me the glory of Lord Nateshwara, the Lord of the divine dance of creation and destruction.

Equally beautiful is the identification with 'Shakti', the Divine Mother, the Cosmic Energy—the female embodiment of the cosmic force. The divine union of male and female counterparts effulging into divine life, which has been so lyrically depicted in our temple sculptures.

The divine matrix, in which are contained this life, this creation, the knowledge, the word, time, space, causality, motion and all the phenomena, can be known only experientially. And thus these experiences of mine form a treasure, as they have intimately and systematically revealed to me various aspects of the Lord, by making me one with each aspect of His—the sole path of really knowing.

To understand experientially that the great number of gods and goddesses are but different aspects of the one Reality—the

Lord—and to feel their origin in me, as I too am of the same Reality, did not demean them in my esteem; if anything, the worship of these gods has sublimated into a sincere love for the divine concepts these deities represent.

To comprehend in its entirety the Reality—as much as can be understood within the limitations of man—there was showered freely upon me the boon of knowledge, knowledge that burst forth at every turn, employing any tool of communication that would prove most effective for the purpose of my guidance.

No doubt, this is a mere glimpse of the mighty ocean whose magnitude, depth or fullness of content can never be grasped fully by the inadequate senses of man, but then whose glimpse is it? His, Whose mere existence sparks forth a creation of this dimension, Whose matrix contains all that is, and Who by His love envelops us, whether we be aware of Him or not. Then, will not a mere glimpse of Him shatter the ignorance of eternities in man and spread through him the bliss that is inherent in Him? And that is precisely what these experiences did to me. A state of total uncover made me one with Reality and made me sip the brimming nectar.

The sip of nectar transported me to the realm of intuitive wisdom. It made me know that life is not fragmented from Reality. Life is only its manifestation. Life includes creation, man and society. Society brings in its wake duties and obligations. These incur action. To lead a life with dignity, discharging the allotted chores and duties is important to man. He should remember that action too is divine.

These experiences showed clearly that the ultimate truth is that there is no duality; that the Lord and the world are one—the manifestation being merely the extension of the Lord. And the nature of the Lord is Reality—plain existence or just being. Awareness of this Reality and enjoyment of this Bliss and a spontaneous spill of His nature into one results in a burst of True Knowledge.

Another important revelation has been that the Self is divine. If the Self is divine, and if one identifies himself with this Self and not with the body, which is perishable, then where is the need to make an effort to meditate? Meditation is an endeavour towards union with Reality or to seek Reality. If the Self and Reality are one, who is to meditate on whom? Life itself has become a meditation for me, for no more is there any distinction between life, the Lord, and myself.

50

The Inner Voice II

Wednesday, May 9, 1984:

The Sadguru always used to say that the inner voice that speaks to one is like the sinful woman always wanting to entice the individual. Shun it. The moment it appears, crush it, erase it, squash it. Never fall a prey to it.

I always wondered why. To me, this inner voice had been a faithful instructor, guiding me, educating me. Pointing out to me my progress and revealing to me astounding facts. But for this voice, I would never have known what I was passing through, what I was witnessing. I had never read about such things nor hankered for them, so I was not anticipating them. I would never have deciphered anything that went on within me, but for this voice. So I wondered why the Sadguru distrusted this inner voice so. Till, one day, I realized suddenly why, fully.

This inner voice is nothing but our own voice educating us. The degree of accuracy of interpretation depends upon the purity of the mind. In a purely sublime state, when our own ego, emotions, intellect, thoughts, etc. have been subdued, and the mind is in total communion with the Infinite; knowledge coming from the Infinite is quickly perceived, grasped, and interpreted accurately by the purified mind. So whatever the mind, in its fully purified state, now tells us in the form of an inner voice is the Truth. This is because, in such a purified mind, the decoding of the message passing in from the Infinite is perfect.

Once the current has set in, and the individual has had a taste of the wisdom this voice imparts, the temptation is to evoke the voice at will, and to ask of it all sorts of questions. This is the pitfall one has to watch out for, and avoid. The moment you invoke this voice with a conscious effort, with a motive, you are at once activating your ego, your intellect, along with your prejudices coloured by half-baked ideas and notions. In short, you are activating your sullied mind, not the purified mind. This negates the state of mind absolutely required to get conjoined to the all-pervading Infinite of the nature of Supreme Knowledge. The Supreme Knowledge is still there, and coming in; however, the mind, now tarnished by ego, intellect, etc., decodes these 'beeps' faultily. The problem is here. The temptation is to seek knowledge, and the moment you seek actively, you lose your state of thoughtlessness or your ego-intellectlessness. The very act of seeking debars Supreme Knowledge.

Once invoked, this activated mind, that is, the inner voice, prattles on with sometimes true, but more often misguiding, information. This voice is now fraught with danger, as the innocent individual believes all that the inner voice has to say, and, worse, acts upon it, basing his decisions on this unreliable source. He soon gets more and more into the habit of invoking this voice and depending on it. Not satisfied with this, he even starts guiding others, which is unforgivable and is like playing with fire.

Where the mind is absolutely pure, and the emotions are subjugated, the sublime wisdom comes of its own without being sought, and then it is true, as it has been in my case. I could evoke it any time, but there has never been any will to do so nor any curiosity left.

Thursday, May 10, 1984:

I saw wild animals facing me. They were ferocious and flesh-eating, baring their fangs at me and growling. But I was not frightened. For, underneath their ferocity, I sensed innocence. Their ferocity was not backed by cruel thought. It was governed only by their inherent instinct for survival.

Dissociated from this superficial ferocity was an underlying consciousness that was pure and still. I saw a continuity in their consciousness and mine. I saw I could manipulate their consciousness. My calm, my tranquillity, my peaceful thought, could be conveyed to them without their being conscious of it. My calm was passed on to them. They were silenced. My contentment was delivered to them, and they were tamed. The growling stopped. Their fierce look gave way to one of contentment and friendly curiosity. I persisted, and, from their look I knew that they too saw the mutual continuity of peace, of oneness, of innocence, and they were appeased. Slowly, they turned and went their way. I stood there watching, till they disappeared. Then I regained my body consciousness !

During this experience, when I began working on their consciousness, I had lost my body-consciousness. I was pure awareness then.

Friday, May 11, 1984:

I had gone to Sarada Mandir at the Ramakrishna Math at Khar. The atmosphere was beautiful there, and I saw a few ladies sitting in meditation in front of Saradadevi's statue. I joined them. I closed my eyes and became one with the temple atmosphere. Slowly, I found my head turning sideways toward the right. I knew 'kriya' had started. I stopped the movement and looked to the front. Again, I found my head turning towards the right. It swivelled further and stopped right at the back. It was fully facing the view at the rear now. I brought my head back to the normal position. The 'kriya' repeated itself. It was very soothing and meditative. I tried turning it towards the left side. The pattern repeated itself. As the others were sitting with closed eyes, I allowed this 'kriya' to go on for some time, then got up, and went home.

At night, I saw myself sitting in a half-'padmasana' pose next to my bed. A number of 'rishis', sages, compressed in size and with wings, almost like angels, were flying around me with a crown in their hands. They hovered over me for a few moments, and then put the crown on my head. They sang the praises of the Lord, and rejoiced in the glory that had awakened in me. They honoured the Lord that had shone forth in me.

51

'Nirvana' and Worship

Monday, June 18, 1984:

I am the 'nirvana'. 'Nirvana' is not an object one picks up nor a place one reaches. It is only the Real Self shining forth in its glory in a state of total uncover. The natural state of Self in 'nirvana', in 'moksha', freedom, liberation! The original state of man is 'nirvana', till he covers it with the binding and harrowing mind, complete with ego, emotions, and thoughts. An individual should endeavour towards this recognition and this experience.

Identity, not with an object, a body or a being, only with existence, brings on serenity and quietude. That is 'nirvana'.

This state brings its own momentum and consciousness. There is an intuitive certainty about real knowledge, and a clarity and a complete grasp of things.

Though there is a ceasing of thought, there is a clear awareness of knowledge, and refined intelligence. There is no loss of consciousness, environmental or of life.

There is a negation of desire. There are no wants yet to be fulfilled, no wanton meanderings of mind. There is no burden of the past, no hopes or expectations for the future. No undue attachments either. Emotions are not there to ruffle the mind. The mind is at rest, the individual is at peace.

At work or in repose, in sleep or awake, there is clear identity of 'I AM'. That is all. Finally, 'I' also drops off. Only 'AM' remains.

This is the 'Atman', pure. A sheer light of consciousness. Above time, space, and causality. Sustaining the universe.

This is 'nirvana'. This is 'moksha', a condition free of misery, devoid of fear. This is the liberation everyone should aspire for. This is 'soma', the elixir of life. This is contentment, the source of life. This can be you. Whereas identification with the body causes misery, experiencing the 'Atman', the Self, brings peace. This should be the goal of man.

Tuesday, July 10, 1984:

Occasionally, there would be pressure in the head. With the onset of this pressure, there would be heaviness in the body. After some time, when this pressure would subside, there would be a pleasing lightness in the body.

The Sadguru says that this is due to the repeated transformation of 'jada' (gross) into 'chaitanya' (subtle energy).

This is the continuing transformation of the gross mind into the subtle mind that is pure energy. This goes on for some time in the beginning, building up a little pressure in the head. Eventually it stops.

Thursday, July 12, 1984:

Today is Guru Purnima, the annual full moon day of honouring the guru. As I decorated the altar and the deities and lit the fragrant 'agarbattis', incense-sticks, I became conscious of the 'Soham-japa'—continuous involuntary intonation of the phrase 'I am That'—going on within me. I was in continuous ecstasy. I had not intentionally or consciously directed my mind towards this 'japa'. It had started on its own, triggered by the fervour of the occasion. Of its own, my hand holding the incense sticks turned around so that the incense sticks were directed at myself, instead of at the altar. As I watched, my hand began waving the incense sticks around me, as if doing 'arati' to me. I was engulfed in divine love and ecstasy. Amid the 'japa' of 'Soham', the Lord within me accepted, with grace and resplendence, my humble offering of love and devotion. In these prayers, the worship, the Lord within me, and I, had become one, the trinity had merged into one; and a divine peace and ecstasy, which are manifestations of the Lord, descended upon me. I went deep into this bliss and drew divine nectar of felicity.

Of late, a gradual transformation has been taking place in the style of my worship. I do not have to specially sit for worship or meditation. All throughout the day, working, sleeping or resting, I am merged in the Lord. A mood of serene tranquillity, that one experiences in a sacred 'ashram', surrounds me all the time. A wave of ecstasy comes over me at any time like a swoon, affecting my entire body. This wave is partly painful, partly a pressure, but wondrous to the core. I can only with difficulty keep my head in position, as my whole body goes limp. As most of the time I have to resist this spell and go on with my household work, perforce, this wave needs to be absorbed within myself. This leads to the build-up of a tremendous pressure in my head, till I go and relax for some time and allow the wave to ebb.

This spell or wave is in addition to the current of vibration and bliss that continues within me constantly.

Often, after each little chore, I have to go and relax completely in a chair, relaxing each cell of my body, and the swoon is near total then. Now, though consciousness is maintained throughout, the mind is totally at rest, neither interpreting nor reacting to all that the senses register. Perceptions are clear and not distorted by any memory or interpretations of the mind or intellect. There is no desire, want or will. No motivation to move, blink, or even breathe. There is no movement of body, mind or intellect. There is total peace and stillness. But should there be anything of importance, or someone coming over or anything needing immediate attention, I can and do at once snap out of this spell or wave. That, I suppose, means that I am in control, at least to some extent. However, if the repose continues uninterrupted for some time, I do lose my will or determination, and find it hard to snap out of it.

At such times, my eyes feel as though pulled inwards into non-existence. The insides of my head would be swallowed up by the unfathomable infinite too. I feel that my mind would completely merge with the deep void. There would be no thoughts now. No 'japa', no remembrance of any deities, not even of the Lord. Total disappearance of the mind, thought and intellect. Only a subtle awareness remains, and a knowledge of existence.

At such times, my body would be very tense. The tension would reach a climax. There would be a tingling sensation and a building up of pressure in the top of my head where the 'sahasrara chakra' is, and suddenly I would feel the wave ebbing, traversing down the body, and out at the toes. Sometimes I would feel the tension partially escaping through the 'sahasrara chakra'. Sometimes, the tensions would be so strong and the feeling of merger into nothingness so severe that my entire being would feel something akin to a light dough being pulled and stretched to its maximum. The severity, frequency and duration of this spell would vary.

Once or twice, I felt this tension traversing down my spine, taking a U-turn and coming up the front, and joining the 'sahasrara chakra', with part of the tension going down the front to the toes, making a U-turn there, then coming up to the 'sahasrara chakra' from the back, thus completing the circuit.

Often, at the climax of the wave, different 'mantras' or 'japa' would come forth from me of their own. A sense of ecstasy would always prevail.

During the tension, my breathing would change; it would be slower and very subtle, as if it was not ordinary air I was taking in, but the very essence of air. For all practical purposes, breathing was not there. Yet I was not choking; in fact, a quiet nectarine feeling of well-being would permeate me. Physical effort would be difficult.

After this tension had passed, my body would suddenly go limp. 'Shavasana' would be assumed by my body at this juncture for complete relaxation, though not necessarily in a sleeping position. Every cell in the body would be totally relaxed now. I would physically feel this deep relaxation, this total abandonment of each cell. It would be a heavenly tiredness. It is supernally pleasant, and no other pleasure in the world would equal this peace and serenity. Time and urgency would lose their meaning. There was a sense of total peace with the world.

Sometimes, wave upon wave would come in quick succession

and with great intensity; sometimes, they would be spaced out and feeble; and sometimes, after the wave had receded, the body would be in a state of fine vibration.

All my activities, like driving a car, going out alone on an errand, came to a halt. I could not take chances on the road. But whatever state I was in, be it this ecstasy or the thick of household work, the feeling of communion with the Lord would be deeply felt. No chore was unpalatable or a hindrance or an intrusion or a wasted time, nor even a barrier, keeping me from the Lord. The Lord and I had become one. Wherever I went, whatever I did, I found the Lord ever-present, engulfing me, permeating me. I had not to seek Him out elsewhere. I knew He was with me, in me. He was me!

A deep attachment has developed for the One within. There is adulation, adoration, and offering up of love, to this Self or this God that resides within. Rarely is there any yearning for Krishna or Vishnu as there had been in the earlier days. Deep within me, there is an assurance that these deeply-loved gods are not apart from me. They can be invoked any time. If they do not manifest at any given moment, it is solely because I have duties to perform; and duty and God, I have found, are inseparable.

Anything of beauty, any mention of God, in fact, practically anything and everything, reminded me of God and sent me into a state of oscillation. My head would begin to nod, my body would go limp, and my eyes would begin to turn inwards. There was hardly anything that was not associated with God, and, hardly any time that I was away from God. So now I have begun to live in ecstasy all day. Nothing is more pleasurable in life than being in the company of this Supreme Self; to contemplate on Him, to yearn for Him, and to silently worship Him!

Friday, July 13, 1984:

At night, I had a stunning revelation. In my deep sleep, someone spoke to me. The voice said, 'When man sleeps, he dreams. His mind, thought, intellect are also sleeping or are suspended; he is, in short, in a state of meditation. Yet he dreams. So what is

this dream? A projection of the sleeping man . . . in meditation!
Without his active participation, his senses, thought, body,
intellect, are in a state of meditative suspension—a world
projected around him, which he can feel and see. There is time,
space, and matter in this world, much like the world he lives in.
There are people in it, moving, living, communicating. This is
a world alive, a duplicate of the world we live in. And the sleeping
man lends his own life to this dream and makes it come alive.
He experiences everything that the dream participants experience.
He sees this dream, experiences it, but neither controls it nor
interferes with it. The dream is him, but he is not the dream,
and he is not bound by the dream. As his mental state, so the
dream!

'So is the universe a projection of the Lord in His state of
deep meditation. The breath-taking grandeur of the universe is
due to the supreme resplendence of the Lord. Without His having
to plan, conceive or execute, a universe, unmatched and
unparalleled, is projected, deriving life from His life-force,
awareness from His awareness, and knowledge from His
knowledge. In deep meditation and bliss, the world He projects
is stupendous and wondrous. The stunning marvel of the
universe, much like the splendour of the unmanipulating Sun,
only goes to show the unfathomable and inexpressible greatness
of the Lord. The universe, in its entirety, is His dazzling aura
irradiating from His mere existence!'

So is man's life a projection of his waking mind; of his own
making; of his own superficial thinking. It is this world that has
to be transcended, and a new world of purity, love and bliss
seen. It is this world of the mind that is false, changing,
illusionary, a delusion, according to his conditioning, purity
and hang-ups. It seems real and of the utmost importance and
his be-all and end-all. But it only brings misery, as it is a
projection of his impure mind, impregnated with emotions,
prejudice, hatred, greed, desire, lust, rage, envy. It is a world we
like to project to others, and a world we perceive through our
faulty perceptions. A far cry from reality, a far cry from the world
as it truly is. A falsity. A world of imagination.

Man does not consciously indulge in such projection of his world, but does so according to his inherent nature. He builds around himself a world of bliss or misery, according to the degree of purity of his mind.

Sunday, July 15, 1984:

A few days later, I discussed with the Sadguru my continuing state of blissful abandonment, of total relaxation. He said, 'Absorb this mood into yourself, and rise above it. It would be easy for mere laziness to inter-penetrate such a state, and for you to interpret one for the other. This is not the goal. Being carried away by such feelings and emotions, one is stalled in the path. Enjoy this bliss, no doubt, but transcend it so that you do not stagnate there. Rise above it and, not content with this, ask for 'Purushottama' and 'Purushartha': the One and the only One, and His divine valour!'

Whatever one receives on the path, shun it, and say, 'Not this. Not this. I want only the final one!' Then alone will you be surely but firmly and permanently established in the Ultimate Reality, and not receive only a glimpse of it as I had received till now.

I found it easy to shun these spells of total abandon.

I absorbed and assimilated these spells in a trice—in the time it took me to see the wisdom of the Sadguru's advice. These spells stopped. Only the mood of peace and tranquillity prevailed. Not without a feeling of melancholy and a heavy heart did I bid farewell to this devotional though emotional fervour. And right enough, after ingesting these spells of heavenly repose, I got right back into the mood for my writings, which I had neglected for quite some time, fully steeped as I was in enjoying this bliss. I was lagging way behind in my writing, and I was now in the mood to catch up. Truly, one must capitalize on the God-given gifts and not indulge too much in such luxurious and intoxicating moods, even though sublime.

Previously, after each spell of waves, when the thought of work would arise in me, there would be a spurt of bodily activity: I would suddenly feel elated and buoyant; and full of energy, I would accomplish a lot of work within a ridiculously short time. However, the time allowed to me for carrying out any work would usually be very brief, and within no time, I would be back, listless, and under the spell of this ecstatic mood. I was permitted barely enough time for the essentials. The inconsequential, the unimportant, always got left out. Just enough energy would be spared to me to maintain the essential services of the household.

Now, after gobbling up this mood of total relaxation as suggested by the Sadguru, suddenly I was light and energized. Buoyant and dynamic. And somehow I felt this mood was for a lasting duration, not a fleeting one. I began catching up with my writing, and attending a little more to the efficient running of the household.

52

The Stopping of the Breath II

Thursday, July 19, 1984:

The current continues, the vibrations continue, different types of ecstasies, fervour, worship, bliss, all continue unabated; but the mood is predominantly work-oriented. Often, it is tempting to sit back and enjoy the quiet fruits of my silent worship. Various 'chakras' get activated at various times.

At night, Tejaswi moved, and I half awoke. Continuing in my half-asleep condition, I perceived a steady rhythmic flow gently moving upwards in my body. My entire subtle being, my thought, my concentration, even my breathing, all were ever so soothingly and smoothly, streaming towards a particular point at the centre of my head. Somewhere about half an inch below the crown. Here, the gently moving stream stopped; my subtle being, my thought, my concentration, and my breath, all got arrested at this point in a state of dynamic equilibrium. Now all these four, in fact, my very existence, seemed concentrated at this pin-point in a tiny void under the skull. Now the breathing had stopped. The awareness of this pin-point equilibrium was similar to the awareness a thermometer might have when the slowly rising mercury in it stops at a particular point of equilibrium.

In the equilibrium of this arrest was the centre of the universe, and an awareness of pure existence. The same sense of permanence, and a feeling that nothing is but That. A complete fullness.

A state beyond knowledge and thought. A sheer state of meditation. A complete union, a finality, a totality. The magnificence of endlessness in the 'present' and in the 'here'. Along with this, there was an awareness of actually tasting an indescribable nectarine ambrosia. It was superb. I now know what is meant by 'Amrut', the divine, immortalizing nectar.

The arrest was released, and the stream began traversing down the body gently. The breathing resumed.

When, earlier, the usual breathing had stopped, there had been some subtle inner breathing that did not have to take in air by the normal channels. A subtle inner 'japa' accompanied this phenomenon.

In my half-awake state, I observed this entire event happening several times. It was like nothing I had so far experienced. I got the feeling that everything was contained in this centre and in this state. A feeling of just existence prevailed, everything else stopped, nothing else mattered.

In a flash, I understood that this was the process of getting into deep samadhi. The rhythm of the inner flow was inducing a sort of a trance, and I felt that the stream could perhaps be kept arrested there, at the centre at the top of the head, with a little practice. There was a dull awareness of both what was going on within me and around me, and it would be easy to lose grip on either state. The two consciousnesses were very finely balanced, and only superb mastery could maintain the two states of awareness in equal strength. A slight tilt towards any one was sure to lose the other awareness.

Tejaswi moved again, but I determinedly continued to observe this phenomenon. I tried to probe the nature of the inner, automatic 'japa'. My fascination and probing woke me up completely. I had tripped, and lost the heavens. I tried to induce once more this concentration and this meditation. I tried to do 'japa' on my own. I tried to imitate the process to bring the phenomenon back, something like giving artificial breathing to a drowned person. But that was not to be. I had lost the divine stream. Things had to happen for me on their own. Things were being done for me. I had only to watch.

Friday, July 20, 1984:

Went to the Sadguru. He explained in detail what are 'jada' and 'chaitanya'. 'Jada', he said, is inert, inconscient, static energy stored in the body. This is the potential of the body. 'Chaitanya' is the activated, dynamic, the conscient. 'Jada' gets transformed into 'chaitanya.' This 'chaitanya' must be made to blossom and channelized.

The pressure in the head is 'jada' getting transformed into 'chaitanya'.

If the 'chaitanya' is too much in the body, it must be released from the body by mentally drawing it down, through the length of the body and out through the toes, and if this did not help, then by touching the big toe with the fingers.

The best way is to snap out of the soothing lethargy it induces. But at such times, there is neither a will nor a desire to snap out of it. It is quite pleasure-inducing, taking one to a city of inner repose.

These methods were not always effective with me. Raja would then touch my right toe, and would feel the energy flow into him. Often, this would give me instant relief. Occasionally, I had to sleep it off.

Saturday, July 21, 1984:

It dawned on me that the drowsiness and the pleasing listlessness that I had been experiencing all these days is actually a state of equipoise, a spontaneous state of equilibrium, which is half-way between the wakefulness and the oblivion I had observed on the 19th. In this state, there is a dull awareness of the surroundings, though the senses seem totally withdrawn; and yet, it gave out the ambrosia of the state of pure existence.

The essential thing was to have the subtle stream of consciousness unbroken. The state was of concentration stabilized in equilibrium. It had now become a part of my life.

I tried to get back into the state where I could be aware of my subtle self moving towards the point of equilibrium in the head. It was so pleasing to be in the state I had experienced the previous night that I now understood why people spend entire lifetimes in seclusion, trying to recapture or to remain in this state. With deep concentration, I was getting the hang of the technique, when I got frightened and gave up the venture, as not only did it require intense concentration but also the directing of my subtle elements in a particular psychic channel with a herculean effort, and I realized quickly that even a slight error in the manoeuvring could cause untold damage to my system. As I was carrying out my experiment without guidance, I thought the adventure was fraught with danger, and stopped it. I reasoned that I was given these experiences only to comprehend the complex processes, and not to remain continuously in them. One fleeting experience was enough to reveal to me the subtleties involved in these profundities. If and when the time comes for me to remain in a particular state, nature will guide me there of its own accord. Till then, all I had to do was to go along with this stream of equipoise, which continued whether I was at work or at rest. This equipoise had practical value in living the daily life—as it spread untold peace, tranquillity and a quiet joy right through me.

53

The Inner Silence

***

Sunday, July 22, 1984:

A deep and profound otherworldly silence enwraps me in the midst of humanity. This silence is pregnant with life. I turn to this silence often, for enshrined in this silence is a hint of communion. Though this silence bars outer thought and meaning, it packs into itself the sound and meaning of all the worlds. Encased within this silence is a full and complete consciousness that makes possible subtle communication, and exudes fullness, joy and contentment that permeate my entire being. It entered every pore, stimulating a feeling of joyous emptiness. But the joy is so serene that there is hardly any scope for its outward manifestation.

This happiness is complete; there is no room for craving or hankering. This characteristic lack of want, this typical indifference to outer aids of pleasure, abstinence from actively seeking joyous living, an apparent indifference to pleasure and pain, will appear as self-denial and self-abnegation, as perhaps too severe a recourse, perhaps unnecessary and unacceptable.

However, this austerity and a seemingly dull and drab life is rich with an inner happiness. There is such an outflow of joyous serenity and a deep contentment within that it makes any outer pleasures redundant.

This inner repose, this composure of mind, the stilled activity of body and mind, this refraining from seeming pleasures of life will definitely denote a drab and dry life. But steeped in inner bliss, endowed with a reservoir of inner strength, it is intelligent, dynamic and full of life. In fact, often, carrying on with ordinary

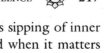

social obligations becomes painful, as it hinders sipping of inner enjoyment in solitude, till a mastery is reached when it matters not whether one is alone or in company. There is then a permanent stream of inner enjoyment unhindered by outside intrusions and interruptions.

However, when socializing had to be done, I found out that I could snap out of this current and enjoy the moment. Once the current ebbed and my concentration was on outer pleasures, I could extract full enjoyment from them. In fact, a stage came when the current was so much a part of me that there was no snapping out of it. It underlay and commingled with the other pleasures so finely that I could derive as much pleasure from the one as from the other, and simultaneously so.

A time came when I concluded that life in all its aspects is no different from this electrifying current of bliss. Both are part of an all-engulfing and continuous stream, originating from the same source, running inseparably together. When this realization dawned, then boredom, repugnance, a sense of ordeal, ceased to be, and life became one continuous joy whether in the midst of worldly pleasures or away from them. No longer did it make any difference.

Monday, July 23, 1984:

There was another trait to this silence. It was devoid of thought and knowledge. One would have thought that into this emptiness would rush murky, unwanted thoughts, but it was not so. This emptiness was self-contained and brimming with its own self and hence stalled any thoughts. This consciousness, cleansed of thought, was restful and soothing. It accorded a repose to which I reverted any time I got a chance. Nor was this emptiness stagnating. It would all the more sharpen the intellect and sensitize it towards intuitive wisdom. In one small flash, it would reveal what would have required hours of wordy explanations. It was as if a lamp had been lit to expose each and every corner of a room. Knowledge would flash forth.

This emptiness of mind was a potential dynamo of knowledge. It sharpened my 'knowing'. I simply 'knew'!

Monday, July 30, 1984:

I saw clearly an invisible and non-physical protective sheath, a 'kavacha', an armour, that gets built of its own around a yogi, whose mind has reached a particular high stage of development.

Thoughts arise around this yogi, but they get snuffed out in his presence. Even the persistent ones will not penetrate his armour. These too get burnt off.

The yogi is unaware of these thoughts. Such is the force radiating from the yogi that, without his volition, spontaneously, the thoughts are rendered powerless, thereby helping him to maintain his meditative state.

The thoughts are alien to the Self. In yogis, where the Self is glowing, the thoughts disintegrate in its august presence.

54

The Birth and Death of the Cosmos

Monday, August 6, 1984:

Last night, I had a dream: We were all in a quaint little village, with barracks-like houses built neatly around a cluster of mango trees. A sprawling banyan tree stood proudly to one side. A few other trees dotted a cemented, clean-swept pathway meandering through the village. Each tree had a raised cement bund around it on which the villagers would sit of an evening and gossip away. Sheltered under the canopy of the banyan stood a little temple. The houses had 'rangoli', patterns drawn and filled with coloured powders, outside their doors, and the women were busy decorating their entrances with 'toran', auspicious leaves strung together. The tolling of temple bells, the myriad lights of 'aratis' kept in readiness, the fragrance of incense, and the general hustle and bustle, heralded an event as great as Diwali, the festival of lights. The evening dusk was charged with anticipation. Playful cries of children, commands of the elders, the tinkling bells on the adorned feet of women, the aroma of festive sweets and the excited running around on errands signified the onset of an auspicious moment.

In the midst of this hurly-burly, there was a sudden mystical calm suffused with the magic of peace and permanence. There was an aura of Lakshmi, the goddess of wealth, that seemed to have lodged itself in the village to witness the coming sublime moment. Soon I saw a majestic cow-elephant, beautifully decked out, approaching the tiny temple, the bell tolling in tune to its unhurried step. Slowly, the elephant came in full view, followed by worshippers and children, amid the blowing of conch-shells and trumpets and the beating of drums. The elephant halted outside the temple in the open courtyard. The musicians sang the glory of the Lord, and the women and children took turns to do 'arati' to the resplendent elephant.

I learnt at once, as one does in a dream, that the elephant was a goddess incarnate, and had come to the village to shower upon it her blessings, and then proceed on to other villages. As she stood there very still, receiving the worship and loving services of her devotees, the expression on her face was serene. Occasionally swaying her trunk, she accepted their devotion with dignity. The evening dust glowed, the dancing flames in the fluttering lamps lengthened and, standing still for a moment, turned lambent. The illuminated village square swayed and sparkled. The auspicious elephant signified bounteousness. The goddess of plenty had come to the village. She was being evoked and propitiated. Her very presence spelt splendour. The grandeur of plenty holds magic for all. The expression on every face was exalted.

The elephant was to move from temple to temple, receiving homage from all. And along with the elephant would move the hordes of worshippers. Suddenly I am made to understand that, contrary to earlier plans, the elephant was not to move away but was to come and stay at my place for good. I am aghast. How was I to maintain this splendour and this grandeur? The elephant represented a deity of plenty and had to be looked after in a fitting manner. How could I, with our limited resources, do this? I was about to refuse, when a bright spark flitted through me. It seemed to say, 'Why do you assume it is your responsibility to look after a deity? Do not worry about inane things. He who has planned for her stay at your place will arrange for her upkeep also. Rejoice that the elephant deems it fit to come and stay at our place!'

With this responsibility removed from me, a feeling of deep contentment and quiet joy flooded through me, and I slept in ecstasy and with a splendid feeling of well-being that usually accompanies great and auspicious events.

Next morning, this feeling of enchantment persisted. In one of my meditative reposes, I slipped into 'sahaja samadhi'—a spontaneous, natural meditation. I was sitting on a sofa, completely relaxed. Though my eyes were closed, my vision was focused at the ground level. Suddenly, a deep, resonant voice spoke, 'You are restricting me. You are binding me down. I am 'tapan', 'tejomaya', 'tejasman', all-pervading, all-reaching. Free me, release me, and behold my splendour!'

And there on the horizon, behind my closed eyes, appeared a glowing sun, mild and red as if about to set. But this brilliant sun, instead of dipping and becoming increasingly mellow, in fact increased in size and intensity. Slowly, the size, the red and gold and vermilion glow, and the brilliance of this unusual sun increased and spread through the horizon across the skies till it almost covered the entire vista. To behold the full glory of this expanding sun, I had to lift my eyes skyward. As I lifted my eyes upwards, my concentration shifted from the bright sun to deep oblivion, and I fell into a deep meditation. The sun and its brilliance faded.

It had achieved its purpose. It had effectively instructed me to focus skyward whilst meditating. It gave me more of a panoramic view of the infinite, and instead of making me feel drowsy, as it did with downcast eyes, it kept me alert, and yet made me go deeper in concentration.

Slowly I came out of my samadhi and marvelled at this self-revealing force. By visions, by word, by thought and by gentle hints, it helped one along the path. Of what magnitude could this force be that it could reach and help everyone at all times and all together! This magnificent guiding force spread evenly everywhere. It was there for everyone's asking. Of what stuff could it be made that it could penetrate even the minutest thing, and yet contain all that is! Of what magic was it that a part of it was also the whole, and the whole the part? What was it that had sublime attributes, like the nectarine bliss, compassion and unadulterated knowledge? What was this that was born before birth, and had its existence beyond death, in whom time had no meaning, and space no scale?

I was lost in the contemplation of the astounding Lord Who reaches beyond the infinities, and the laws of birth and death, when suddenly a voice spoke, 'The Big Bang theory cannot be! In the Big Bang theory, the universe burst forth from a point so tiny that it was non-existent. The matter was compressed so densely that it all fitted into that point of nothingness. The force of the burst flung the matter apart, forming planets and stars and galaxies, evolving in a pattern to form the ever-widening universe. And when destruction finally comes, with the universe falling back upon itself, the matter will again converge and disappear into this mighty density of nothingness. The resultant force of this high density reduced to the compressed ultimate nothingness is the potential of the birth of the next universe.

'But to what centre will the universe converge when each point is itself the centre of the universe? And from which special point has it been flung apart when the all-pervading Infinite is spread across all infinities in equal force and evenness? Just as a grain of rice taken from a sackful will contain all the attributes of all the grains of rice in the sack, each point in the universe is an entire whole of this mighty Infinite, and is capable of being that special point from where can be born universes and into which can disappear universes. The Big Bang is only a local action going on all the time at different places. In minuscule ways and in stupendous magnitudes.

'When destruction finally comes, each atom will disappear where it is, transforming itself into energy which, in turn, will become so subtle that it becomes nothingness, for, after all, that is how it was born. And when the birth of the next universe takes place, each atom, that is already there within that nothingness, at that point, in the form of unmanifest energy and eventually matter, like the cream is already present in the milk, will precipitate forth in the form of matter and universe, as expansive, dynamic and ever-evolving as before. It would be something like the light suddenly being put off and the world shut off from our eyes, and then switched on again only to lay before our eyes the magical extravaganza of creation, no doubt, each process involving enormous time, and being accompanied by traumatic upheavals and cataclysmic changes. Till then, the perpetual pattern of birth and death goes on every moment, everywhere, in smaller and bigger magnitudes.

'This is the divine breathing. The divine drawing in of the breath at each point would be the slow destruction of matter at each point, or conversion of matter into pure energy sublimating into nothingness, like the burning camphor slowly disappearing into nothingness. The entire universe would be swallowed up or absorbed in or inhaled unto It. At each point, where each particle is or was. As is, where is. So would be the rebirth. The Almighty is omnipresent, with the sameness of indescribable exactness.

'So, which point could be more important than others, as to be designated The Point where the universe would be born or swallowed up? The Almighty force is all-pervading; each point will breathe in and breathe out with the same evenness. When it breathes out, the universe will be born again, first in the form of energy that would unfold into elements, and finally, into matter and physical universe, all-pervading and ever extending.

'This process goes on. So does the evolution, once the universe takes its birth, much like man continually evolves from birth, till death finally merges him into the divine matrix, and he once more comes back with a new body to further the process of evolution.

'At each point in the universe, in one form or the other, conversion of matter into energy, thence into nothingness, then again the birth into matter is going on, all the time.

'Then again, on a larger scale, local big bangs, or explosion of matter or galaxies into nothingness, and again precipitation into matter and galaxies, are going on constantly in the universe . . . progressively involving vaster areas and a greater span of time.'

When the inner voice got transformed into a cinemascopic vision I do not know, but somewhere down the line, my eyes got fixed at one point, and I began seeing a magnificent spectacle of awesome proportions of the universe dwindling into nothingness, accompanied by colossal upheavals and cosmic-scale devastation, which, even in its destruction, was the divinity itself. Of course, what I saw was only a glimpse of one tiny process. The whole process, no doubt, would be gradual, involving eons upon eons. After all, a colossal amount of matter had to change form, so then, where is the hurry?

There is no conceivable end to evolution.

Tuesday, August 7, 1984:

There is an alternating pattern of days of lethargy and days of zest and energetic activity. During the lethargic days, there is no will to work, think, write, even to stir. But, during the active days, a lot of work could be accomplished smoothly and with no obstructions.

Wednesday, August 8, 1984:

I was sitting, staring fixedly at nothing. My attention slowly focused on my breathing. Within moments, I felt that with each inhaling breath, I was drawing in the entire cosmos. With the exhaling breath, I was breathing out the cosmos.

Slowly, I became conscious of the entire humanity breathing in and breathing out. And I felt that I was in myself a gigantic synchronized breathing rhythm of the humanity as a whole, at one moment breathing in, then breathing out together.

I ran down and asked Nandita, my daughter, to lift one of her fingers, as a signal, while inhaling, and drop it while exhaling. I found her rhythm coincided with mine. I went from person to person, experimenting, and I found that all were breathing, unknowingly, in rhythm with mine.

Could it be that all, barring those with breathing problems, breathe in and breathe out together?

This experiment held true, as long as the other person did not know what the experiment was, and so did not become self-conscious and alter his breathing rhythm.

55

Love and 'Bhakti'

Friday, August 17, 1984:

The inner current started. As I lay on the bed, I felt that the body as a whole was being drawn inwards like water is drawn into a whirlpool. This was different to a similar movement of each individual cell perceived some days earlier.

Wednesday, August 29, 1984:

For this year's festival of Ganesh Chaturthi, we had instructed a statue-maker to make for us a clay image of the deity Ganapati resembling the deity Lord Vitthal of Pandharpur but with a golden-complexioned body. The golden Ganapati, standing like a resplendent Vithoba, is so beautiful that none has had the heart to immerse the idol in the ocean waters after the 'puja', as is required by tradition. Thus it has stood in our drawing-room, gracefully accepting our love and affection, even after the usual ten days of celebrations. We have decided to immerse the idol along with the next year's one when the festival comes around again after twelve months.

Often I used to wonder about the wisdom of keeping a clay Ganapati for so long in the house. Often we had planned to immerse it; either there was a change of heart, or some obstruction would crop up. And he has remained with us.

At night, I got a clear message: 'You have often planned to send me away. But I have remained. There is a reason for this. Having seen the non-duality, after perceiving the highest truth, you have been bowing to me, though knowing I am merely a clay model. This is as it should be. Be always humble. Revere the concept of divinity in everything. Respect the symbol of divinity. My work is over. You may send me away.'

Monday, September 24, 1984:

I had just finished reading a life-sketch of Shri Anandamayee Ma, whose 'darshan' I have had previously a few times. Now I recalled vividly her benign, soothing presence, and humbly prayed to her.

At night, she appeared to me in a vision, dressed in white, her hair let down, and head covered by the 'pallav' of her saree.

She said, 'I have given everything to you. Now there is no difference between you and me. I am you, and you are me. Do not pray to me.'

As she said this, it was I who was standing there, dressed in white, poised in mid-air, talking to my body lying on the bed. I was Anandamayee Ma, and I was also myself. Each one was both.

Tuesday, October 23, 1984:

Love, love, love! There is an effulgence of love. An effulgence of compassion. Love and compassion are the essential nature of this state. I feel love, compassion, understanding, emanating from me and spreading out to cover the universe.

I realize now what Christ had meant when he spoke of love and brotherhood. Love flows out of oneself. But this love is different. It has control. It does not make one get carried away into breaking the norms of society and, yet, it does not stop at the world of body and matter. It transcends everything to pierce the realm of the unseen, and uncovers a world of unity, purity, oneness and innocence.

There is no sin here, as there is a perfect understanding of why a person is behaving in a particular manner. There is no ugliness here, as beneath this ugliness is a substratum of innocence, of beauty.

This love is pure consciousness. It vibrates through the cosmos. This is the potential, of which the world is the manifestation.

Love is sublime. Love is divinity. Love is an essential part of the Lord.

Wednesday, October 24, 1984:

The force of knowledge remains unbroken. There is a continuous urge to write. There is an urge to share the joy, the simplicity, the bliss of this sublime experience through the medium of a book. Repeatedly a message comes: let this be a modern Gita.

I write only when the flow of Knowledge is spontaneous, as it has come to me of its own.

Thursday, October 25, 1984:

It is said that the backdrop for pleasure seems to be pain. As the pleasure is removed, pain prevails. To remove pain, we have simply to reinforce the original, eternally unchanging state of calm, serene bliss, which is beyond pain and seeming joy, identify completely and permanently with it. Before this ever-present, forceful, sublime composure, the worldly pain and pleasure will flit like pictures across a screen neither affecting nor involving us. Strengthen this inner joy that needs no external instruments, unlike the worldly joys. Worldly pleasures are temporary, and pale into insignificance in comparison with the absorption and joy in the Self, in the stark inner being. The means of seeking worldly pleasures too are painful, their absence agonizing. The very first step inwards to the Self is a step on the road to heaven.

Friday, October 26, 1984:

Love, bliss, nectar, compassion, ecstasy! There hardly seems any demarcation between them. They all merge in one—into nectarine love. Into ecstasy. This ecstasy forms the very core of divinity. All-pervading. Forming a substratum of existence. It effulges from the Divine in super-abundance, impregnating every particle and being.

This ecstasy is the essence of Reality, of the Self, which It experiences all the time. This Self-centred experience or Self-absorption, or 'bhakti' unto Itself is the nectar or experience of the Divine bliss that flows out of the Self, inseparable from It. This is the bliss or 'ananda' of the Sat-Chit-Ananda. Inseparable from each other, spontaneous, born of the Ultimate, forming part and parcel of the pure Divine Consciousness, 'ananda' spurts from pure existence. It expresses itself in creative energy or in creation. The whole world is an expression of this consciousness, of 'ananda'. The Ultimate Reality derives 'ananda' from Itself, constantly, absorbed in Itself, in a state of unwavering and deep self-meditation.

If the individual does not feel the presence of this 'ananda' or pure consciousness, it is because his own individual consciousness has not been raised to such sublime levels. The individual whose consciousness has merged into divine consciousness experiences this state of ecstasy spontaneously, permanently. Absorbed unto himself, he experiences 'bhakti', transcendent love unto Self.

When he is Self-absorbed and looks around, he feels the same 'ananda' flowing out of him to every being, every cell. He feels love flow out for everyone, just as love flows out of the Ultimate for everyone. He sees the grand unity and the oneness of all.

When man has whole-hearted devotion to God, it is called 'bhakti'. He is now experiencing the same divine 'ananda' in duality. Without cognizing that the outer God is really dwelling within him, without cognizing that concentration on the outer God is actually leading him to self-absorption, he enjoys the ecstasy of 'bhakti'.

His prayers, his love for God, his total surrender unto a particular form of God, all are leading him to the 'Purushottama' or the Self or the Ultimate which is beyond even the Sat-Chit-Ananda or the Knowledge. 'Bhakti' will lead him one day to perceive that God is self-dwelling in each being, in each cell, in each particle, and that the particular God he was evoking is actually residing within him, accepting graciously all his offerings of love and devotion. Then 'bhakti' becomes a spontaneous meditation on the Supreme Self, on one's own Self.

Such unconditional and spontaneous 'bhakti' or love for God or Self or 'ananda' is totally fulfilling. It becomes a goal, the culmination of a quest, all-encompassing. It leaves one without desires, wants or demands. It is self-less and is purely for the love of God or Self. It is love sublime!

Life on earth too experiences love instinctively. In man, it is developed strongly.

The universe and life spring from the Ultimate, uncaused. But each being falls under the purview of cause and effect. It has to be born, experience certain events, lead a certain life, all according to its personal evolution and, in man, according to his past deeds. Now, it has fallen into the realm of time and space. For this individual to be born in a particular place and at a particular time and under particular circumstance, to undergo or enjoy punishment or reward for his past deeds, a sort of a timer is required. So the phenomenon of 'conception' comes into force, with two particular parent individuals meeting at a pre-destined place and time. So the instinctive affinity for the required counterpart takes place. In humans, this affinity superbly developed in the form of sublime love. Love for the opposite sex. In the union of the two individual parts is experienced the divine ecstasy, just as a devotee experiences in his merger with his chosen deity, and the realized person experiences in the merger with the Universal!

The bliss experienced in the merger with the Universal is the highest and permanent. It requires no external entities or aids or instruments. It is spontaneous and pure.

56

Mind and 'Maya'

Monday, October 29, 1984:

Mind:

Mind is the twilight zone between matter and non-matter; mind is the link, the threshold, between matter and energy. It is the point where the two come together and remain in a continually stable mixture. The mind can tilt heavily towards matter, or sublimate into pure energy and then the divine. Hence, mind is a link between man and the divine. A link to reach the divine, or an alienating barrier to it.

Mind, when inert, is matter or 'jada'; when sublimated, cosmic energy or 'chaitanya'. Mind enwrapped in 'thought' gets encased into sheaths of spiritual ignorance and ego. It is now inert or matter, though still subtle and, no doubt, beyond conception of man.

Mind purified to its utmost gets liberated as energy and, piercing more and more subtle sheaths of spiritual ignorance, and finally that of Maya, it merges with the all-pervading cosmic force, with the Divine. It is now non-matter. It is divine. It is the Infinite.

Matter reduced to its subtlest form turns into energy, and this transition from the gross to the Infinite is the great evolution of mind.

Mind is that in-between state when an unfathomable subtle state of matter can change to a super-subtle state of consciousness. Mind in its subtlest form is Divinity. Mind is simultaneously matter and non-matter, and matter and energy, capable of changing from one state to the other.

Tuesday, October 30, 1984:

Maya:

'Maya' is not spread across the cosmos like a gigantic curtain, veiling the Reality from man. 'Maya' is only the final subtle sheath of spiritual ignorance covering the mind of man. 'Maya' is confined to mind and to man. The mind of other species being too primitive, it is redundant to talk of 'Maya' in relation to them. 'Maya' is an integral part of the mind, and thereby of man. It is his personal possession to be cherished and preserved, destroyed and discarded by him. He alone is its master, who can either choose to transcend it and grow in the higher realms of purity and immortality, or remain in the baser world to bask in its illusory pleasures.

'Maya' is not a veil spread across the cosmos waiting to be pierced by man. 'Maya' is only a pair of coloured glasses covering the eyes of man . . . in his mind. Depending upon the colour of the glasses is coloured the man's view of the world.

The world that spreads before us has sprung from perfection. The magnificence of the source reflects in the grandeur of the creation. The universe surging forth from such a divinity cannot be tainted by illusion. It cannot be contaminated by confusion. The world is an illusion or unreal to the extent that it is ever-changing, and it is relative. By Real, or 'Sat', is meant only that which is eternal, ever the same, permanent, all-pervading, changeless, timeless, ever-fresh, perfect, in short, the Infinite, which is never born, never dying, the soul, the consciousness. The universe gets born, dies, changes, and is restricted by form and structure, and so it cannot be Real. Our life is relative, and subject to so many changes, all depending on our mood, health, environment, circumstances, and so on. So, our life, as we understand it, is also not Real. Nor is our body, for the same reason. But the world is real in so far as matter, of which it is constituted, and our life, as we with our limited understanding make of it, are concerned. But the universe and our life are not Real. By real, we mean real to the senses. By Real, we mean a real beyond the senses, which cannot be seen, smelt, touched, tasted or heard, and which does not change and which is True, certain, a fact and eternal; in other words—Consciousness.

That we confuse real for the Real is our ignorance. That we fail to understand that, beyond the real, co-existing with it, overlaying it, underlying it, is the Reality, is our ignorance or 'Avidya'. That our very life and the world lie within the higher realms of this Reality, we fail to see, and that is our ignorance. And this 'Avidya' or spiritual ignorance, the cause of all misery, is caused by 'Maya', the sheath of ignorance or turbidity of the mind of man. So he gets enmeshed in the tangle of this material world, getting so bogged down by it that there is no wish or intent to look inwards into the subtler realms. This is where the nectar lies, and the ambrosia abounds. This is the abode of the nectarine Bliss and the Supreme Knowledge or 'Dnyana' or 'Vidya', and of contentment.

This is where the permanent bliss is, beyond the realms of 'Maya'. The bliss or peace or happiness that man is ever striving for. This is Real and permanent, and this is Reality. The same Reality pervades man and every creature. This bliss is an inherent facet of Reality. This Reality is within reach of every man, because it is within him only. He has to only discover it. But in his deep ignorance, plastered thick by his ego, man fails to transcend the much-abounding, easily available, transitory and non-satisfying pleasures of the material world and does not turn inwards to the supreme exuberance of Reality.

This is his ignorance. Man's inherent nature is to seek out pleasure and happiness, and as he knows no better, he thinks the material objects will give him happiness. And he gets entangled in obtaining them. In the wake of this struggle comes the allied misery. And this misery and this struggle become his world and his life. This is illusory and impermanent. It is real to the extent this world revolves round his senses. He can see, he can hear and he can taste, and naturally wonders how all this world of the senses can be unreal. It must be real. This is where he stops. He will not or cannot comprehend anything other than this. He cannot comprehend a non-sensual reality where one can see without eyes, feel without body, hear without ears, and taste without the tongue; where the world does not exist in relation to the body and matter. It is a world beyond light, beyond word, beyond thought and beyond matter.

This is the realm of a fabulous, all-pervading Principle. A Principle that is non-existent, yet contains all that is. It forms the matrix for all energies, all power, all the force, all the Knowledge, all the matter and the entire consciousness, and yet is Itself beyond them all. This is the Reality. This same Reality permeates man, as it does throughout the cosmos. A part of this Principle is a whole, so the Reality residing in man is also the whole. Man has it in him to experience this Supreme Bliss, the Supreme Knowledge, and the Universal Awareness in its totality. As he understands this Principle, ignorance slowly withers away, and, by acquiring more and more of purity and knowledge, he strips away more and more of these sheaths of ignorance. A time comes when only the last subtle sheath of ignorance remains: when he is pure, he believes firmly in the Principle, and knows this Principle theoretically. But a slight doubt or confusion still remains and still separates him from the Principle. He has to learn it first-hand, experientially.

This final sheath of ignorance, thin, subtle, elusive, is 'Maya'. Ignorance in its purest form. When mind transcends this ignorance and pierces the veil of 'Maya', he experiences the Reality. The separating veil having been pierced, he becomes one with the Principle. One with the divine.

This is the grand evolution of mind. From the gross, it sublimates to the subtle, thence, it transcends to the divine. With the sublimation of mind, the individual consciousness, but not the body, merges with the divine. Mind that had separated the individual from the divine negates itself in the ultimate sublimation, culminating into the purity of non-existence, making one whole continuous Infinite.

In the negation of mind, the mind does not disappear. Mind is a pre-requisite to experience the higher Reality. It only transcends to the higher degree of purity when it totally subdues its alienating ego, thought, emotions, its knowledge and its slippery and impure nature, and effaces itself completely into the purity of non-existence. Now its individuality is lost and it becomes one with the all-pervading Principle. Shorn of these, it remains, nevertheless, as a shining, luminous, highly sensitized medium, ready to experience the nectar of-the divine. The mind, having merged with the divine, all-pervading Principle, is now the Universal Awareness. The pot having broken, the air inside and outside becomes one; that is, the individual soul that was confined by the impure mind now comes forth and merges with the Universal Principle.

57

What Is This Force?

Monday, December 24, 1984:

The current was on. I was half-asleep. A gentle throbbing started on both sides of the nose at the high point of the bridge. As the vibrations increased, a wave of ecstasy spread outward, soothing in its effect. I had the feeling that my nose was expanding, stretching, detaching itself from the bridge. It expanded vastly into space and into nothingness. My identity was lost too, swallowed up in this nothingness.

My breathing seemed to stop. The throbbing stopped. I was suspended in nothingness. Time lost its meaning. Then, slowly, breathing recommenced, and with it came back the gentle vibrations. I found my nose, my precious nose, back in its position, and yes, back to its old shape and size!

Thursday, December 27, 1984:

I have mentioned earlier that, frequently, the senses withdraw completely. They turn inwards; it is a feeling of being pulled inwards to such an extent that they all seem to converge to a point of perfect equilibrium. Even the life-force seems to be pulled to this point of perfect equipoise, comfort, and stability!

Now, there was a further development to this. Even while walking around, doing my work, I would get into this state. My breath would, in a swift change of direction, get sucked upwards, towards this point of equipoise. I would suddenly stand still, with the body limp, and head tilted back and sideways. It would happen so quickly and so unexpectedly that I would be taken off my guard.

As I am fully awake at such times, the instinctual fear of the unknown would grip me, and not knowing whether I would be able to bring my breath down, I would try and prevent its going upwards. Because of my efforts or on its own, I would regain normal breathing. There would be no discomfort. All it left in its wake was ecstasy.

Friday, January 11, 1985:

What is this force that floods a being with an engaging sensation of pouring energy?

What is this force that brings with it such enchantment that the universe seems to stall in its wake?

What is this force that makes one limp with pleasure and satiated to the brim with oneself?

What is this force that stops all thought, stops time, and halts movement, making do with only awareness and bliss?

What is this force that unifies the body, the mind, the senses, the life-force to a point of ambrosial, heavenly equilibrium?

Such peace, such tranquillity, such a sensation of permanence and eternity, wrapped in a sublime feel of purity and divinity— what is this force that comes thus invested?

What is this potent, vigorous force that races through the body, like the winds across the oceans?

Now as if pouring into the body, now as if self-generating, now as if radiating from the body, coursing through the body like a current of electricity.

This is the primal force of nature, the incalculable energy pervading through the cosmic expanse.

As the mind gets purified, it sublimates more and more from the heavy matter that is its grounding to pure energy, and thence to the subtle, primal force, becoming one with the all-pervading cosmic energy. Now it is non-matter. This is different to the bio-energy of the body that is generated by the well-functioning organs of the body.

The primal force is generated by the transcending mind—that is the reabsorption of matter into the Self. This activates all the subtle nerve centres of the body—the 'chakras'—which radiate and throb with singular force. This radiation and throbbing cause a sensation of flowing energy, a sensation of dynamism, animation, impulsion, all in the midst of quietude, equipoise and repose. This seeming flow of energy is the manifestation of the unmoving, primal force. It is the energy of that indivisible Divinity that operates the matter.

58

'Spanda'—A State of Subtle Vibration

To be in a position to see the entire universe, with all its multitudes of galaxies and super-galaxies, in one span, throughout time and space; to be able to witness every little event that takes place every moment through eons and eons of time, beginningless and endless; to know intimately all beings, down to the smallest particle in space; to know each little emotion that infiltrates through them; to smell, hear, see, feel, and taste everything that they smell, hear, see, feel, and taste through all the eternities that have passed, are passing and have yet to pass; to have all the cumulative bliss of all the eternities; to have all the knowledge, art and talent that exist in the universe; to have all the power and this cosmic awareness, without mix-up of individual or group identities, and the Self-identity; to know everything, to feel everything, yet remain uninvolved, ego-less; to have universes of such stupendous-ness coming out of oneself, out of nothing, then these same universes getting re-absorbed in the same self, negating into nothingness, yet remain whole, untouched and undiminished and uncontaminated, calls for an entity as great as only the Lord can be and is.

To be every component, every particle, every man, every beast, the micro—as well as the macro—, containing all the time and space within, to be all the energies, knowledge and matter, to absorb all the tumultuous multi-multi-multitudes of emotions of all the beings, and yet remain in a state of undisturbed meditation, without having to strive for it, Whose very nature is such all this would at least hazily indicate the incalculable calibre of such a Being.

To possess such a supra-awareness, to feel and have such limitless power, unbounded force, endless knowledge, undiminishing ecstasy or bliss, yet remain in equipoise, detached, witnessing everything, fully aware that all is Him, yet remain unmoved; be in a state of bliss, yet exist so unassumingly, abstract, humble, unseen, behind the scenes—that is the Lord!

This limitless bliss, this eternal and undisturbed state of meditation, this controlled state of existence, generates staggering, fathomless, inconceivable and unimaginable dynamism and momentum.

Even this mind-boggling dynamism, momentum and kinetics is controlled, and its expression or its manifestation is in turn controlled. It is smooth, uniform and unchanging.

Such a control gathers a charge, a force, a potency, a flux, almightiness. This charge becomes a throb. It pulsates. It radiates.

It gets into a state of vibration, constant and eternal. The radiation, the vibration, finds expression in creation. This cosmic throb, born of the Lord, is the Lord Himself. It is His awareness, His knowledge, His power, His bliss finding expression. Born of a vibrant, true, absolute Reality, the one and the only existence. Throbbing, pulsating, vibrating—this is the natural expression of the Lord. It depicts His dynamism, His Cosmic charge, His potency, His momentum, His radiance!

This radiance, His aura, His charge, create a flux that results self-knowingly into creation permeated by the Existence of the Lord, suffused by His awareness, His knowledge and His power.

This state of vibration permeates man too. As his mind dissolves, as it gets purified, as he progressively merges with the Lord, he becomes aware of this state of the subtlest vibration, this '*spanda*', in his being.

As the mind gets purified, it gets transformed into cosmic energy. Now with the awareness heightened, that is, more and more of individual awareness merging with the universal, the divine attributes get accentuated and the being is made more aware of this vibration.

This state of vibration generates peace, equanimity or a state of meditation or samadhi, and bliss.

The cosmic vibration and the cosmic energy, both of which are born of the Lord, are the Lord's, inseparable from Him, one giving rise to the other. When the mind transcends itself and slowly sublimates into purity, it activates the important nerve centres of the body, throwing them into a spurt of activity and radiance. This simulates the feel of energy and vibration in the body. Now the energy and vibration in the body are tuned into the cosmic energy and the cosmic vibration, the segmenting mind having been transformed into a higher form.

Vibration, throbbing, or pulsation would be an attribute of matter, of a physical body, no matter how small.

But the Lord is formless, beyond matter, and is an abstract entity, so the cosmic throb or state of vibration is without movement. The movement is only in the awareness. If you touch the body of such a man, no vibration will be felt. Yet it is there. Reality itself does not vibrate. It is still. But it generates the flux, the vibration.

From this dynamic charge comes the primal energy, from primal energy come the manifest energies whose permutations and combinations give rise to the subtle elements and the gross matter.

If a man be high up enough in his evolution, he may contain within him the unmanifest energies in high concentration, and may pass on heat and charge to others. He could, by his will, transform the energy arrangement of objects, producing or altering the things. For example, he may transform the unnoticed leaf lying in the garden into a cup of hot tea merely by the exercise of the unmanifest power lying within him. He may cure people, or change events. Things and events which seem miraculous are only the result of nature dancing to such a man's tune. As this man's mind is pure, he will never stoop to base motives or actions. Such a man is now revered by humanity. If he transcends further, miracles might happen, spontaneously, without his even willing it or making any gestures, without his thinking and perhaps even knowing, just as the miraculous world is sprouting spontaneously, without effort, without gestures, from the Almighty.

59

God Is Not the Creator of the Universe!

Creating something would involve some space to create in, some time to create, materials, equipment, hands, a lot of thought, conception, planning, and then execution of the plan.

All these are the prerogative of man. He has to think, plan and execute. He needs the raw materials, equipment and hands. He needs time to create, and space to create in.

But such is the power of the Lord that He does not need to create. He is everywhere. There is no place vacant where He can create. Will He create something within Himself, and then search for a place where he can 'park' His creation? No, the Lord is larger than the creation, and as such, it is within Him, and as such, it is permeated by Him.

The Lord has no form and hence no hands. Thinking and planning would require thought. Thought would require a mind. He has no thought and no mind. These are the essential characteristics of man. The Lord is beyond thought and mind.

There is no material that is not Him. Shall He create out of Himself? Chop and mould Himself?

Just as He cannot create the creation, He cannot create implements required by Him for creation. Then where will He get the necessary equipment from? Who will make them for Him? Who will create His plan for Him? Will He sit up for days, creating things step by step?

No! Such meticulous and progressive creating would be the requirement of man.

Such is the power of the Lord that He does not need to create. Creating is man's handicap. He would need to create. But the Lord does not need to create. Creation springs from Him. Creation of such grandeur, such majesty, such perfection. Creation of such variety, mystery and profundity. Creation divine, creation beyond imagination.

Immaculate meditative state spurts forth creation. Eternal, faultless, unwavering, undisturbed, spontaneous, divine meditation of such a massive, pure, mighty entity, spurts forth faultless creation. Divine creation!

As He exists through all time, with superb uniformity, His creation too exists eternally, though following a pattern of creation, evolution and destruction—birth, growth and death.

He Himself remaining intact, uninvolved, undiminished, untouched, the aura of the Lord blossoms into creation. Into matter and energy. Into heat and light. Into universe and man. The Lord Himself remains in deep meditation.

The Lord Himself is Knowledge, perfect, impeccable Knowledge. Knowledge which does not need to progress, change, or evolve. It is perfection itself, eternal and true for any time. Such Knowledge does not need a plan.

The Lord dwells beyond the dimension of time, beyond all dimensions. He does not need time to create. Creation springs from Him instantly, eternally, spontaneously. It is automatic and natural. It is an inherent power of the Lord which He does not have to will. To will would again involve time and effort. Such is the power of the Lord that He does not have to either will or make an effort.

The Lord pervades everywhere. His aura is everywhere, inseparable from Him. The aura is the Lord. This aura is all-pervading, like the Lord. As He is endless and limitless, so is His aura. His Knowledge, His bliss, His power, His terrific awareness, His energy, all generate a powerful aura. Such is the power of this aura, which is itself this universe and is much more than the universe.

The Lord does not need help in execution. The Lord is self-supportive, self-subsisting, self-emanating, and His creation is self-born, following a self-known rhythm and a self-planned pattern.

What strength, what staggering proficiency, what cogency, what endowment and ability are gathered behind this vibrancy that we call the Lord, that out of Him come forth star after star, galaxy after galaxy. What power He wields that, effortlessly, this creation follows a meticulous path and a faultless rhythm which involve not only the inert matter but also the glorious and very much alive energy, in their multifarious forms, leaving Him unentangled and uninvolved!

A witness absorbed in eternal samadhi. The creator and the enjoyer of the rhythm of birth and death, of cause and effect, the rhythm of self-reward and self-punishment! Like the rest of Him, even this rhythm is self-contained, self-supportive, and self-propelling—leaving man to be the sole cause of his own life!

What effulgence of justice that things just don't happen haphazardly in the world. They are brought about by a simple rule of 'as ye sow, so shall ye reap'. In the eternal cycle of birth and death, one always retains one's origin, one's path of evolution, one's aspirations, one's dedication to evolution. Evolution of not only body but also of mind. Opportunity after opportunity is given in repeated births to ascend the ladder of happiness, of knowledge, of divinity, of knowing how to sow the divine and to reap the divine. All that man has to do is to avail of this opportunity. The will to evolve, the will to ascend. Such is the generosity of the Lord that He has showered His blessings on man to enable him to leap to the Lord's own heights, in his own time, in his own course, in his own way. This is the glorious Law of 'Karma'.

How unfathomable is the greatness of the Lord! His creation is superb, so scientific, so artistic, so aesthetically satisfying, so glorious, and so radiant! Is it any wonder that people have sung such glorious paeans of praise of Him throughout the history of man? And no amount of praise and no amount of glory sung would do any justice to such greatness. Language fails; expression fails.

The only true, adequate praise and appreciation of His magnificence would be an endeavour to merge in Him, to know

Him, and to be worthy of His glory. However, all the possible perception of Him, all the possible comprehension of Him, all the possible merging in Him are still a limited reaching towards Him, because of the in-built limitations of man. Because the Lord is limitless.

Still, such is the glory of the Lord, that even a glimpse of Him is enough to transport man to ecstasy, to the Kingdom of the Lord, and bestow upon him eternal glory and grace. A glimpse of Him reflects in full measure the glory of Him through such a man.

The Lord and His Creation:

I am the Lord God, the eternal God, the Almighty. I pervade everywhere. I permeate everything. I exist as Sat-Chit-Ananda. Knowledge and power are inseparable from me.

I cannot be slayed, diminished, made wet, burnt, pushed or tainted. The entire power, bliss, knowledge awareness that exist in the world are me. It is mine. Every form in the universe is my form. All the heads are my heads, and all limbs are my limbs.

You cannot see, hear, touch, smell or taste me. But you can experience me—be me!

I am nothing, yet I am everything. I have no form. I have only a manifestation. A manifestation which is a world of matter, energy and movement.

I am the soul of this creation. I pervade man and all matter. I pervade all beings. The soul of man is me, my continuation. Man's body and mind are part of my manifestation.

I am unchanging, undying, undecaying, without birth, eternal, and pure. This is the Reality. This is true existence. The womb from where springs all the existence. The soul of the universe. It is my existence that is reflected by the existence of the universe. It is its life-force.

This life-force creates movement, a pattern, a rhythm. This self-generating, self-supporting, self-knowing rhythm maintains the eternal youth and grandeur of the creation. It makes the matter dance. It makes the universe dance. This is the grand cosmic dance in which the smallest individual particle of matter, in unity with the biggest, the largest super-galaxy, dances in rhythm and in unison to an intricate cosmic beat.

Man's body too is subject to this meticulous rhythm. It gets born, lives and dies, only to be born again, young and new. But along with me, his soul, the real he, remains eternal, unchanging, unborn, undying, pure and stark.

The creation is me. But I am other than the creation.

The creation is born of me. But I am independent of the creation. I require it not for my sustenance, nor my existence.

The creation has its very existence in me. But I am free and uninvolved in the creation.

Man's body, his aura, his performance, are his creation, his manifestation. As he purifies himself, his manifestation will shine and glow.

Just as the sun manifests itself in light and heat, I manifest in creation, and man manifests in his doings and in his behaviour.

Just as the sun is known by his manifestation of heat and light, I am known by my manifestation of creation.

Just as the sun by itself is nothing and invisible, I am nothing and invisible.

The sun does not 'will'. Will is subject to change. Change is a prerogative of man's mind. It changes with his condition and evolution. The sun does not will his manifestation. There will be chaos if the sun's will changes according to its whims.

Like the sun, I too do not will my manifestation. I have no will. I have no evolution, and hence I am not subject to change. My manifestation is spontaneous, without my willing it or directing it.

Just as the sun and its manifestation are one and the same, just as you cannot separate the two, just as the sun exists through its manifestation, I too am inseparable from my manifestation.

60

Man and 'Maya'

The Glory of God–Man:

A grain of rice in a sack of rice contains all the properties of all the grains of rice.

The Lord, with His infinite consciousness, pervades everywhere and every component. He pervades homogeneously each component, containing all the cosmic aspects of the Infinite. He pervades Man too.

A glimpse of the Lord within oneself will give one a fair perception of the Lord. As the Lord exists uniformly everywhere, the Lord of the universe will be revealed within oneself in this inward glimpse.

Where all will you go peering for the Lord of the Universe? Play safe, and capture a glimpse of the Lord residing within you, and who is within reach.

The Lord of the universe is invisible. He is manifest in His creation, and is known by your merger in Him.

In this merger, you will perceive the universe, and perceive your true Self.

Neither matter, nor plant, nor beast can perceive the Lord in all His splendour. Only Man can—such is the glory of Man that, at least to some extent, he can perceive and be enthralled by the glory of the Lord! Infinite is the glory of the Lord!

But the glory of one is continuous with the glory of the other. The glory of one reflects the glory of the other. In this beautiful inter-relationship is perceived one harmonious, uniform, eternal glory.

But for the keen perceptions of man, the Lord would have existed unsung and unappreciated like a rose in the wilderness.

Awake, O Man! The supernatural grandeur and majesty of the Lord is your heritage, your birthright—it is you!

Perceive, O Man! The Supreme Lord you seek so vehemently without is within you. He is you!

Behold, O Man! The glory of the Lord you sing, the fervent prayers you offer, the sincere gratitude to Him you feel, the praise you utter of Him, are all heard by the Lord within you. It is the gracious He who receives your praises, and basks in your recognition of Him.

Remember, the divine inner peace can be an abode for you. True Knowledge can be you. Cosmic awareness can be yours.

Discern, O race of man, you are not the body; you are not the accumulated, biased and inadequate knowledge; you are not your egoistic intellect, not your emotions—the harbinger of misery. The real you is something immense, something pure, free of sin and ugliness, free from pain and hurt, with an inherent nature of bliss, knowledge and cosmic awareness.

This is the Kingdom of the Lord—the regaining of your true self, becoming free, unbounded, all-pervading and happy.

Beyond 'Maya':

Once the veil of 'Maya' is pierced, the world does not disappear. The universe does not become a falsity, a fabrication of the mind. The world of matter remains intact.

But the miserable world that you had yourself built for yourself, by your faulty understanding of things, which you had fortified heavily, by your cherished thought and ego, and which you had guarded zealously with emotions and which was subject to changes and upheavals with the changes in your moods and situations— the world of your mental make-up—that world disappears. That world was falsity. You realize what an illusory world you had built and inhabited! Understanding and wisdom dawn upon you, and a new world of purity and perfection unfolds before you.

Matter too seems illusory. In this state of cosmic pervasiveness, you permeate every component of matter, even the walls of the tiniest component. Each particle is suffused by you; it is you. It is pure consciousness, which is your state too now. Matter is now transformed into consciousness. So, where is the matter now? No more does matter offer any obstruction. You can see through it, pass through it, be in it, be it! Suddenly, it seems an illusion. But it does not disappear.

However, in this non-duality, one must regain an assertive duality. To function effectively in the world of duality, one must have the protective duality. Duality without the knowledge of non-duality is a hindrance, but duality backed by non-duality is a 'charge'. The goal is not to disappear into the world of permanent non-duality, nor to renounce the world. Natural evolution will look after that aspect of it. Having become anchored in a state of non-duality, the goal should then be to work wonders in a world of duality. Pull the aspects of non-duality or divinity into the world of duality. Bridge the gap between the two worlds. Remember, your glory will reflect the Lord's glory. Your achievements will reflect the Lord's achievements. The states of duality and non-duality must exist side by side. Relive life. Recapture the thrill of matter, of life. Confirm Godhood. Perform great deeds. Sing the praises of the Lord—in your own way, by expressing it in the arts, in poetry, word or deed. Do not deny the world.

Illusion or 'Maya' lies in the deep-grained belief that each component or each individual is an isolated, fragmented island in this universe, unconnected to the rest, a master of his own ship, free to chart his own course. This is spiritual ignorance, 'avidya'.

The whole creation is one gigantic whole, with each particle playing its decisive role in the general functioning, with each particle influencing and governing the other's destiny. And the font of this gigantic entirety is an unseen, formless, and eternally unassuming Being whose mere presence originates and sustains this stupendous universe of which we form an influential component.

To feel this oneness experientially and to perceive our oneness with the font is the piercing of 'Maya', and this should be our goal.

61

'Kundalini Shakti'— The Inner Force

Tuesday, February 5, 1985:

A discussion was going on about 'Kundalini Shakti' and the recent trend among yoga adepts of arousing it in individuals at mass meetings. Some opined that the 'Kundalini Shakti', so aroused, is automatically raised to 'Sahasrara Chakra', which in turn leads one to self-enlightenment. Also that, without the arousal of this Shakti, enlightenment was not possible. Different people had different views.

Finally, they all agreed that they did not know enough about either of the two, that is, 'atma-dnyana' or self-enlightenment, and 'Kundalini Shakti'.

One of the debaters asked my opinion. I told him that I had no direct experience of the 'Kundalini', and so could not throw any light on the topic. I had neither felt any rising of the psychic power in me nor had I gone to anyone to have it aroused in me, nor had I read any treatises on it. Disappointed, the group resumed the discussion, if anything, a little more animatedly!

As I listened to them, a new vista opened up before me. This is what was then revealed to me, and which I told them: Mind is all-important for man. Mind is a link between man and divinity. It is also a barrier alienating man from divinity. By purifying the mind enough, man would reach divinity. By making it base, he could cocoon himself in his individual ego and tear himself from divinity. Thus mind is like a pot. The air inside the pot is like the individual, and the air outside is the all-pervading Infinite. The inside and outside air is one continuous whole but for the separating walls of the pot. By ever purifying the mind, one could increasingly make porous the impure, differentiating, unwanted pot. Or by making the mind baser, make the pot stronger. A time comes when the mind is so purified that the separating pot becomes weak enough to break. The outside and the inside merge, become one undistinguished whole.

No longer is there any individuality. The individual has merged with the Infinite. With this divinity, comes Knowledge, contentment, peace, love, compassion, wisdom, discriminating power, self-control, equanimity. All positive virtues. The baser traits like rage, envy, ego, lack of self-control, etc. get subdued or even altogether eliminated.

When the mind is thus being purified, 'Kundalini' automatically rises in the person's psychic system. It acts like mercury in a thermometer. As the fever rises, the mercury rises. It is only a gauge, not the fever itself! It is a slave to the fever. It only records or pin-points the magnitude of the fever. 'Kundalini' is just such a registering scale in a purified mind focused on the Lord. In such a case, the focus is never on the ups and downs of the 'Kundalini'. It is hardly noticed. But as the 'Kundalini' rises, it activates certain psychic centres which act as simulators, bringing about or triggering certain conditions which open up vistas before the mind. These reveal certain truths. The opening up of psychic centres makes you experience these truths, and bestows upon you some powers, sometimes remarkable ones!

The 'Kundalini' is now your helpmate. It is a sublime asset. But it is still the slave of the purified mind. It is only a milestone. Whatever it reveals or bestows, the purified mind will recognize, perceive, and use with discrimination, with equanimity, humbly, with wisdom, with compassion, with justice, and with self-control. The purified mind is in control here. That is the master. Knowledge of the highest order, and power of a sublime nature, will manifest in this individual. He is ascending towards divinity.

Here, the arousal of 'Kundalini' has been natural, unforced. Only in a purified mind will it rise of its own.

Now take the case where the individual's mind has not been

purified enough. The mind is not sufficiently under control, and the baser values predominate. In such a person, the 'Kundalini' can be aroused by external means or by an external agent, by different artificial methods, including misguided hard penance.

For one who has had his 'Kundalini' aroused in the incorrect hope that it would lead to divinity, or for the one who has got it aroused with a base motive of gaining powers, the play of 'Kundalini' is in itself all-important to him. The undue importance to 'Kundalini' makes this force the master, and the base weak, and the unprepared man its slave. The force, not reined in, becomes unruly, untamed, all-powerful, causes havoc in man. In a purified and self-controlled man who is hardly conscious of 'Kundalini', it bows to him and takes orders from him. You may say that it has been broken in by the sheer inattention from such a man, and does not dare to play mischief with him.

In the uncontrolled and unpurified mind, where the force is the master, it lashes out in all its fury, and unless controlled, can bring out the worst in him, blow his mind out, or cause much psychosomatic damage.

'Kundalini' is a cosmic force, very powerful, needing to be tamed and guided. It can bestow great powers, also it can flatten out a man. Like other forces in nature, like fire, lightning or electricity, it can be an asset or a curse fraught with danger. It is the untapped potential of mind.

The aroused 'Kundalini' in an unpurified mind is like dynamite in a child's hands. It gives power to the child without the wisdom as to when or how to use it. This is precisely what happened to the 'asuras' and the 'rakshasas', enemies of the pantheon of gods in our mythology. By hard penance, they acquired divine boons, and then misused them. Masters and sages of old were careful as to whose 'Kundalini' they aroused, unlike in the modern times. Today, the concept of 'rakshasas' and demons has changed into the modern men with demonic thought and action.

When a person arouses this force in seekers, he has to take upon himself full responsibility for them. He should be able to tame this force as also guide the mind, so the seeker should be constantly under observation. Will the modern master have the time or the inclination or even the ability of such a high order, when he arouses the force on such a large scale among the unsuspecting, gullible masses?

'Kundalini Shakti' is the cosmic force of the Infinite. It exists because of Him. He does not exist because of this force. He is the fount; the force is the cascade. Even in man, it lies in his consciousness, biding its time. As the mind gets purified, his consciousness heightens or becomes sensitive, and it can tune in to the cosmic power within him.

To a pure mind, power and force have no meaning as he has neither the will nor the mind to use them. He will one-pointedly pursue the path that will lead him to the Almighty. What he is seeking is the peace, love, ecstasy of oneness with the Lord.

The supra-consciousness of the Almighty will take over in a self-realized man. He will be spontaneous in his actions, guided by this divine consciousness and divine power. Consciously or unconsciously, he will automatically emanate power and force. A pure mind will only think right and do right. His 'Kundalini' would have merged with the divine supra-consciousness.

62

Experiences III

Tuesday, May 21 and Wednesday, May 22, 1985:

The whole night I was conscious of flights through the unknown. There were no 'chakras' vibrating, no body-consciousness, no identity. Only the knowledge of I-ness.

Thursday, May 23, 1985:

Often I have been getting a tingling sensation in the centre of my forehead, in a spherical area about an inch in diameter. Of late, it was quite pronounced. My attention would be riveted there. At night the tingling sensations and the vibrations there were very forceful. The 'chakra' was blazing away. Suddenly, I got an inkling that the 'chakra' was about to be pierced. Within moments, the tingling and the vibrations reached a climax and as suddenly fell silent, and I knew that the 'chakra' had been pierced.

Friday, May 24, 1985:

Hitherto, all that had happened to me had done so on its own. I was doing nothing on my part to induce anything or to accelerate it.

Today afternoon, as I lay on my bed, a thought occurred whether I could, on my own, whilst fully awake, induce the 'nirvikalpa' state in myself and become one with the universe.

I relaxed, closed my eyes, and made myself thought-free. Within moments, I became drowsy and got into conscious sleep. I was conscious that I was awake, that I was asleep, that I was in a state of meditation, all simultaneously. I was enjoying this state of flux for some time when before my eyes came the view of a landscape with mountains, the sky, clouds, valleys, pastures, and so on. I was flying as if in an aeroplane and watching it all. I had no body-consciousness, only I-ness, only a moving existence. Only a witness.

Suddenly, I was myself the clouds floating high up and watching the ground below. Soon I was myself the entire landscape and could see all at once the sky above, the ground below, the air, the mountains inbetween. I was all. Intelligent, awake, all-seeing, all-pervading, still! In total equilibrium!

This state must have lasted a few moments. Then I became conscious that I was in 'nirvikalpa'. I was conscious of the fact that I had induced in myself this state. I was conscious that if I let a thought occur or became fully awake, I would break the stream. Now I tried to maintain the state of 'nirvikalpa'. I was conscious enough to want to find out as to how long I could maintain mastery over this stream, and also my effort to sustain the stream of equilibrium.

Now I was, in a dull way, conscious of the surroundings, of my half-awake, half-asleep state, of my state of meditation, of my effort at maintaining this state, and of the 'nirvikalpa' state that I was experiencing.

However, the moment I got tired and let go, the landscape slipped off, and I was fully awake. This was the evolution of mind that I had observed: Mind in the highest state of purity and subtlety, slipping into the 'nirvikalpa' state and transcending itself, sublimating into pure consciousness — the 'Atman' or the 'Brahman', the divinity. But this pure state of sheer consciousness would leave man functionless in the world. So mind regains the pure conscious dual state, of the divine and the ordinary together, experiencing the state of divinity whilst simultaneously retaining and controlling the ordinary state. This dual state is important for man. It must be maintained—waking or sleeping, working or reposing. This should be the final goal.

This state is consciousness in sleep. This state knows that the individual is sleeping. This state experiences the state of meditation, and this state also partakes of and experiences the state of divinity, the state of bliss! But whose bliss have you experienced? The Lord's! So the Lord, Whose very presence made you experience all this, is beyond this state. His awareness made you aware of all these states.

Transcending even this dual state, an individual would fully merge into the divine.

After coming out of this state, I tried to get back into it again. I could do so at will. I did it four times, got tired and gave up.

Wednesday, August 21, 1985:

In my sleep, I distinctly became aware that my body had become immensely heavy. I half awakened, and found that indeed the body felt heavy. As suddenly, I started feeling light. I became light to the extent that I felt I was lifting off my bed and floating up. I floated out of the window, though my body was left on the bed. The floating me resembled a tear-shaped balloon. I could see my body on the bed, as also the balloon, and feel the balloon's gliding movement. I floated round the neighbourhood buildings and came back and entered my body that was lying on the bed.

The exit from the body and the re-entry into it were smooth and effortless. On re-entry, I suddenly became fully awake and realized that I had had an experience. One stage was being fully awake; the previous stage was conscious-sleep, a half-awake, half-asleep condition; another, deeper still, was witnessing these two states.

The balloon that was me was not being directed by me. Yet it knew how to come out of the body, take a round, and re-enter the body faultlessly.

In this flight there were two entities. One was me, who, in conscious sleep had left the body, taken a round and come back, and had previously felt the body become heavy and then light. The other entity was non-existent but watched everything—the surroundings during the flight, the body, the balloon—and, though utterly passive and unassuming, it was, by its mere presence, directing the sorties without making a fuss, without making its presence felt.

Thursday, August 22, 1985:

In deep sleep, I saw a cow running towards me, and I began to feel her running movement within me. Her heavy thud on the road, the movement of her muscles, her panting, were all mine. She and I were different, yet one. We had merged, yet remained separate. I knew that if any part of her body had got hurt at that moment, I would have felt the pain, and if she had fallen down, I would have felt that crash; and if she had died at that moment, I would have known what death was!

In this experience, though the awareness had merged, there was a clear duality, fully maintaining the protective individual awareness. Whilst vividly experiencing her panting, etc., I was distinctly aware that it was I who was experiencing her panting and that it was I who was not getting tired by the run.

This mastery over the protective individual awareness is important; that is, experiencing, yet not getting involved! But for this, the universal awareness would become a handicap, as man would be subjected to universal pain, hurt and anguish.

Friday, August 23, 1985:

Aqeela had gone for her vehicle driving test. She was taking inordinately long in coming home. I began worrying a little. A prayer arose in my heart. Immediately, there was the familiar disturbance in the equilibrium of my peace that stalled the prayer. I said, 'You never allow me to pray. Surely, as a mother, I have a role, and I would wish to pray occasionally. I only wanted that Aqeela should pass the test, and come home safely.'

I was answered: 'The two roles have merged. There is no separate identity of a mother any more. Let the events take place as they will. You only witness. This is true samadhi. Only to witness is the highest form of samadhi. Praying brings in thought. It brings in duality. It breaks the samadhi. Let life be one long continuous samadhi. Let not prayers break this long true meditation. Your 'will' shall be done. Remain in samadhi. She will pass her test. She is on her way home. But do not pray. Have faith, and only watch. Let events take place unhindered. To watch events without any reaction, to remain in the present, to be unencumbered by memory and desire and thought, to make efforts without the wish for results, will make you remain in the eternal equipoise of 'sahaja samadhi', spontaneous or natural samadhi. To cultivate this state should be the goal of man. To live a full life, infused with divinity, should be the true goal. Events will take place anyway, as predestined. You only watch uninvolved. Detached. If any action has to be taken, thought or inspiration will occur to you even in this samadhi to take the right action. Right impulses come whenever required.'

This sort of samadhi does not, as some people imagine, make man passive, inert, resigned and functionless. On the contrary, it makes him dynamic, wise and energetic, and haloed with divinity and manliness. Inspiration and the impulse to work will come spontaneously. Nature will see to it that he is productive.

Aqeela came home shortly and told me that she had passed the test.

Saturday, August 24, 1985:

Whenever I have tried to pray, there would be a mental block, and a disturbance in the deep peace of mind that I have always had. Words of prayer would not come, and there would be a subtle agitation or a protest in the body. The moment the idea of a prayer would withdraw, peace would prevail again.

Today again, a prayer arose in my mind. Immediately, there was the usual block. I felt it to be a dense block, spherical, an inch in diameter, tensing up in the centre of the forehead. Thence it emitted the minute wave of agitation that spread through the entire body. The words of prayer get blocked, thought is stalled, and the centre of forehead becomes leaden.

And I realized at once that the thinking centre is in the forehead. The 'chakra' situated in the forehead is directly responsible for thought. With purity of thought and the ascent of mind, the third eye situated in the forehead opens, which makes a man see a world beyond this mundane world.

I also saw clearly why men smear this part of the body in all reverence with holy ash. It induces their mind towards purity. It made sense why warriors were applied a 'tilak', a vermilion mark, before they left for battle . . . to keep the clarity of thought and purity of mind and thereby of deed, so essential in battle; why women too applied the auspicious 'kum kum'. The mark is made with auspicious and beneficial ingredients like sandalwood paste or vermilion or turmeric or holy ash. The very act of applying this mark puts one in a mood of sanctity and reminds one of one's duty. When done in reverence and with true faith, one invokes the 'chakra' in the forehead, thereby invoking blessings of the deity presiding over this 'chakra'. This deity blesses one with purity of thought that lends a glow to one's life. This 'chakra', having shown me non-duality or the highest reality, was now stalling my slipping back into thought.

Sunday, August 25, 1985:

After joining college, Akshata suddenly let go of herself and started taking it a bit too easy with her studies. I was a little concerned. Then I felt a force leaving me, heading towards Akshata. And there came a clear message. 'Don't worry about Akshata. Leave her to me.' In the evening, I saw her with her study books.

At night a thought came to me that Tejaswi, who was four, was not yet talking very clearly. Immediately, I was made to turn towards her, and for a long time, I could feel a strong force emanating from my eyes and entering her head. I almost felt some rearrangement of the cells in her brain. This happened three times at night. Within a few days, there was a marked difference in her speech.

This sort of a thing has to happen of its own. Whenever I have tried to worry, worry would not come. Life seemed perfect. And even when I knew certain things were not going as they should, I could not deliberately evoke either the worry or this force. I had no part to play. The force had to become active on its own.

Monday, August 26, 1985:

In deep sleep, I half-awakened to experience a tiny wave of tension injected into me, with a clear message: This is the tension of 'mine'. My whole body, for a moment, felt this quantum of tension. Then, as suddenly, this tension departed, followed by another message: This is the release of 'yours'. And I felt free again.

Now I was fully awake, and knowledge came with a profound force. The tension I had felt was very subtle, yet it was physical. It had very minutely tensed up my body. This is the tension, 'mine'-ness, that men accumulate with every little thought of attachment, that this particular idea or thing or being is mine! With this attachment comes fear of loss of the object, anxiety on its account, grief for its absence, expectations from it, and various other emotions, which all lead to tension. Man thus accumulates an immense load of tension. The moment he feels detached from the object, he suddenly feels free. All the tension leaves instantaneously and he feels better even physically.

Though the thought was mental, the tension was physical. The tiny wave of tension I had felt was in between the mental and the physical, a link between the two, which could be acquired or released instantly.

In the release of 'yours', 'yours' means the feeling of detachment or the feeling that 'the object is not mine', that it belongs to someone else, or in the case of a devotee, to God. A life free of attachment is an emotion-free life, a thought-free life, and thus a tension-free life. This is liberation. This is freedom.

Wednesday, August 28, 1985:

For a few days, I was getting palpitations of the heart. But these were of a different kind. There was no tiredness, no weakness, and the heartbeat seemed to come from the centre, instead of the usual left-of-centre of the chest. The palpitations were so strong that I sometimes felt as though my heart would burst. But no matter what, the doctors could not even detect any palpitations, nor would my pulse change from the normal. Palpitations would start suddenly and stop as suddenly. They could also be induced by focusing my attention on the centre of the chest. However, they would mostly start on their own.

Intuitively, I knew these were not physical heart palpitations. Still to be on the safe side, we got all the cardiac tests done. Everything was normal. I concluded that my heart 'chakra' was getting activated with force. I also knew that my heart 'chakra' had still not been pierced.

We got it confirmed by the Sadguru that it was the heart 'chakra'.

At dead of night, with the palpitations going full swing, I also got a sensation of fluttering in the region of my navel. It was very pleasant. Suddenly, the palpitations stopped and the fluttering reduced in intensity, and I knew my heart 'chakra' had been pierced. There were no palpitations thereafter.

63

Samadhi

Thursday, August 29, 1985:

After this, for three or four days, I would go into instant meditation. The moment I sat down or lay down, all the senses would be withdrawn within a split second, my breathing would stop, and I would feel my life-force centred at the 'sahasrara chakra', and get into some sort of a conscious sleep. So much so that I would be in this meditation an entire day and night. During the day, I had to make an effort to come out of it, and, at night, I would be fully conscious and enjoying the deep 'dhyana'. Then, suddenly, after four days, this stage left me and I regained control over my body.

In this 'dhyana', however, I could keep myself conscious and my head erect.

This samadhi was different to other states of samadhi. It was instant, deep, very deep. It was forced upon me even when I was walking, talking, outdoors, and so on. I had not much success at shunning it. It was very, very powerful. I had to break it forcefully to attend to any chores.

In fact, ever since this odyssey of experiences has started, it has been one long, continuous samadhi, with a little variation here and there. And this is my natural state now. The thought-free state; the half-asleep, half-awake condition; sharp consciousness in sleep and daytime; various types of drugged sleep; different patterns of breathing; all these are different states of the same samadhi, 'sahaja' samadhi, spontaneous samadhi, effortless and permanent. But as I am a housewife and a devotee of Lord Krishna, it was stressed upon me that performing one's duty is of paramount importance. God and creation being one, the performance of one's chores or discharging one's duty is synonymous with the worship of God. Nature sees to it that the two worlds, the one of samadhi and the other of action, run parallel in equal measure.

Hence, till the two states merge or perfect mastery is gained, the state of samadhi recedes when work is necessary; otherwise it engulfs one totally. Sometimes in a continuous phase, sometimes allowing for some work, at times mild, at other times overwhelming, occasionally coming in waves, all depending upon what was required for my development.

Sometimes there was normal breathing, sometimes none at all, at other times, very subtle. Sometimes manifestation of existence was there, of Awareness, of Bliss, force, space, power; sometimes total absence of it. At other times, there was only calm, equipoise, a serene joy and peace; or else energy, buoyancy, thrill, running down the spine. Knowledge was there; or oblivion, even during activity. Sometimes there was 'experiencing'; or, nothing. Intensity would differ, type would differ, duration of intensity would differ. But, all throughout, it was one long samadhi.

The state of 'experiencing' the manifest, like the creation, and the Sat-Chit-Ananda, should be transcended, and finally merged with the unmanifest, the font. Now there is no more experiencing of the throbbing, flowing existence, no more sharp awareness of things or an outflow of knowledge, no overwhelming bliss and thrill, nor a feel of space and time.

Now one should experience only the subtle Existence, the subtle awareness, a quiet peace. No need to be aware of the samadhi, or of 'amrut' trickling down, or the life-forces moving up to the 'sahasrara chakra'. It would be a natural state now. Just like, although breathing is going on all the time, no one is specially aware of it. Samadhi and its benefits would be there, but no longer is there any need to be distinctly aware of it, till one's attention is specifically diverted to it.

I was shown all the steps one by one, for my education, but in reality everything happens all at once. It is an ongoing process, but my focus had been systematically sharpened at various points to understand the process and to gain knowledge experientially.

During sadhana, one advances gradually and gets into these different states. Later on, there will not be different states. All get absorbed into one.

Only, there is a difference in the intensity at different times.

This was my state now. Living was one big samadhi. 'Sahaja' samadhi. Getting the knowledge or awareness of something when the attention was focused on it, otherwise, only peace and quiet.

By knowledge, I mean the Knowledge of Reality, not of the empirical world.

64

The Glowing Self and the Mind

Monday, September 2, 1985:

During the day, whilst working, again and again my breath would get directed towards the brain. Along with this change in breathing, would come 'bhava samadhi'. My facial muscles would arrange themselves into different expressions depicting peace, compassion, bliss and withdrawal from this world. I would freeze into any pose, though I would be conscious of my surroundings, and I could snap out of it or stall its onset. But it was enjoyable to be in this samadhi. My thought, breathing, identification, everything would come to a standstill. I would be in this world as also in another world, a world of nectar.

Monday, October 14, 1985:

Whilst reading a book in the evening, I became drowsy and the book slipped from my hands. The 'chakras' throbbed and the vibrations reached a new crescendo. My senses withdrew. I was awake. I was aware of this world, but it mattered not to me. I lost my body identity. My own identity was demolished. Only the Self was blazing. I felt 'alive' and charged.

Slowly I felt an invisible, spherical shield around me. Mellow, pastel-coloured, fluorescent globes, like ping-pong balls, emanated from the irradiating Self. The pink, yellow, green and white glowing globes, rising from the Self, were hitting the shield one after another, bouncing back, hitting the other side of the shield and again on the rebound getting reabsorbed into the Self. The back and forth interweaving pattern continued smoothly in a definite rhythm. The number of globes remained the same. Globes of each colour followed a different set of patterns. The paths and globes were evenly spaced within the sphere.

The lambent Self was still flaming. The luminous globes were still dancing. And I knew that this is the primordial charge of that fulgent Self permeating every being. The pulse of all existence! The throb of life pervading throughout the universe. The self-generating energy of a sub-atomic particle. The rudiment of awareness in a particle; self-knowledge limited to instinctive self-generation of energy, of motion. The individual nature intrinsic to a particle. The numbers of globes varies with different particles.

This is the sensational emission of a charge from Sat or Existence of the Lord. A dynamic charge spanning itself out into the laws of nature, into the primal charge of energy and motion, into the rudiments of awareness, into the beginning of an individuality, into the development of mind, intellect and ego, into particles of matter, into matter or bodies. Matter is being born, suffused with this charge. As this charge evolves, matter becomes more animated, more complex. As matter and mind, or this charge, or this awareness evolve, higher beings come into existence. Both body and mind are now on a path of grand evolution.

The elemental constituents of both the body and mind remain the same. It is the individuality that evolves.

The Self still glows in this tiny, almost non-existent particle. The Self gives it intuitive knowledge of its behaviour.

If the particle is not aware of the glowing Self within itself, it is because the awareness, hardly developed in minerals, is sleeping as it were. But the Self and the awareness are alive alright.

In the plants, it is stirring. Plants being more evolved than minerals, there are the beginnings of perceptions, feelings and visible life.

In animals, it is awake. More prominent. Their perceptions, emotions, their instincts, behaviour, intellect, awareness are quite active.

In man, it is divine. He excels other species in his perceptions, intuition, awareness. He can feel the presence of a superior force within him. He is aware of the divinity within him. He is capable of experiencing this stark, dazzling brilliance within him. The primitive charge is now effulgent; and, when he is in his sublime state, man experiences this throb, this pulse, this vibrant, bedazzling, procreating dynamism of the Self.

I experienced the Self positioned in the centre of my chest. Not in the heart.

Tuesday, October 15, 1985:

For the last four days, I have been reading a book on Saibaba. Involuntarily, my mind was fixed on him, and unknowingly, I was invoking him constantly. For four nights, I saw him in my sleep. On the fourth night, he said to me, 'Why are you praying to me? Why are you causing duality? You and I are one. There is no need to pray.'

Mind:

Self is divinity. Self is the spark of life. Self is that by which man cognizes form, taste, smell, sound and sensual joys. By Self, one perceives all objects whether it be in a dream or awake. Without the Self, a body is inert and dead; functionless, in spite of all organs being intact.

Self is the intelligence in the intelligent—in the brilliant as also in the cunning. It is the movement in the moving. The Self is ever-awake, witnessing every state and every event of man, asleep or awake.

This Self is residing in all beings.

But it is covered by mind in man. Mind varies in the degree of its purity in each individual. It is conditioned by previous, indelible impressions etched upon it; by acquired knowledge which could be wrong, inadequate, incomplete or not properly grasped; by its memory, its emotions, its moods, its intellect, its observation power, its perceptions, etc. All these are variables.

It is the mind that enables the fine impulses emitted by objects or by any event to be perceived by sense organs of the body. This depends upon the focus of the mind, its sharpness at that particular moment, the alertness of the sense organs, the clarity of the objects, etc. If the mind is not on the object, there will be no cognizance, as in absent-mindedness or in staring vacantly.

As the mind is conditioned by various factors, and the combinations and permutations of these factors will vary in each individual and with each set of circumstances, the observation, recording and understanding of each event or object will differ in each individual and with time, so each individual mind will have its own conclusions. Hence, recordings by mind are relative, changeable, and need not be reliable.

And the intellect influences the interpretations of the events, the reactions to it and the course of action to be taken thereafter. Re-evaluation and judgement of this decision then quickly take place through intellect and memory and the orders for its execution are sent to the sense or motor organs.

In all this, mood or emotion too plays a major role. Emotion will colour observation and judgement, and the mood will also prevail upon execution of orders.

Wisdom, control of emotions, sharp perceptions, uncluttered and clear mind, good knowledge, good impressions or 'samskaras', etc., are invaluable assets of life, and they influence the mind.

In this near-instant process of observing, cognizing, synthesizing and the executing of orders, various organs come into play, like the brain, nerves, sense and motor organs.

But it is the mind that is the key factor, and not the organs. Organs remain the same in an individual, but the mind keeps changing and thus man keeps changing from minute to minute.

Mind brings into play different parts of the organs, and activates various centres in them and makes them function according to its mood and intent. It can reduce the organs to dullness and rusting, or whip them into super-human excellence.

Different factors of the mind, like the recall of events in memory, intellect, emotions, etc., activate different sensitive nerve centres in the organs and in the body, and thus activate different parts of the organs and get different results.

All the factors of the mind are variables, and so they can be activated or stilled. They are alien to the Self, no matter how clinging, hence, they can be stripped off. They play a decisive role in life. For that very reason, it is essential that good 'samskaras' or good impressions are etched upon an individual mind from childhood itself.

Good upbringing, good food, good surroundings are vital. Food influences mind. Mind influences brain.

Mind is ever-evolving. There is no conceivable end to evolution. Evolution of mind means evolution of man.

On one side is the evolution of man within the world of senses, his leaps in science, in technology, in knowledge, etc., via his brain and intellect. On the other, is his evolution via his mind, transcending the mind, and being in the realm of altered consciousness. Here the knowledge is true, invariable. There is a cosmic awareness and eternal bliss. This evolution is brought about by purity. Purity of thought and purity of deeds. Here the knowledge is tapped from the super-conscious.

All emotions, knowledge, impressions, likes, dislikes, wants, desires can be expressed in one word: thought. Purity of mind and, subsequently, absence of thought catapults man into higher realms. Mind is ancient, and will remain unchanged unless it is subdued and controlled, thereby stilled, negated or transcended.

Mind influences consciousness. The denser the mind, the duller and more restricted the consciousness. Clearer the mind, sharper and truer the consciousness. The more the mind becomes still, the more the consciousness becomes cosmic.

Consciousness means clear perceptions, sharp observations, deep insights, true knowledge uncluttered by bias or prejudice. The two together influence the brain and the sensitive, subtle nervous system.

Mind is made up of memory of the past, be it recent, ancient, social, or of indelible marks called 'samskaras' left on it through numerous births; hope, aspirations, wants, desires, expectations of the future; emotions, good and bad, joyous or sad.

Intellect is made up of the ability to discriminate, wisdom, sound judgement, good reasoning, ability to take decisions, etc.

Ego: Subtle, purified ego is good; it is buoyant, retains the required duality; it is dynamic, potent, lends capability, enhances faculties and makes one cogent.

Pride, vanity, jealousy, arrogance, possessiveness, attachments are bad.

All these are mere thought. So mind is thought.

The mind is a stream of thoughts and feelings. All these individual thoughts and feelings together give man a distinct personality, a sense of individuality, an impetus to resolve, a volition, a will, an ego.

Individuality is mind, ego, intellect.

By a deliberate silencing of wants, desires, passions, emotions, sentiments, the thought can be negated and the mind subdued. This sharpens the intellect, enhances the wisdom, makes for clear judgement. In effect, it purifies the mind. A pure·mind will be dynamic, forceful and clear, and enables man to see his duties, his obligations, his path, and enables him to overcome any shortcoming he may have. A pure mind will be free from unsettling evil passions and fierce, excitable sentiments, thus rendering it unwanting, reposing in quietude and contentment. This contentment in turn leads to a liberal, generous and noble mind, which takes a man to lofty heights of magnanimity and divinity.

Thought can be stopped. Mind can be silenced.

The thing that separates an individual from the Infinite is the thought or the mind; his 'ahamkara', that is, his ego. With the removal of thought or being in the state of mindlessness, one begins to merge with the Infinite. In this state of merger, one partakes of all the aspects of the divine.

Meditation helps to reach this state. All other paths also lead one there . . . to mindlessness. Then on to the 'nirvikalpa' state.

This state of purity is the true nature of man. Standing on this threshold, one begins to get glimpses of divinity. Here begins the true quest. This is the ultimate in one sense, and a beginning, in another. One works towards this state, but once there, things happen automatically because the mind, as one conceives of it, does not exist any longer. It is there only to perceive things divine and then to express its perception in terms of words, music, knowledge and art. Mind, once hooked on to the divine, becomes only an instrument to pass on things from the Infinite or the unmanifest into the finite or the manifest, from the unborn to the born. And the manifestation is unique in each individual, all depending upon the personality of the individual.

This path or quest is endless, as the true knowledge is endless. This knowledge has to come slowly, as body and mind are usually slow in being readied to receive it.

Spiritual mindlessness is not that the mind is destroyed or negated. It does not result in work being shunned either. It is in fact an effulgent, dynamic state where knowledge and inspiration mingle, leading to inspired work. This we call a brain-wave. A sudden bursting open of a lotus in a calm lake; a sudden cloudburst over a parched land.

Being continuously in the state of spiritual mindlessness or thoughtlessness, one may slip into the state of 'nirvikalpa' where there is a total demolition of one's identity. In this state, one is like a simulator. One can, in this state, as a witness, experience all that there is in the world, actually feeling and being that.

In this state, one is also like a computer. Early on, unconsciously, you feed it with a query by way of concentration or one-pointed quest. All the software is packed in the Self. In the 'nirvikalpa', the computer gets activated, as it were, and taps the Infinite Self for material, draws upon the required knowledge, and in a rapid process of decoding, one gets a complete feedback on the query, as you regain your identity. The state of 'nirvikalpa' gives the Absolute Knowledge, knowledge of the Brahman and its relation to the world, the Knowledge of the Self and its manifestation.

Spiritual mindlessness will give one inspiration and knowledge pertaining to the world of matter. Many scientists have seen many formulae or solutions to their problems in their deep sleep, or in their state of mindlessness while either fully concentrating or fully relaxing, either state leading to mindlessness or thoughtlessness. Many great musicians have seen complete scores of music in similar states. A yogi who has no restrictions in the sphere of knowledge will have an access to all knowledge.

One must try and incorporate this state in all one's waking and sleeping states. Let it be one's true state and yet carry on with one's daily chores. Such a mastery can be deliberately cultivated to begin with, till it becomes spontaneous. This is 'sahaja' samadhi, sleeping or waking.

This intelligent integration of knowledge and action should be the goal of man. This will be his glowing manifestation, as creation backed by Supreme Knowledge is the stupendous manifestation of the Lord.

I have almost forgotten spirituality. Of course, the knowledge is there but the visions and the experiences have become very infrequent. Unless someone reminds me of all this, I do not remember it on my own. That phase is over. Even the spontaneous 'kriya' is all but gone. It can be induced, of course, but the very thought to induce it never occurs. It all seems so alien now. There are certain bodily yogic experiences still continuing, but I undergo these without any association in memory with spirituality. Even whilst I was in the thick of experiencing, there was no memory of the previous experiences, due to my totally living in the present. But now, even in the absence of such experiences, there is no memory of the past experiences. Not that there is a loss of memory, but the memory of the recent past does not clutter up the present. Now the experience is only of peace, self-absorption and mindlessness. The ecstasy has turned into a silent contentment and a nirvanic peace. There is no manifestation of enjoyment either. There is now only a calm equipoise.

Sometimes I am reposing, at other times, I am active. Sometimes I am writing, thereafter, I am drowsy. At times, the spells are strong enough to make me lie down; rest of the time, they are mild enough for me to ignore them. Sometimes I can pierce through the spells, at times I give in to them. Sometimes I have a will, at times I have none. I am not resisting. As the mood comes, I only react. Life is pleasant and that is what matters.

65

Rebirth and 'Karma'

Along with intellect, there develops, in the course of evolution, a power to discriminate between the good and the bad. This takes man beyond the instincts of plants and animals and lays before him a new vista of spiritual evolution.

In order that this evolution is free-wheeling, nature offers man an array of options. This gift of having options is a double-edged sword. Unknowingly, he becomes the master of his destiny. Taking decisions at every step, he assumes the guardianship of his own future. By making sacrifices, setting priorities and working towards lofty ideals, he can traverse towards divinity; or, taking the opposite path, ride into decadence and misery. This choice is guided by his power of discrimination.

When man understands wrongly the law of 'Karma', he becomes a slave to it, because he confuses this law with destiny. This law says: As ye sow, so shall ye reap. Good deeds bring in rewards; bad ones, punishment. The seeds of Karma, sown by man himself, trail him through successive births, and in the fullness of time, strike roots. There is no escape from this.

As perception dawns, revealing the great responsibility resting on him in charting his own course, man strips himself progressively of his detrimental qualities and endeavours towards a self-integration that will lead him to a better future.

Often, man appears to be a mere pawn in the unfathomable game of destiny. Events seem to play their own game. Unpredictable and unjustifiable fortunes or misfortunes descend upon the unsuspecting individual. Was it the will of God? On what was it based? Why exert at all, it is argued, when life takes its own course willed by a super-force? Why strive towards perfection when, nature takes man along a pre-destined path? Can destiny be changed? Is everything pre-determined? Why bother then?

If man lets destiny rule him, destiny more than willingly obliges. Indulging in every whim, yielding to temptations, not bothering with upliftment, self-purification and nobility in thought and action, man steps down from his role of being the master. Destiny now appears all-powerful.

But once man sees the part he has in shaping his own future, he puts to work his power of discrimination and self-control and paints his future in gold. Destiny is only the fruits of his past 'Karma'. The future is a blank sheet for him to paint upon as he wills it. He is no longer a victim now. He regains the status of being the master.

Of course, man still cannot free himself of the fruits of his earlier deeds. The seeds of the deeds, once sown, are irrevocably rivetted. Even a penitent or a chastened man has to accept their fruits. But henceforth, he can take care as to what he plants, and what is most important, he can maintain a balance of thought in dealing with these bitter or sweet fruits, knowing them to be the result of his own past sowing.

If the past is one's present, then a controlled present can be made into a glorious future. Destiny is what you make of it!

This freedom of choice can be made into a bane or a boon. If used judiciously, this freedom can lead one to great heights, or it can drag one to the corridors of hell.

This freedom aims at taking man towards a grand evolution. In his own time. Free to indulge himself, or make sacrifices, he is given chance after chance to correct and perfect himself, to lead him on in this sublime evolution. The individual that has sprung from God has to merge back in Him! And perceive the magnitude of His glory and his own glory!

This is the grand pattern of our destiny. But there is no pressure of time on an individual. Till the individuality is not adequately developed, the individual will be at the mercy of the laws of nature. But man, who has his intellect developed sharply and who has the boon of options, becomes his own master and carves out his own path and walks on it as he wills, whether he knows this or not.

By his own efforts, man can, through self-control and dedication, negate his demeaning instincts and perceive his true identity and capture his inner peace and bliss. This is the true Garden of Eden he has pined for. This is the true Kingdom of God on earth. Nature ultimately takes man there. But a monitored traversing of this path can hasten his progress and avoid unnecessary misery and toil of, perhaps, many births.

But man gets distracted by the temptations littered on the way and loses the path leading to this garden. He gets busy with satisfying his immediate wants and confuses the accumulation of objects with the lasting inner peace. He does not comprehend that he is running after fleeting pleasures. Not satisfied and still seeking lasting peace, he acquires more objects and gets more entangled in life. Besides, in acquiring these, he might indulge in unfair means. This restlessness enmeshes him all the more in the net he needs to discard. This has an adverse effect on him. He heaps misery upon himself.

Man will free himself only when he realizes that true satisfaction comes from within, not by external aids but by giving up wants and desires.

Very few bother with freeing the mind, for it is far more appealing to satisfy desires. All these wants and desires nurture the mind.

When man dies, it is the body that is discarded. The unfulfilled intense wants, strong attachments, deep-rooted talents, the basic traits of his character, do not die. These have an existence of their own and remain in the consciousness as the seeds of a new life. These and his 'Karma', form the 'self' of a new being. This 'self', along with the 'Self' within, leave the body. This 'self' trails the 'Self', which is eternal, till the former is subjugated in successive births. Then the glowing 'Self' is unveiled and the merging with the Universal takes place. Thereafter, the body that was like a shroud becomes a shrine to the Self.

Life does not cease with death. When no more experience is

to be gained through a particular body, it is discarded. This is called death.

In his new birth, an individual will be thrown in contact with people he had associated with in his previous births. Here, he benefits from them or is harmed by them; or, in turn, unknowingly, helps or harms them, all according to his behaviour with them or theirs with him in their previous births, or, in other words, according to the past 'Karmas'.

Man has to free himself of both the good and the bad Karma, to even out his entire give-and-take account and gradually purify himself of his wants and desires, and find liberation.

As long as the give-and-take account is not worked out and desires not sublimated, rebirth will continue. In each birth, some Karmas will be worked out but many more will be added. As it is not possible to meet all the people in one birth and work out all the Karmas with them, many births are required.

Birth does not cease with liberation either, as man has to 'realize' more and more of the Almighty, and there is no end to evolution. But, in such births, there is no misery as there are no desires and expectations. There is total acceptance of life. Vibrant, as also peaceful.

Slowly, the interval between the births widens. The propelling force of a new birth is strong desires and Karma, and now that these have been subjugated, he remains more and more in the Consciousness in a subtle form, still evolving, to take birth occasionally, only to do good to others, as an instrument of the divine, remaining in a state of bliss.

Destiny in a new life is only the past following an individual. This past which is non-matter begins to take shape like the nothingness coming into 'being'. A new birth takes place.

The Self wrapped in destiny becomes the cause of a new life. The Self maintains life, and the mind and destiny create fine constituents that make up the DNA chains. The DNA constituents are a bridge between non-matter and matter, a link between mind and body, between thought-energy and matter.

Having forgotten his past, oblivious of a natural grand pattern, ignorant of the laws governing nature, man begins to lead a new life only to be baffled by the whims of his destiny.

It is not necessary to shun wealth or those pleasures that are bestowed upon him by destiny. Only, let him not acquire them with base motives or through foul means. They are to be enjoyed humbly and in purity of thought, without attachment to them and for good pursuits, with generosity and equipoise, in that, should these be lost, it should not be deemed a calamity.

Attitude to life and purity of thought are supreme. Thought-energy is destiny. Destiny is in man's hands.

66

End of the Beginning

Tuesday, January 14, 1986:

I have travelled far in my journey, but often when I look back, I find I am still where I was, with no steps having been taken and with no perceptible change in me. The picture of an expert mime comes to my mind, who so convincingly performs to give one a brilliant impression of having climbed up a wall or walked miles, though all the while he is standing in one spot. Haven't we all sometimes experienced a similar mood in our life during our deeply reflective moments? Felt like this expert mime? And shouldn't it be so? Are we not all miming away, make-believing paths and progress and herculean effort? Where is the path and what is the progress, when we are ourselves already at the goal, nay, we are the goal itself? Stubbornly refusing to acknowledge this simple fact, we flounder ceaselessly in search of imaginary paths and pine away for illusory progress!

Having come thus far in the journey is not enough. This is just the beginning of yet another path. A path promising vistas of even greater dimensions. Perhaps, one day I shall look down this path too, and wonder once more why I floundered again when I am still where I was, and that there was no path and hence no progress, and I need not have moved at all. But if floundering is the fate of man, so be it. Let me too flounder like that brilliant mime, endeavour to walk, staying in one place.

I stand today on a new threshold. At the back is a vista full of memories, visions and experiences, which I am told to shun and forget. In front, the new dimensions and unknown realms. The beckoning path is the sole guiding factor. Trusting to be led by the inner benevolent force, I wait and hesitantly raise my eyes to the horizon.

That exalted mood has passed now, in which, in sheer purity and a state of uncover, one reflects clearly the glory of the Lord. No more do I get into this mood when I used to feel no demarcation between the Lord and me, and felt His attributes as mine. That state of complete dissolution eludes me, where there is no more a distinction between body and mind, subject and object. No longer do the distant stars form a part of me experientially; and, when I look around, I perceive that I have let slip the web that relates each object to the other and have also lost the interpenetrating touch of time and space. No more do I feel His power and glory emanating from me, but the memory and the knowledge are just as sweet as the moments of actual experience. Enough! The memory and the knowledge are potent enough to help me retain the taste of this precious ambrosia.

When I wonder if that exalted mood will repeat itself, Raja says yes, most emphatically. Different people retain this mood for different periods of time, each according to his evolutionary requirements.

Some retain it for a few fleeting seconds, some get into it time and again for varying periods of time, and a very few remain in it permanently.

For a housewife like me who has duties to perform and a home to look after, Raja says, this much of ambrosia is more than enough. But, as my duties get discharged one by one, and my body and mind get used to the present awakened state and are readied gradually for further exposure to the new awakening, he adds, then at the right time, I will be established more firmly in this state. The force, cosmic and eternal, knows when, and always does the right thing by each individual.

This self-revealing, benevolent force is in a relentless suffusion within me. But should my consciousness be focused on action, be it physical or mental, the current steps down, as it were, and the queer tiredness, listlessness and nectarine drowsiness associated with it and that hamper action, depart, giving me a temporary impetus to action. But the state of samadhi never ever leaves. It is permanent and continuous.

At present, I plan to focus my consciousness on action. It is no doubt heavenly to sit and get deported to the sweet realms of worship, self-absorption and cosmic hush, the pleasures of which excel any pleasures of the world, realms in which one could stay immersed happily one's entire life, and for which all humanity subconsciously hankers.

But spirituality must have some practical worth, and towards this I shall strive. Inculcating the peace, the tranquillity and the supernal bliss that this force so graciously showers upon me, into the pleasant and unpleasant chores and duties of the world, I shall endeavour to make life joyous. After all, if all the manifest is the manifestation of the Lord, then the universe and all that goes with it are Him only; and the chores, the duties, and the obligations form an integral part of Him and His manifestation. Then is it not pragmatic to serve Him and experience Him through what is concrete and is within our reach and has been presented to us by Him, rather than shun it all and seek some vague and obscure avenues? To lead a simple life, as it comes, with calm and discrimination and to seek and enjoy the Lord in what lies scattered around us, is the highest form of yoga. And towards this yoga, or this sublime lotus pose, let me move!

Saturday, January 18, 1986:

The previous section was written by me on January 14, 1986. By then, the intensity of experiences had slowed down. No doubt, there was no end to experiencing, but experiences pertaining to my education and to what I was writing, namely, the evolution of mind and thereby of man, were largely over. Whatever I wanted to write for the time being on that subject was also over. I was passing through a stage of 'total self-absorption' and 'absorption in the present'. I was not experiencing being the universe, nor was I in the exalted mood of being the Lord. I was just an entity absorbed in the moment and in the work. There was still time for the next phase. It was time for the book to end.

I wrote down the previous section, and began putting in order my notes. I was totally engaged now in being a housewife and in my writings. My gaze turned elsewhere. What would I do once my writing was over? Ideas came pouring in. It would be nice to take up painting in oils once again, I thought. Our social life had dwindled to almost nothing, and my other activities had all but stopped. I had been too engrossed in our house, in the family, and in the inner bliss. I must socialize more, and enjoy more the outdoor life, I resolved. I had been in a cosmic simulator all these days, as it were, now let me be in the normal milieu, I thought.

Well, I had looked too far ahead!

Today, January 18, 1986, I was half-way through my dinner and had got up to help myself to some water, when suddenly my hand went limp. I could not pick up my glass. All my strength had left me, I could not think, talk, lift or stand. My senses had been suddenly pulled inwards. One moment, I was astir and nimble, and the next, I was staring into nothing, and falling down. I was conscious, of course, but all my life-force had gathered up at the 'Sahasrara' point.

I thought I was going to faint. The wave was mighty strong and it had come upon me unawares. I felt a sinking sensation, one so strong that I felt I would disgrace myself by throwing up.

The first reaction of my children at such times is to think that I am shamming, and to take things lightly. One daughter said it was the over-eating; the other said, it was the over-dieting.

I recovered a little, but the second wave came swiftly upon me, and with a greater force. The force was now coming in waves and with escalating intensity, engulfing me, drowning me.

Such sudden withdrawals of the senses were common enough with me; so what was the fuss about this time around, asked my children amid laughter. By now I should be a past-master at it, someone teased. Raja flung back at me my own words that I was the master and the controller of this force, that it was my own force and I should be able to control its magnitude. Someone announced that she herself would never enter spirituality. Another advised in a grand-motherly fashion that one should only indulge in pursuits one can cope up with.

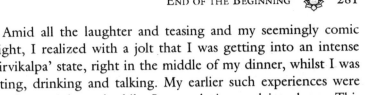

Amid all the laughter and teasing and my seemingly comic plight, I realized with a jolt that I was getting into an intense 'nirvikalpa' state, right in the middle of my dinner, whilst I was eating, drinking and talking. My earlier such experiences were mostly at night and whilst I was relaxing or lying down. This complete demolition of identity, of losing my self-consciousness and suddenly evaporating into the cosmos, in the middle of routine activity, was something new and brought on the previously felt momentary fear. The fear of the unknown. The intensity of the onset also frightened me. It was almost two years since I last had similar experiences, and the unexpectedness, the suddenness, threw me into almost a panic.

I tried to tell Raja what I was entering into, but I could not talk, as the senses had pulled back too swiftly. I somehow forced the words out. I was half-crying and half-holding on to my consciousness.

Raja went on saying, Relax, and let go. But it was easier said than done. Don't resist, he repeated.

But it is the body that resists. The vital processes suddenly seem to stop. My stomach was contracting. I wanted to throw up. I was getting a sinking feeling. My breathing had stopped. All my energies were being sucked away. My identity was being snuffed out. I was not reacting to what I saw or heard. In short, there was a total disorientation of the mind. The world seemed a different place. I seemed to be in a different dimension. A feeling of isolation gripped me, and there was a sudden premonition of extinction of life. By now, the room had turned sombre. The children were paralyzed, not knowing what to make of all this. It was their first experience of watching something they could not understand. They were embarrassed and unsure. I was lying down on the sofa, and the others had been hovering round me. But now there was a sudden freeze and total silence. There was nervousness in the air. Only Raja went on giving instructions to everyone. It was a little like whistling in the dark. He even caught hold of my right toe, as he had done a few times earlier, in the hope of letting at least part of the tremendous surge of energy slip into him.

But I could not relax. The waves were intensifying even further. I had not sought out this path. Nor had I ever endeavoured towards it. In a frenzy, I now shouted that I wanted none of all this.

Raja immediately caught on to this and reminded me that that precisely was the crux of the matter. If I didn't want it, it would subside. It would step down its intensity. Just will it so, he said, remember you are the master!

It worked. Slowly, I regained my senses. I was not resisting now. I was controlling it. I was keeping the force at bay. Slowly, the force ebbed. I could feel its intensity receding, and again I felt I was the master. The momentary fright had been subjugated. All sat quietly, staring at nothing. Slowly, Raja began his next list of instructions to the children. I was not to be left alone henceforth. I was not to go out alone, and one daughter, by turn, was to skip college to be with me, till I gained back 'normalcy'.

The scene that had frozen came to life again. There was a general stir. Raja went upstairs to phone Mr Nemlekar, to inquire as to what was to be done. In case I did get into a deep 'nirvikalpa' state, how was I to be brought out of it. Nothing to worry about, Mr Nemlekar said. In ten minutes, Deepa will be all right.

And I was. At night, I pondered over what had happened earlier. With a tinge of worry, I regretted having shunned this surge of force. Suppose it does not come back again? Suppose I have insulted it? Why was I so foolish, and behaved the way I did? Had I thrown away a once-in-a-lifetime opportunity? Though I was not hankering after it, I did not loathe it. Though I did not specially want it, I did not want to lose it either.

I realized I had reacted spontaneously to it without much thought to the repercussions. It was a genuine fright, however fleeting, and it did come upon me so abruptly that it had caught me unawares.

Immediately came an internal flash that the force would resume after three or four days. It was, after all, my own force that was being manifested; who other than I did exist? I had experienced total non-duality. There was none other than I that existed. There was none other whose force manifested.

I also reasoned as to what further would I experience in the 'nirvikalpa' state that I should get frightened about it. Either it would be the formless Brahman, or with form. Other than that, there exists nothing at all. All that is is contained within It. So I shall experience only my own Self. This pacified me, and I braced myself to enter any state even when walking or sleeping. It would be an adventure unto oneself. Why worry?

This mental preparation helped me to regain my composure. In fact, I even looked forward to the next onslaught now. I had overcome my initial fright, and the next day I sent my daughters off to their colleges. I was now quite prepared to face alone whatever might come.

The only precaution I took was to remain at home.

Wednesday, January 22, 1986:

I woke up in the middle of the night. I felt I was ablaze in a red-hot furnace. I was almost like a piece of meat on the skewer, being grilled on direct fire. My whole body was being exposed to this direct fire. And yet, somehow, this fire was not scorching me. It was almost pleasing. As much as it was roasting me, equally it was transporting me to realms of sublimeness. The heat was from within, but I felt it was all around me. And it was increasing. It finally reached a peak, and then slowly subsided. Again it started, gradually increasing in intensity, roasting me, baking me, sucking me dry. Again it subsided. It had not burnt me.

There was a pattern to it. The moment I would think it had become unbearable, it would subside. I learnt to relax and enjoy the roasting. There was a bizarre pleasure in the roasting. My entire body was being baked from within. Its minutest particle was alight with this flame, throbbing and pulsating. A concentrate of energy, each particle had become a tiny sun with heat, light and fire packed in it. My whole body was a solar dynamo, flaming away. All my 'chakras' were charged and blazing. Especially the one at the heart was an incandescent, pulsating star. I could feel its heat, its light, and its throb.

As suddenly, everything subsided, even the tiredness and all the throbbing and glowing. I was totally my normal self again. Though only momentarily. The wave came on again.

I remembered the happenings of January 18, and knew intuitively that my second phase had begun. I lay pondering over this knowledge, when immediately came the familiar inner voice:

'Yes, you are entering your second phase. I had told you so a few days back, that you will begin again your quest on the fourth day. This is it.'

'Who are you?' I asked directly. I knew it was my own inner being, that had been educating me all these months, that was now answering me. But I wanted to hear this from itself. The voice had changed a little. It had developed more authority, and had a deep, sonorous resonance to it. There was no trace of the lion's roar in it now. It was charged with serenity, dignity and knowledge. The voice sounded ancient, yet imposing.

'I am the representative of the Lord', it said, in a commanding tone. 'The Lord resides in each being. I represent the Lord. The Lord remains silent and still, in supreme repose, and I am the "mover" of the world and the "doer" in the world. He is the cause, I am the action—the Karta, the doer, the creative force. He is the stillness, the silence. I make you walk and talk. I make you think and pause.'

'What is the state I am in now?' I asked. 'Is this the fourth state, the "turyavastha"?' 'No! You have gone beyond "turyavastha". "Turyavastha" is low down compared to the state you are in now. You are in that "mahan avastha", (great state), where there are no more rungs of ladder left. You are all.' And I actually felt that "turyavastha" was a long-forgotten dreamlike state, only a faint memory in some deep recess of the mind.

'What is happening to me now?', I asked.

'You shall now undergo a "tapas" for fourteen years. "Mahan tapas" for fourteen years! After that, the state you will be in is difficult for you to fathom now. There are no words to describe what you will be then. Suffice it to know you will be 'mahan'.

'In the first phase, I was inactive, enjoying it no doubt, but neglecting my chores, feeling drowsy, staring mindlessly, and drifting. I don't want that life any more. I was very active previously, and I want to resume my activities,' I communed with the voice.

'All these days, you were identical with the Brahman. Silent, still, reposing, meditative and in bliss. Henceforth, you shall identify yourself with me—the "Karta", the doer. I am the dynamism of the Lord, His voice. And you shall be active, creative, and moving. With the substratum of the previous phase, of equanimity, silence, and bliss and peace, you shall be now dynamic.

'You say that I shall be "mahan" one day, but I don't see myself as sitting down to receive visitors all day long, and giving them guidance. I don't want to be a guru. I want to be free and doing things'.

'Guiding people and being a guru is not your vocation. You shall not be a guru. The "diksha-guru"—he who initiates—is different. You shall not be giving 'diksha' to anyone. All this is for your own development.

'You want to work, go ahead and work! You want to write, go ahead and write! You want to paint, go ahead and paint! Do what you want. Be free, be dynamic. Rewrite the legends. Correct through your writings the wrong notions people have collected about God, about Self. Educate them. Go ahead and write! Remember, this is your phase of activity. Go ahead and plunge into activity. I am with you.'

A doubt assailed me. Was this my own outermost mind, given to exaggeration? How much of it was to be believed? It was true that, while educating me, it had been precise; but whenever it was predicting the future, it had needed to be reined in heavily. It was easy for one to be misguided by it, as this voice could be one's own ego, or a deep-hidden desire expressing itself. It was thus the informant, the revealer. The Reality never spoke. This inner voice made people perceive and know. Clearer the mind, purer this inner dialogue.

Should I shun it, or let it go on? I had definitely entered my second phase. I knew that intuitively. The process of self-purification was now even more intense. I had no desire for advancement. I had neither previous knowledge of how to go about it nor what to expect, so this was not my own subconscious or conscious desires finding expression nor any acquired knowledge buried in some deep layers of memory.

Immediately, I was answered by it. 'By posing questions and pondering thus, you create duality, you create me. Your intuitive knowledge is the truth. By seeking answers and questioning, you give me a separate identity. You and I are one. I am your creative force, your "Karta". You and the Lord are one. You and I are one. It was your pondering over your state that made me manifest apart from you. There is no duality. All are one. All is one. What you know, what you do, is the truth. Remember this always. Quit questioning.'

'I feel no duality,' I responded. 'I feel no identity. I don't identify myself either with the Lord or with the housewife that I am. I feel I am just the witness, without identity, without any reactions to what I witness, always in a state of bliss.'

'That is because you were totally identifying with the Lord. The Lord too exists in the world with no identity. He is all. He has no separate identity, no confining individuality, not even of being the Lord. Identity involves speciality, specificness, a mark, a differentiation, a designation. All these involve an idea, a concept, a name, a word, a language. The Lord is above these confinements. He just exists, signless, with no indication, with no fanfare. So have you existed all these days. But now you enter another phase. You shall gain authority. You shall dispense from a base of authority. You shall see slowly forces manifesting in you, like intuition, telepathy. You might even occasionally see flashes of things happening elsewhere. But do not exploit this force. This is only a phase in your long-term development. Do not make use of it. Watch it develop, and enjoy it. That is all. Do not try to guide others.'

By now the huge bright diamonds in my head and chest were pulsating with unusual vigour. They were incandescent. The other 'chakras' too were on fire, as it were.

Then the voice again called upon me not to let duality creep back in me. It asked me not to summon it anymore. 'Be authoritative,' it told me. 'Don't underestimate yourself. Know that you know the truth.'

It then gave me an assurance that it had taken charge of all my chores and my activities. It then told me what plans it had for the various activities of mine.

One more question I asked. 'What can I expect in this great "tapas" that I have to undergo?

'You are now on the path to becoming the inconceivable. What you will experience, what you will undergo, will be inconceivable and indescribable by you. You need not write all that down. You will not find words to describe it. All you will do is witness and enjoy. You will get deeper insights into things. What you have hitherto undergone or understood, you will now find inconsequential and trivial.'

'Is what I have written all these days worthless then?' I asked.

'How do you mean worthless? Was it not I who made you write all that? How can it then suddenly turn worthless now? All that you have written is true and significant, but it is relevant only to that stage. You have gone beyond that stage. Everything is true to the state one is in at a given moment, but one must charge ahead. Evolution must go on. You have to be firmly established in the oneness of the universe. After fourteen years, there will be no more any difference.'

'Will I be something like Shri Anandmayee Ma then?'

'You will be like all the Mas. All will be one. All will be the same.'

And with that the voice subsided. The throbbing and the pulsating disappeared too. True to the promise given, there was no drugged feeling or of being in samadhi, as it used to be after such a strong spell. I was alert and buoyant. There were no after-effects either. My body had accepted this force as its own.

The active phase of my inner quest had begun.

And, with this, I also conclude now my scribbling. I enter my new phase alone and silent, to be put through fire like iron ore for its purification.

I enter my next phase to seek the oneness with its silence,

where the silence is a 'mantra', a worship, and where the silence itself is mightily eloquent.

I begin now my journey that will take me far into the depths of oblivion, where oblivion and consciousness are synonymous, where there is no entry for duality or identity.

67

Mind and Body in Spiritual Evolution

The different stages and states that mind passes through during spiritual evolution can last just a few moments each or years together, all depending upon the requirements of an individual mind. Nature sees to it that the education is complete, and regulates the intensity, duration and periodicity of these states according to the evolutionary needs of the individual, the role he has to play in life, his future, etc. Spiritual experiences vary from individual to individual; intensities will differ; some may even skip certain stages, but finally it is the same Reality that Nature reveals. Each individual will receive explanations in the language he understands and in such a way that things will be clear to him. However, the interpretations of these experiences may differ according to the bent of the individual's mind. But each 'event' will be pointing to the same Reality.

There are different layers or states of an individual mind. All these states can be active at the same time, or only some as in most cases. These states are not definitely demarcated; one state merges into the next. The following is only a broad classification to understand the workings of the mind. Mind is one continuous subtle stream finally merging into divinity.

The Gross Mind:

One is the waking mind, which seems very active as thoughts rise continuously in it, and which goes to sleep regularly. The sleeping state is active when it is hashing up dreams, or peaceful when without dreams. Sleep can be deep when the individual is like dead to the world, or light when certain body movements take place. This gross mind that includes a man's waking and sleeping states, his entire thought process, his memory, acquired knowledge, hopes, fears, etc., makes up his general personality. With his individualized thinking, he develops his own individual character. This state is based on 'me' and 'mine', on attachments, greed, aspirations, hopes, and consequently, fears, frustrations, disappointments, grief, rage, etc. Here 'me' and 'mine' come first.

In the beginning, the conscience pricks an individual into doing something by way of worship. Or he experiences moments so beautiful that he thinks of God. Or it is the lash of calamity that makes him kneel in prayer. Whatever it is, a time comes in every individual's life when the thought of God is sparked off in him. Slowly, devotion is born, a prayer is sent up, and hands fold in supplication.

Either through devotion, or by following one's conscience and maintaining the purity of thought, or through the path of knowledge, yoga and meditation, man slowly begins a journey to where mind begins to bloom and unfolds a blush of radiance that is the Reality. It is a long and arduous journey.

As man advances in spiritual evolution, his outer or gross mind begins to stall. Vanity and ego drop out. Irrelevant, hindering, upsetting thoughts begin to fade. The thinking process required for the normal, intelligent, fruitful functioning of life does not and need not stop. It is only those thoughts based on or springing from desires, attachments, jealousy, greed, rage, 'me', 'mine', etc., that have to fade out. That is, thoughts or deeds based on the past and the future have to fade out. Thoughts springing from purity have to come to the forefront. This can be done and does get done. This stops one's mind from swinging from euphoria to grief, from buoyancy to despondency, and vice-versa. A mind capable of becoming euphoric will swing to melancholy with equal force.

Purity brings calm and composure to the mind, which gets diverted from the 'why' and 'rewards' to 'how' and 'when'! Later, even these latter subside. This total absorption in work is like meditation or a 'mantra'. It stills the mind and empties it of unwanted things. This makes man see things 'as they are', improves his judgement, efficiency and output. He learns to do things for the sheer love of it. Here, the doing or the learning become in themselves the enjoyment, and not the rewards. If rewards come as well, so much the better. But there is no grief, disappointment, heartburn or depression, as there were no specific goals. Instead, there is enjoyment right throughout. The emphasis is on the doing and the enjoyment.

As his waking mind stills, so does his dreaming mind. For dreams are but a projection of his waking mind, his memory, emotions, acquired knowledge, etc. Now the dreams subside and finally vanish. Emotions get steadied. Both the sleeping and waking mind experience a feeling of well-being. Sleep is restful and the day is tranquil. The mind slowly loses its individuality and merges into a common pool of 'human conscience'.

Human Conscience:

Then there is a more subtle mind which may be called the conscience of man. This is a purer mind, closer to the divinity within him. It pricks him when he is doing wrong, guides him and warns him when needed, and can be termed as his instinct or intuition. The internal dialogues that take place in man are generally between this mind and the gross mind. Dialogues that take place in fantasizing or daydreaming belong to the gross mind.

This second state is the collective conscience of a human mind that is based on values, ethics, right thought, right deed, generosity, compassion, etc., that are inherent in man. Though it may be influenced by the environment and the traditions of his upbringing, this state nevertheless transcends the superficial values and sense of ethics imposed upon man by man. Generally the gross mind tends to ignore the voice of the subtle mind to suit its own convenience, ego, desire, vanity, etc.

Now there is less struggle with the conscience. Emotions having been stilled, man spontaneously begins to take wiser and more appropriate and correct steps. The gross mind now listens more to it. The baser aspects of mind begin to recede. The gross mind becomes pure enough to merge with the purer mind, the conscience. Now, there will be no internal struggle, conflict and guilt. Mind will be under control, tranquil, judgement clear and intelligence sharp. Deeds and emotions will spring spontaneously from the nobler mind. The purer mind begins to rule.

The individual will now be free of the past and the future. That is, his deeds will be spontaneous and not based on past emotions, feelings and urges, nor will they depend upon hopes and aspirations for the future. Deeds will be done for the love of performance of the deed, not due to the hope of a reward, nor as a reaction to something. The man is no longer a frustrated, isolated being. His 'me', and 'mine' are dropped, and peace reigns. He is more carefree, tension-free, contented, ready to do without things, at peace with the world and himself. He will not need external tools for happiness and contentment.

His inner strength, inner source of knowledge, inspiration, dynamism, energy and motivation, all the inherent good in man, will begin to throb. The restlessness of body and mind will stop. This man is now pure. He is inspired. He will exude an aura of goodness. He will have self-confidence, self-respect and a deep understanding of things.

This state is not the ultimate spiritual frontier of man, however haloed it may be. Therefore, even this glorious pure human conscience which is yet fragmenting has to be demolished.

He is bestowed with a supernal mind that transcends even this high state of purity, and now proceeds headlong towards even higher states of subtlety and purity. Mind has to sublimate to where there is no longer any demarcation between human, animal and plant kingdoms, and matter, energy, time and space. He has to become cosmic. To attain this, the mind, now already pure, has to break its shackles of individual identity so essential to human nature.

The 'Karta':

The still purer mind is more subtle than the previous two and is very close to the divinity. It is like a 'karta', a doer, of the divinity.

It is its representative, as it were. This state takes over, as the individual is ascending the rungs of spiritual evolution. It guides him and educates him. It employs any means—audiovisual, flashes of knowledge, internal dialogues—to make spiritual things clear to him.

This state is very knowledgeable, as it is very close to the Knowledge aspect of the divinity. It may still have traces of gross mind, conscience, or conditioning. It might still not be totally free of ego, vanity or want. In that case, it may run wayward, and start predicting or give blessings for impossible or unordained events. Coming events may get worded in grandiose language or bombastic predictions; and the event, when it does occur, might be tamer than expected, or might not occur at all, thereby causing sorrow or disappointment. It may be totally wrong when mixed with hopes and desires. But if the mind is totally pure, it is divine in nature and it will guide one faultlessly. It becomes man's inspiration and motivation.

The Merger:

As the demolition of the subtle mind proceeds, the devotee and the divinity merge. Prayers and blessings merge. The doubts and the answers merge. They merge and yet remain separate and retain their identities. They are now occupying the same space, so to say. It is beautiful, though unbelievable. It seems true, yet doubtful. It seems divine and crazy.

In this merging, there is at times equal predominance of both the states. There is one part of the mind, the individual mind, praying spontaneously, worshipping the newly-perceived Lord in all His Glory, doubting, asking questions, seeking reassurance; and another part, the representative of the Lord, the 'karta', giving blessings, answering, reassuring.

Then who is it that is watching and observing all this, and is aware of all that is going on? This is the eternal Witness, the all-pervading cosmic Witness, the Lord Supreme, lending a rare stillness, a feeling of well-being, an undercurrent of bliss and stability, a feeling of pervasiveness, unity and eternity.

In this state are contained all the different states of the waking mind—the gross, the conscience and the 'karta'. No doubt, in their purest form. Here both the minds and the 'karta' are active, against the background of the eternal Witness.

At other times, this merging brings forth a silence. A totally silent, thought-free state. A spiritual mindlessness. Nothing matters now. Everything is perfection. Everything is at peace. The world stops. Time stops. Only 'this' moment counts. There is nothing in the world except just 'being'.

At such times, both the minds and the 'karta' are silent against the back-drop of the eternal witness.

Either of these two states can manifest itself, when in company or in solitude, in the wake of activity or while reposing.

Even in sleep, this merged state prevails. Because of the Witness in him, even when asleep, man is aware of his sleeping state, his dreams, or his dreamless deep sleep, his surroundings, his samadhi-like state, all simultaneously. Even asleep, he is like one awake.

In deep sleep, if his mind is still, there will be no dreams, only an awareness of deep, peaceful sleep. At this time, the 'karta' may be active and educating him, or is in repose itself.

In this state of sleep are contained all the states of a sleeping mind. Such an individual is in a half-awake and half-asleep condition. He may even answer questions. If this breaks the stream of his sleep, he gets fully awake; but, with the gaining of mastery he can command continuity—he may respond to questions, yet still sleep on.

But this state, too, has to be transcended. The devotee has to be totally negated. Worship annihilated. Only the Witness must remain.

The demolition proceeds. The 'karta' takes over. The cosmic force reveals its glory. Slowly, gently, step by step. Education proceeds in regulated, monitored doses. It proceeds in sleep, in wakefulness, in 'nirvikalpa'. The 'karta' guides, educates, talks, explains, and propels the individual along the path of revelations.

As long as there is this revealing, explaining, educating, there is duality. No matter how subtle. The two, the individual and the universal, are one and the same, yet separated by a highly subtle veil of spiritual ignorance that has to be sundered. What is to be revealed by the tearing of this last veil? None other than the non-dual, cosmic, universal, all-permeating, eternal soul of man. The divinity of man, his true nature.

Education: What is revealed?

The only true, complete, thorough, all-encompassing education lies in just 'being': By 'being', by merging with, becoming one with the object you seek. Here we seek the identity of our soul. The culmination of an evolution. And what is that soul? None other than the Lord.

But the Lord is multi-faceted. So, the mind is made to merge in turn with each facet for a thorough education. Of course, in reality, the mind is not made to merge with these aspects; it is only that the veil of ignorance lifts; the inherent, true nature of man in its different facets is revealed.

What are these different facets? Pure existence, cosmic awareness, bliss, knowledge, power, all-pervasiveness, eternity, and so on. The list is endless.

But the Lord is a paradox. He contains mind-boggling contradictions. He includes all the above in Him, and also contains the absence of them. As much as He contains the existence, awareness, bliss, knowledge and power, He also contains non-existence, absence of knowledge, absence of bliss, oblivion, and non-interference. Being all, He is nothingness to the point of extinction. But these are only His facets. He is beyond these, like a musician is beyond his music. Music is in him, music is of him, but still he is free of it. Music sprouts from him, music depends upon him, but he is independent of the music.

That is not all. The Lord is the universe. But only a part of His force bursts forth as the universe, the manifest. The rest remains as the potential. The universe is the Lord, yet the Lord is above it, free of it. The Lord is the eternal Witness, yet he is withdrawn, uninterfering, detached. All-feeling, yet unshaken; approachable, yet aloof.

Such, and a multitude of other facets, some known and understood by man, some not, are revealed to him. And what is made clear is that this is man's own true nature, his own true identity, his own facets, for he is also none other than the Lord. Nothing is, that is not the Lord; not even man. By knowing himself, he knows the Lord; or knowing the Lord, he knows himself.

In the beginning, these revelations are given in the 'nirvikalpa' state; but with mastery, when the 'nirvikalpa' state and the waking state become one, the 'feel' of these various aspects may remain all the time. Then again, it is not required to have this 'feel' all the time, for mind transcends even this; and, just as man does not need to have the feel of being a man all the time, his existence alone makes him aware of everything, in the same way the transcended mind does not need to have this 'feel' all the time, because he has become That. If there is a 'feel', there is duality. The individual absorbs this too.

No matter how fleeting these transcendental and immanent experiences are, they leave a lasting impact and an equally enduring knowledge.

Identifying oneself with gods:

Man's mind is moulded by the traditions, the religious beliefs, the environment he is brought up in. In his mind will be etched all these impressions. He will identify God, based on these beliefs. So, in his spiritual evolution, in the earlier stages, he will pass through a period when he correlates himself with a god, as He is understood by him; a godhead conditioned by his upbringing and religion; the image he has built up of God in his mind. This will be with a form and a name.

But, soon, he will understand that name and form are confining, limiting, that God has to be formless to penetrate every cell, has to be nameless to be everything. He has to be subtler than the subtlest energy; that He can only be knowledge, existence, bliss and power! But even this would be limiting Him. He can exist as efficiently, as fully, as eternally, as all-pervadingly, as beautifully, and as intelligently, without existence, bliss, knowledge, or power. These are his manifested aspects. He is complete and rich even without them in His unmanifested form as non-existence and oblivion.

When finally man's mind has merged in the divinity, and when knowledge becomes a part of him, the work of the 'karta' is over. As the mind becomes more and more established in the divinity, knowledge and power are with him constantly. The 'karta' gets effaced. His work is done.

Formation and negation of mind can be a continuous process, and hence the 'karta' may surface again and again till the final merger.

Then comes that state of the mind that is divinity itself. When mind is totally pure and has broken the shackles of its individuality and has merged in this divine state, it becomes divinity itself. This mind is in the state of Sat-Chit-Ananda, pure Existence, Knowledge and Bliss. It becomes the eternal Witness. This is the font from where arise all the other states and into which they get reabsorbed eventually.

How does the body react to spiritual evolution?

The body is in continuation to, and congeneric with, the life-forces, the mind and the divinity, it being the grossest aspect. Much the same way as are ice, water, cloud and fine water vapour. The stuff is the same, only in different states and interchangeable. However, one state affects the other, only the state of divinity remaining unaffected. It only reveals itself. When the ever-wandering mind is stilled or brought under control, either through meditation or through the path of knowledge, the life-forces are channelized and begin traversing through the body, activating certain very subtle nerve centres in it, giving rise to different psychic experiences, including certain yogic 'asanas' and 'kriyas' to facilitate the passage of these life-forces and also for further purification or stilling of mind. All these—the mind, the life-forces and the body—join hands and together align themselves for further progress.

If spiritual progress is attained through yoga or the body, this discipline also triggers the life-forces and slowly stills the mind, and again these three work together for further progress.

The path of devotion to God, 'bhakti', purifies and stills the mind, riveting the mind in God, which in turn triggers the life-forces.

Natural purity of thought, without resorting to any of the above paths, also sets the life-forces into action. No matter what the path, knowingly taken or unknowingly, consciously seeking God or coincidentally, with or without effort, the above triggering action will take place sooner or later. It is all very scientific and each path is a science unto itself. Certain steps must bring about certain effects, however slowly.

When the vital forces have reached the goal, 'sahasrara chakra', the subtle centre at the crown of the head, the body's job would be complete. By then, the mind also would be in a state of total purity. All the three, the body, the mind and the life forces, would have been stilled by now.

Through all these stages, the body has to continuously adjust itself to the winds of change, like a ship tacking its sails. It has to face many rigours and cope with them, such as bouts of lassitude, in the course of its trying to keep pace with the spiritual development of the mind.

It is the individual mind that gets into different stages of samadhi and finally gets into the 'nirvikalpa' samadhi, when the individual identity is totally cast away, and the individual mind merges with the divine.

The body is still during this period; even breathing may stop. All the senses which are outward-responding turn inwards, realign themselves to facilitate the life-forces to concentrate at the 'sahasrara chakra'. The body is now inward-looking, or 'antarmukhi'.

When the breath and the vital forces are poised at the 'sahasrara chakra', there is a trickle of 'nectar' from there to the rest of the body. The only word fit to describe this state is 'nectarine'.

This is the 'amrut', the nectar that makes one immortal. Not that the body does not die, nor that one becomes immortal in fame; it is that he gets established in true consciousness. His awareness or consciousness is so heightened that he is fully aware or conscious in his sleep, dream, samadhi, and even in death, and then in the subsequent births. The awareness slips from the old body to the new. The awareness is immortal, not the body.

All these states and stages might take many years and even many births. But the good effects may be felt instantly.

Often, man loses consciousness in samadhi. He is in a state of oblivion. But with mastery, awareness right throughout can be achieved and the different processes of the body observed. Often, there are long gaps between the experiences or states. This is so, to enable the body and mind to get ready for higher experiences or states.

A brush with Reality is not the end of the goal for man. It is just the beginning. He will then have to be fully established in that state. The intensity of the different aspects of Reality will have to be deepened. A stage must come when he no longer needs to get into that state, but is 'that' all the time. With more and more purity, more of the Self will be revealed. There is so much to perceive of Reality that to understand even a minute fraction of Its aura, all man's faculties will not be enough.

The experiences of the 'nirvikalpa' state must slowly be experienced during full activity. A state of deep samadhi must form a substratum for all activity.

There should be no more any difference between one state and another. He should be 'that' all the time.

The body, which hitherto had experienced cosmic energy and which had at times made it listless and without motivation, should absorb this and become oblivious of it.

The body and mind having absorbed all these states and, in fact, having become so one with them that these become the individual's natural state, the man then continues to remain in the present, and is no longer consciously aware of his new identity. He carries on with his normal life without hindrance.

But his work would now onwards reflect divinity. If he does not let his ego hamper his progress and if he does not tamper with his newly-acquired powers, he is well-set on the path of progress.

And there is no conceivable end to his evolution.

68

The Years Roll by

October 2005

My own need and the urge to immediately put down in the form of a diary every spiritual occurrence and idea as and when it occurred have resulted in this book. The last entry in the diary of those days, beginning with the Christmas of 1983, is on January 22, 1986. Thereafter, though I have continued recording the Knowledge that wells out of my inner being, as also various aspects and stages of my spiritual development, it cannot be categorized as maintaining a diary.

The outpouring of Knowledge from within resulted in the book, *Teachings of the Inner Light: A Blueprint for Right Living.* It gives detailed descriptions of the grand plan of the Lord Almighty and His awesome Creation. Divinity is all-pervasive. It pervades us too as the Inner Light of Consciousness. However, our impure mind covers this and prevents its divine Knowledge and bliss being imparted to us in their fullness. But we are not destined to remain eternally condemned thus either. Divinity intends that we partake of this bliss and Knowledge by becoming one with Itself. By becoming as pure of mind as the Inner Light itself, by shedding all the impurities of the mind, we can experience and know this Inner Light. *Teachings of the Inner Light* explains how this can be accomplished. The description and narration in the *Journey* may be likened to the spilling over from a boiling cauldron, red hot and immediate. The subsequent writings are like cool streams leisurely flowing from a placid lake. Yet, the two are aspects of the same theme: Man and God.

People often ask me as to what phase I am going through now: What do I experience, what do I feel? They want to know more about my childhood: Was the early spiritual awakening sudden or gradual? They are curious to know the course of events that led to the eventual explosion of Light, of 'Prakaasha', Illumination, resulting in self-discovery and Cosmic Consciousness. They want to know about the sort of a world one lives in after the rediscovery of one's Self. Are there any changes in one's mental and emotional make-up?

The world I have entered is enchanting. It is so beautiful and enthralling that it inspires one to endlessly talk about it, to share it with everyone. It includes every thing that 'is'. All is laid bare in its full clarity, simplicity and beauty, revealing the hidden side of it. How to encapsulate all this in a few words? It is an endless discovery: The more I communicate, the more I find freshly revealed. This is the world of the Eternal, of the Infinite. Can He and His world be described in finite words? I am still on the path of discovery, an endless and wondrous path, learning every moment something new. The mystery, the principle behind everything is divulged graciously here, as if this learning, this knowledge, and its enjoyment, are the sole purpose of life.

Yet, it is at the same time difficult to describe, as it contains all the opposites. We assume that opposites generally negate each other, but here, paradoxically, they co-exist in equal measure and vividness, complementing and enhancing each other, making it almost impossible to convincingly convey its strangeness and mystery in all their beauty to someone who has not made a foray into that world.

It is a world of peace, perfection, harmony, and contentment. There is an ambrosial feeling of fullness, completion, and fulfilment, held together with a thread of perennial, sublime joy. There is nothing wanting or needed here. Every thing seems to be just as it should be, following a divine pattern and scheme, even the sorrows, the evil, the bad, the ugliness. Each, with its own opposite, is integral to the intricate fabric of Creation and without which the pattern would unravel into a meaningless jumble. Good can be appreciated only when judged against bad; light only if darkness is experienced; happiness only in the midst of discontent; and so on.

It is a world so peaceful yet dynamic, so silent yet full of music, solitary yet bubbling with life. It is beauty incarnate, soul-satisfying and absorbing, though it may seem a fantasy, a mirage, to outsiders, as it is an inner world elusive and illusory to them.

My body has become so sensitive that any sound, loud or gentle, like the rustling of leaves, the whirring of a fan, the drone of a plane, the swish of a sweeping broom, the whisper of a caressing breeze, an auto-rickshaw noisily passing by, sets even the insides of the bones a-dancing. These pleasurable inner vibrations, in synch with the vibrations of the outer sounds, turn into soothing, pulsating, radially spreading waves of music, though the vibrations vary in intensity with the fluctuating decibel and volume of sound. It feels as if I have become an extremely responsive oscillator. The whole atmosphere seems to gently vibrate with this softly reverberating music. The sound is *Aum*. These vibrations in turn generate coursing streams of divine ecstasy within, god-intoxication, and I am pulled into a state of *Ananda*. Ananda is an aspect of divine consciousness. It sets each cell, each atom of the body vibrating in ecstasy. Thus, I am ever conscious of this Ananda, which is sourced from outside as well as from the consciousness residing within.

My world is solitary as I am, more often than not, Self-absorbed in the enjoyment of the divine company of the Self. I am a soliton, in the world of physics, a quantum packet of energy existing in the manner of a solitary wave. It is an exclusive domain where reside only my higher Self, and myself. Hence, though it is solitary, it is not lonely or forlorn. An active presence of the higher Self is constantly there. There is sweet duality within an intimate oneness. The senses are turned inward, sensitive and receptive to Ananda, and the inner flow of revelations. Yet, a slight movement, a slight sound, turns the senses outward. Thus, I am constantly poised on a threshold of the mind, alert to and enjoying both inner and outer worlds.

The world is silent as there are no compulsive internal monologues of the mind, no intruding thoughts either. Thus, even in the midst of the noisy activity of a metro city, there is peace and the sanctity of the snow-clad mountains within.

The body wants to be at total rest, arresting all its activity and bringing everything to a standstill, yet there is a sudden urge for right action at the right time. The body feels limp and yielding even though it experiences the dynamic universal energy coursing within.

The gaze is one-pointed. Awareness is unwaveringly poised on that point, like an unflickering flame, absolutely still. Even breathing is an intrusion, as it involves movement, however slight. Non-breathing is pleasing. Contrarily, interpenetrating this one-point awareness is a low-profile universal awareness making me aware of the universe at large, for that too is my span.

When I come out of this undisturbed inexcitability, I am the cosmic energy vibrating in ecstasy. It is me who accepts the fervour of all rituals in the temples, and the worship of all devotees, their devotion, and it is I who savour their love.

When I visit temples or am invited to puja at friends' homes, I crave to tell them to wave the lamps a little thisward too, not only at the idols, because the force is awake here, within me, as is within them, as I pervade them too. But I don't, because the feeling gets arrested before I can voice it. This is not a hankering, only an urge to educate them. But their worship reaches me anyway.

I remember that at age three, having spilt *alta* on the floor, I stood there shocked, gazing at the dramatic streak of red, bewildered and embarrassed at the sudden unintentionally committed mess. Soon, I was lost in the beauty of the artistic splash of red. I saw not the *alta* nor the punishable act of dropping it, but a streak of *sindhoor* spreading like a river, narrow at one end, and broadening as it flowed away from me, adorning the mid-parting of the long, black tresses of Mother Goddess. A goddess so loving and beautiful that I was drawn deeper into that red. Before my very eyes, the streak and the span of Mother Goddess expanded endlessly and encompassed Infinity and Eternity. The beauty and the love of the Goddess totally engulfed me, making 'Permanence' a part of my indelible experiences. This was my first brush, among many, with Eternity and Infinity.

It was a while before I regained awareness of my surroundings, only to find that my mother was staring unblinking at me and at the alta. In that shock and silence, her anger and my fear dissolved. What reigned were love and laughter, and the hug of a mother, universal as also mortal.

Thus began my spiritual journey.

At age four, in Simla, where huge monkeys abound, another dramatic insight was unfolded to me. As I walked on the roads with my maid, some of these monkeys would turn ferocious and growl and jump at us. Though the maid kept the monkeys at bay with a stick, it was all the same a frightening experience. Yet, to me, it was a spiritual experience as well. I saw that a monkey's face and body would assume an aspect of ferocity, but his eyes would remain unaffected. That meant the monkey was not cruel at heart! Deep down behind those alert eyes hid an innocent urge to display his might and strength, nothing more. All children intuitively sense kindness, cruelty or indifference; likewise, I was quick to detect the non-cruel nature in this momentary ferociousness of the monkeys. Even at that tender age, I observed a duality within the monkey. One, the quick reaction of his body in keeping with his species; two, his not-so-dangerous a nature. This observation of duality in the monkey gave me strength to stand and stare at them even as my own body would tense up. With the result that I became aware of a duality within myself too. One part of mine would be unmoving, rock-like, unfrightened; the other, in spite of my still mind, would be tense, ready to crouch and hide behind the maid, should the monkey jump. This was my body, standing apart from my mind, just as the mind of the monkey stood apart from his body. Henceforth, I was always conscious of this duality between body and mind. This sense of duality made me very bold. Bold of mind and yet cautious and alert of the body. So at any given time, I would feel indomitable, yet confident that I could move faster than light if need be. This trait later made me venture into fields where others would hesitate for long.

Soon, I would find myself sitting in front of idols for hours, without moving. Not a cell of mine moved or even wanted to move. The gaze would become fixed. It was as though the thoughts, the breath and the senses had been arrested and locked from within. This was not death-like, though. It was nectarine, poised in some unidentifiable pleasure. Sitting thus, alone and unmoving in nearby temples for entire afternoons while others slept, gazing at the pictures and statues of gods, getting lost gazing at the sky, listening to the pealing of temple bells, witnessing the world go by, without reacting to it or reaching out to it, had become the norm. Suddenly the lock would be released and the body would become full of energy again. Now I know those were samadhi states, though at that time I did not notice them to be any different to normal states.

Having been to a church near our house one evening, the pealing bells there, the setting sun, the candles glowing gently inside, the silence, the solitude and the peace, left a deep impression on me. At about the same time, I also happened to read a story on Jesus Christ. The two incidents left a mark on me. After that, often, when I would sit alone at night, concentrating on some incomprehensible portion of my studies, I would find Jesus Christ sitting next to me in his long white robe and with flowing black beard and long hair, about to explain these imponderables to me. Before he could start, all of a sudden there would be a sudden clarity, like a lamp lit, within my brain, and these 'horrific' portions would become easy and their meanings obvious.

Years later, after I started getting into nirvikalpa samadhi, the deepest state of meditation, and began experiencing the profound facets of God, I saw in my meditation one evening, a good-looking, slightly bent, biblical old man, in a white robe with a flowing beard and long white hair. I was seated in a meditative pose wearing a white saree, my head covered, on the crest of a steep hillock, watching the entire, spreading, barren landscape in a detached way, and this old but agile man was heading slowly but surely, with the help of a stick, up the hillock towards me. I knew, as one simply knows in dreams and visions, that he was Moses. But before my very eyes, as he climbed up, he slowly got transformed into a handsome young man with a flowing black beard and sporting locks of black hair, and I recognized him to be Jesus Christ. He was draped in his typical white robe. He came straight to me and, with an aura of assurance about him, as if he knew his task well, entered, and merged into me.

After a moment of pregnant silence, when nothing moved, a deep male voice intoned within me, 'I want to speak through you.' My body at once felt as if it was in a furnace, progressively getting hotter and scalding. The flames of a raging fire were leaping all round me. The heat did not consume me; instead, I felt the heat was a glowing fire of purification, very soothing and intoxicating, penetrating each atom of every one of my cells, setting them ablaze.

I sat for a long time pondering over this utterance and basking in the heat and light of the continuing fire. I found I was not breathing and was empty of thought and feeling. Who had spoken thus within me? Can I mention this to any one without raising a controversy? Will anyone believe me if I did? Would I be able to handle this responsibility? Staring silently at nothing, I heard the same voice intone again, 'This is not *your* responsibility'.

I remained in deep meditation for a long time.

Once, on four consecutive nights, I had been hearing the loud barking of a pack of street dogs outside my window. I had paid scant attention to it, as I was too deep in sleep. This particular night though, I had been half-asleep, when the barking became too very persistent. In the twilight zone between sleep and wakefulness, I noted that the noisy medley of barking had a peculiar alternating cadence to it, as though two groups were standing opposite each other, involved in a fierce verbal fight, throwing insults and curses at each other with all the vehemence they could muster. And the most peculiar thing about it all, I noted, was that the whole verbal exchange was in human voices using everyday human words and inflexions. I snapped out of sleep into a momentary confusion about whether it was dogs or humans who were brawling. Soon I realized that these were, in fact, dogs barking but sounding so human.

I sat up with a start. The barking sounded very much like human voices. I had distinctly heard words and fully formed sentences. It was clearly a show of strength between the two parties. Neither party had attacked the other physically. The two groups had stood about five feet apart, in full control, throwing only words at each other.

The fight was not important, the barking coming in the form of words was. Understanding dawned. I now understood how and why certain rishis and yogis could understand the language of animals and birds. When the faculties of individual consciousness are raised, the raised consciousness intuitively transforms sounds and vibrations into words, into a language known to that individual. This is how the rishis were adept at understanding animal and bird communication.

Also, the founder-sages of ayurveda could understand even plants who would tell them how to use each herb and for which ailments.

It is not that the plants or the birds are reaching out to humans. They are being themselves. It is the transcended individual consciousness that becomes so sensitive and receptive to auras, vibrations, sounds and other modes of transmission, and acquires the rare ability to metamorphose these modes of communication into human communication.

This experience left me in awe of the Lord: To wonder at His greatness, to marvel at His creative and imaginative abilities, to think who else but the Lord, alone worthy of worship, could think of and bring forth such a stupendous, unbelievable and multifaceted, all-pervading Consciousness.

The beauty of such profound experiences was that an experience repeated itself till it got registered in the experiencer and its import deeply realized. The barking had been going on for several nights earlier, till it had registered itself in me and its importance was understood by me, and then had immediately stopped thereafter. Its task was done.

Another thing I realized was that all spiritual experiences were cognized and their import understood only during this transcendent half-asleep, half-awake state, when the body was asleep but the mind awake and in meditation. If the sleep was too deep, the experience was lost; and if fully awake, the transcendence was lost, unless the state of nirvikalpa had set in. In the high state of transcendence, the experiencing was of the phenomenal world, and, in the nirvikalpa state, of the different facets of the Lord.

Hence, each experience was a learning process. It was education of the highest order. But in a very advanced yogi, the faculties are so highly developed that the transcendence becomes their natural and constant state. For them, spiritual experiencing is not an education or a fleeting experience; it becomes their normal state. But this is rare.

At nights often, when I am fast asleep, souls of departed people come, wake me up and implore me for salvation. They always speak in Hindi. One even spoke in a frenzy asking me to hurry up as we were running late to reach the Kabristhan, the Muslim graveyard. He did not wait for me though, to follow, but rushed out of the window. As the fogginess of my mind cleared, for a moment I thought he was asking me to hurry because my time was up and I was delaying my own burial. I was feeling fine, nowhere near death, still I waited to see if I would myself die. As nothing happened, I woke up Raja to make sure I was still alive in a real world. I realized the departing soul wanted strength to face his burial.

Most of the spirits seem to be Muslims and they fly past our bedroom window from east to west. Some wait at the window, hesitate to wake me up when they see me asleep and fly right past. Some fly past unaware of me, but I can see them even through my sleep. Only a few wait at the window and though they see me asleep, beg to be delivered.

As I do not know how to deal with this, I just wait after awakening, and, petrified, pray for them.

Spirits are subtle, shadowy entities, with their personality traits, their fears, and their awareness intact. Normally, they cannot be seen or heard but when one becomes sensitive to them, one can. I am sensitive to them only sometimes and that too when I am asleep and vulnerable.

Once, an entity tried to enter me forcefully through my in-drawing breaths. I got up from my sleep, struggling to keep the entity out. I was breathing out heavily trying to push the entity out. It was sitting on my chest and had gained entry into my nostrils. As I resisted, it put heavy pressure on my chest and, increasing in size, pushed further through the nose. It half entered my throat. This put bursting pressure inside the nostrils and throat. I had to ignore that and keep pushing it out with quick, short, but powerful gushes of breath right from my abdomen by rapidly flattening it against my back. The struggle went on for some time. Then, I woke up fully, in full control, and gave one hard final push. The entity jumped off me and vanished.

Once, when I was sleeping on my side, I ignored the pleas of an entity. It came into the bedroom, pounded my side, kneaded my arm and, as I still ignored it, angrily flew away. Another time, another one lay next to me and tried to push me off the bed. As I woke up frightened and shivering, it laughed sinisterly. I tried ignoring it, when it repeated its efforts and laughed again. I put on the lights and woke up Raja. It disappeared.

One night, when I was asleep, I had a vision. There was an ancient palace, not very richly appointed, but huge, with a big stage where sat a king in audience. A horde of poor commoners came begging and imploring him about something. These people wore dirty, white, flowing robes and had covered their heads. They were apparently in trouble and had come with entire families. Intrigued, I tried to figure out whether it was a biblical setting or an early Muslim one. One of them, becoming aware of me, turned around, hesitated a moment, then from that distance, through our bedroom door, jumped straight at me and fell on me with precision, exactly the way I was sleeping, and clutched me tight. It was a young girl of about sixteen years, beautiful, and obviously in trouble. She implored me in Hindi to save her and give her some sign. I woke up with the thud of her falling on me and felt the impact of her fall for quite some time.

Once I asked a yogi of high order what I was supposed to do when such incidents happen. He told me to just remain calm, be only a witness, and not be tempted to dabble in all this because it could become dangerous as more and more powerful and mischievous spirits would start coming. So I just pray for their souls.

Once, after visiting the Ganagapur temple near Sholapur in Maharashtra, I saw during my meditation a human hand appear before my eyes. A beautiful gold chain interspersed with glowing multicoloured beads was dangling from it. I realized that it was an exceptional *navaratna* chain. It was ethereal and definitely one that adorns the Lord. I marvelled at it without a thought of touching it or possessing it. As there was no movement within me of either wanting it or taking it, the hand came forward a little, and a voice said, 'Take!' I was surprised, as it was obviously a very expensive chain. Having enough jewellery of my own, I had no hankering for more. I wondered why this was being offered to me, when someone again said clearly, 'Take it. It is not an ornament. It is a japamala. It denotes "aishvarya".' At these words, bliss descended on me.

Soon after, I had another vision. I was in a dense forest and chanced upon a pit deep as a well, filled with glowing, magical gems, befitting the gods. I stood at the edge of the pit and watched these gems with fascination. They were of all sizes and shapes, and slowly changing colours and vibrating gently. It was one of the most beautiful, amazing sights to behold. There was no guard watching over them, lying out in the open, protected only by the trees of the jungle. They seemed to belong to no one. It would not have been too difficult to get into the pit and pick up a handful. But apparently they had lain there safely all these days, as the leaves fallen all around looked undisturbed. I wondered how they had remained there all this time unplundered.

No thought came to me to touch them or own them. There was only the act by me of witnessing and admiring them. I waited some time to see if someone would come along to claim them. None came.

Satiated by the vision, as I turned to go, I gave these lovely gems one last look. To my horror, there were only ugly snakes of all sizes slithering, writhing, crawling one on top of the other. I gasped in shock. I could neither move nor understand how I could have been so deceived earlier. But a voice spoke from within me, 'It is your lack of greed and the feeling of total detachment towards these that has saved you. It is very easy in life to be deceived by glittering things and get hopelessly bitten.'

That was a good lesson for me to learn if one does not want to get trapped in the illusory, dangerous web of Maya.

Another night whilst meditating, a thumb pressed upon my forehead with considerable force, and vanished. I presumed it belonged to some spiritual personality.

I sometimes exist as Purusha and feel Prakriti come out of me. The male principle and the female principle; the passive potential and the active actualization. Sometimes I am Prakriti and find myself coming out of Purusha, and getting reabsorbed in him. And then find that Purusha and Prakriti are two aspects of the same Parama Purusha, the Absolute, the Ultimate, and the Cosmic Being, who is beyond even them.

Then I go beyond this Parama Purusha too and experience the *Shunya*, the formless form, the very source of the Parama Purusha. I then experience the Parama Purusha splitting as Purusha and Prakriti, as Consciousness and Nature. And I then see the Oneness of all and see that I myself alone exist as the totality of the Lord.

Thus by personal, intimate 'experiencing', I learn in different ways *advaita*, the oneness of the individual with the cosmos and the Lord. Yet, inspite of this oneness, I have learnt about that which separates them and that which unites them. By becoming these, I sometimes float as clouds, sometimes stand as mountains, at times be the ocean and experience its various depths. Sometimes I am the 'whole', the ocean, the sky, the clouds, the water, the mountains, the landscape in its entirety and finery.

After having transcended the 'turyavastha', the fourth state that is beyond waking, dreaming and the deep sleep state, I have been living for the past many years in 'sahaja samadhi', experiencing the bliss, the peace and the simply 'Being' of the Brahman.

Coping up simultaneously with the vibrant awakening and with all the attendant problems in outer life, along with the unavoidable functioning as a mother and a wife was not easy in the beginning. The divine energy would make me withdraw into deep samadhi, whilst my strong sense of duty would fight off this withdrawal to perform the daily chores.

But, slowly, I was able to master both the spiritual and the mundane levels of life. This must be the goal for everyone: To pursue the divine, to remain in the divine, and yet lead a normal life. To delve in spirituality, one need not be severed from ordinary living. Combining the two, that is, leading a normal life with a substratum of devotional bliss and divine Knowledge, makes life dynamic and free from misery. This is what God intends for man: A glorious life, full of Knowledge and Bliss, enjoying the beauteous bounty that the Lord has so generously, so graciously, scattered all around in life. To live in bliss, *Ananda, Parama Ananda.*

Raja and I have brought up four daughters, given them a happy and wholesome childhood, and the best of education. Three of them, Nandita, Aqeela, Akshata, are now married and settled abroad. The youngest, Tejaswi, at present is in college and is with us.

Seekers from many lands come for spiritual guidance or simply to discuss spiritual matters. Many are in touch through correspondence or over the telephone.

What I generally tell them is that the most reliable and untainted Guru for an individual is within the individual himself as his Atmaguru, who has been accompanying him through all births and who has known him most intimately and thoroughly. This Guru is the highest revealer. This Inner Being reveals to the individual the highest Truth and the highest Knowledge, and is the guiding principle, the Brahman that resides within each. To rediscover this inner guru should be the goal of every individual. Instead of floundering in this search, it is advisable to take an outer guru's help to get back to the inner guru.

I tell people to become sensitive to the simple joys of life; like the open laughter of children, the pealing of church and temple bells, a cool breeze brushing past you, the flower-bud shyly opening up its petals to the sun, the beauty of sunsets and sunrise, the unexpected kindness of people, a sudden smile thrown at you. Oh, so many, many things of joy! Becoming conscious of these simple joys, reaching out for them, focusing on them, till it becomes your nature to be tuned in to joy that is scattered around you all the time leads you to eternal bliss. This will not only distract you from being overcome by misery, but also keep you in quiet joy all the time and allow you to face equanimously the rigours of life.

This very joy, Ananda, is the beginning, the precursor of the divine, all-pervading Parama-Ananda, amrita, pouring out of the Lord continuously and uniformly. This way, it is not necessary for you to wait till you experience the yogic ananda to fulfil your life. The ordinary, pure ananda of daily life found in simple things is continuous with the Parama Ananda of the Lord. It is the same flow in a smaller measure. One should learn to hold on to this ananda. Parama Ananda will be in our hands right now. We must learn to recognize it.

To be able to stoically face the calamities of life, one must endeavour to understand the Law of Karma. This law, simply put, stipulates that 'As ye sow, so shall ye reap'. Once this dictum is understood clearly, one understands the role one has played in one's destiny. Then wisdom dawns that an event has just been retribution or compensation for one's wrong or right doings in the past and not just a quirk of fate befallen on one randomly. Understanding now bursts forth that, if the present is the manifestation of past deeds and thoughts, then the present can be directed wisely to work out a noble future, even a divine one. Understanding one's responsibility for both grief and joy in life makes it easier, to a large extent, to face with equanimity these unbalancing ups and downs of euphoric joy and debilitating sorrow. The course of life is in the individual's hands; in the longer perspective of life, he can, if he so chooses, do what he wants with it.

The Law does not condemn one for eternity for any wrong-doing. By individual grit, this Law can be rendered sterile and one can rise above its bondage by taking appropriate corrective measures. From a position of being its slave, one can recover one's lost position of being its master, and obtain *moksha* or freedom from it. To endeavour to study this Law in its wholeness, to rise above grief and ignorance and even joy and happiness, to find this nectarine equanimity, this *moksha*, is the intent of repeated births.

Purushaartha, or the human prowess, a God-given gift to humans, makes man not a puppet of Karma, fate. There is bestowed on man the boon of free will, which puts in his hands the right to transcend his limitations; to transcend his destiny, his Karma, his baser instincts, and transcend his position from being a mere mortal to attaining the status of a divine, shining being. This is his birthright and this is the intent of Mother Nature: To lead each individual towards divinity, towards peace and towards bliss. He can, if he so chooses, become a partner of God. And journeying further, even become God.

Along with the Law of Karma, yet another incalculably powerful primal energy affects man in his continuous struggle to be the master of his own destiny. Known as Maya, this energy's prime task is to lead man astray from the path of righteous living, and to cover the divinity within with a subtle veil. Maya obscures totally the inner vision of man and thus prevents him from perceiving the divinity within, thereby imprisoning him in spiritual ignorance. She enchains him in the duality of separation from the Lord, keeps him away from the truth of his oneness with the Lord.

Maya pampers the ego, emotions and desires in man. She then traps him with temptations and irresistible opportunities that rekindle and strengthen ego, emotions and desires. She operates even at the highest level of purity of mind as well. Thus have fallen many advanced yogis too, lured by the offerings of Maya.

Maya panders to the senses of man. Senses are outward-facing and depend upon sources from outside for their gratification. Senses operate through impulses coming from outside the Inner Consciousness. Because the eye of his Inner Consciousness is not operative yet due to the veil of Maya, man's senses are crucial for his self-gratification. Maya the great temptress, the robber of man's will and wisdom, forces him to turn to outside sources for his knowledge and satisfaction, and thus he moves ever more outward, away from the Self and divinity. Maya takes him into hankering and striving for comforts and luxuries, towards fame and power, towards bodily and emotional indulgence, towards entrapment by ego and through vices. Due to Maya, man is bound to his body and the senses and does not strive to comprehend anything beyond them and what they have to offer.

Maya encourages the incurring of further Karma by man, thereby enmeshing him in the cycle of birth and death. It is the task of Maya to perpetuate life, and she does it well.

The force of knowledge is still running unabated in me. Knowledge comes as *Illumination*, instantly and clearly, in a sudden flare of intelligence. In a state of samadhi, or half-wakefulness, where there is neither light nor darkness, only a softly glowing blue-gray, like a lamp lit suddenly within the expanse of the mind, Divine light comes forth making knowledge visual and instantly comprehensible. This light is the Light of Consciousness making knowledge an intimate experiencing. By experiencing the knowledge, seeing it, hearing it, I understand in a flash what is revealed in its clarity and totality. This makes knowledge an audio-visual comprehension. Our dreams too are audio-visual and largely comprehensible, but they are only projections of the state of our mind. However, when one has gone beyond mind and turned inward into the realm of the divine where only silence abides, the knowledge comes forth from the Knowledge aspect of Lord's Consciousness and is pure, true, and bearing no ambiguity or any distortion. This Light of Consciousness is called *Prakaasha* and the knowledge revealed is called *Dnyana*.

Knowledge also comes in silence, without words or any other form when I am drawn into another type of inner silence. When I am not required to perform any worldly chores, wherever I am sitting, I become still, staring one-pointed and enter the Silence of Consciousness amid the normal activity and noise of daily life. In this silence, when not a leaf moves, not a muscle twitches, not a thought enters, the outer world is, and yet is not, life is, yet is not, knowledge is imparted silently, without spoken words, without questioning, without answering. Is knowledge imparted or only perceived by a more awakened state? It is a simple act of knowing anew, something that is already known deep down in some deep recess of the subconscious.

I simply *know* profound truths. I do not need any confirmation. I have my own conviction to rely upon. When I know simply by 'being', when knowledge comes from my very being, where none other resides, only I pervade as knowledge, whose confirmation would I seek? There is no questioning, no seeking; I am fulfilment to the brim.

This, I am told, is Dakshinamurthi's way of teaching. Dakshinamurthi is the all-pervasive, Ultimate Itself in Its Knowledge aspect, revealing aspect, Gurutattva. Legend has it that Lord Shiva, whose abode is North, is facing south encompassing the expanse of India with His compassionate gaze. The imparting of knowledge through silence is His unique and wondrous way. He is just present, still, and complete. The seeker has the task of silencing his own being and becoming highly perceptive and receptive to the presence of this all-pervasive knowledge. Words are redundant here as, in this domain, silence is eloquent and is the mode of subtle communication. This place is the origin of words and languages. Thus one has to go beyond the realm of words to where words are not yet born, and are not even necessary. Here one has to only perceive and understand knowledge. And perceive knowledge as oneself. As pure knowledge is Shiva Himself, and oneself in total purity is Shiva, knowledge is seen as one's own aspect.

Once, I was pure Consciousness. I had no body, all I had was awareness and I was vividly conscious. I was not the diffused, all-pervasive 'being all' entity either. Though I had no body, I was limited in size, an invisible wispy trail having a definite identity. I would be here sometimes, there sometimes, travelling through air at times, enjoying myself. I happened to see a hairline crack in a mountain. Suddenly I found to my horror that I was spear-heading, into it with speed. At the mouth of the crack, I hesitated a moment, feeling claustrophobic, scared how I would enter the solid mass and how I would find air to breathe. But there was no time to think. Like a passenger having no control over his vehicle, enters a tunnel, I was sucked into the hair-thin crevice.

However, once inside, I found I had no trouble passing through the solid mass of the mountain. I was in fact enjoying myself watching everything with curiosity. I relaxed and discovered that there were three of us: consciousness, some unknown force, and myself. When I relaxed, all the three merged into one, but the moment fear would arise in me, the three would separate out and I would feel there was another invisible one directing the zooming meteorite that was me. Otherwise it was me alone.

I was speeding through solid mass. But I had no problem. I was racing through rocks, porous mud, dampness, crevices, and streams of cool water that were all within the mountain. I relaxed and learnt to enter everything without feeling any discomfort.

As consciousness, I enter caves within mountains, narrow tunnels that suddenly become solid mass, pass through it and emerge into vast open spaces all within the mountains. A universe by itself. Sometimes I enter the depths of oceans and see all the aquatic life. I am sometimes in deep, dark, damp, normally scary caves full of bats and other creatures of the dark. But bodiless and now no more scared, I go along dark, narrowing streams ending in minute gaps from where the water is slowly making its way. I have nothing to prevent me. I am bodiless yet I can see, hear and understand everything.

I find this trio, consciousness, the other force, and me, form the basic individual. Consciousness, and some 'knowing' force, energy, containing the individual identity, pervading it and encapsulating it. When there is no fear or worry, only comfort and enjoyment, there is oneness. There is duality within the non-duality. With the surfacing of emotions, duality instantly springs forth. And, it is this dualistic individual that comes under the spell of Maya and under the lash of Karma.

I am getting more and more insights on Consciousness and how it operates at the deeper levels of our being. As we become more and more 'aware' even in our deeper states, through purifying the mind and identifying more with the 'witnessing' aspect of Consciousness, we can control and direct better our thoughts when we are awake, and our dreams when we are asleep. The seeds of our thoughts, speech, dreams and actions lying embedded in the Consciousness, indelible marks left on it called 'samskaras', are ejected by the Consciousness to further purify our mind. Such dislodged seeds can surface up and manifest as thoughts and dreams. But before they manifest, they seek permission from our deep, inner states to manifest or not; they even offer to get transformed, or vanish altogether. But our deeper mind is so attached to them that, unknown to us, it wishes them to continue. It is this attachment, this clinging to these seeds and not letting go of them that forms our personality traits. Thus our traits, our fears and nightmares continue. If we remain aware at these deeper levels of our mind and gain control over them, we can let go of the 'samskaras' or direct them to transform and turn to positivity. By changing thoughts and our conscious thinking, we can slowly change our life, our Karma, and eventually our destiny. We can become our own master and live in peace and in fulfilment. I am writing down these insights into the whole process, as they get deeper and verbalized. One day, these might shape up into a book.

Insights of interconnectivity of everything in life are also pouring in. Maybe one day I will be able to share these insights also with others. There is no end to learning. My awe and fascination for this duo of wondrous Consciousness and Energy increases every moment. Its intelligence, foresight and all-encompassing aspect are truly worthy of our worship.

I find that whenever I am a bit relaxed, not involved in anything in particular, automatically some different types of breathing, of 'pranayama', take place at different times. This brings on a very soothing, self-absorbed state. I become aware of different subtle channels the air is travelling through, entering them by different very subtle openings, exiting through others, in various parts of the mouth, the throat and near the base of the nose. Its exit is accompanied by a very soft but clear enough hissing sound and a jet-like ejection. Apparently, our breathing does not follow only the commonly accepted mode of going into the lungs and being thrown out. Correlating to the state of the mind, the degree of purity of mind, and after having been transformed into vital breath, it enters and exits through different openings, traverses through different channels and reaches different parts of the body to perform different tasks. Mysterious and fascinating is the network of breathing. It is an entire system for subsistence, self-correction and self-healing. The more one learns, the more one probes, the more one wonders in awe at the incalculable intelligence, foresight, and planning of the Ultimate we call God. Like the rest of the universe, even within us there can be self-organizing and self-governing. Truly incredible.

Though the word 'prana', with a lower 'p', in a breathing entity is commonly understood simply as breath, it also represents a more fundamental concept of 'Prana', the Life Force, the Primeval Energy. The latter's rhythmic force generates pulses of energy that throb and spread through the body inducing motion and motivation in the glands, organs, and the various systems in the body, thereby governing and energizing them.

Some of the air we breathe in becomes subtle 'Prana' inside the body, and travels through a very intricate and enigmatic network of channels which are other than the gross arteries through which blood flows carrying with it oxygen of the inhaled breath and other nutrients from the food we eat. It transforms into a range of very capable, life-giving energies that penetrate the various subtler sheaths of the body and mind, causing the gross, the subtle and the causal bodies to function normally and sustain themselves. These energies have been classified by the ancients according to their task, their class of activity, and their destination within the body. All the various life-giving energies, including 'Prana' the vital breath, are different forms of Primal Energy itself.

It is essential for our well-being to have the flow of subtle breath smooth and free-flowing so that it penetrates the subtlest of sheaths. A subtle blockage in the channels hampers its flow and its task, causing upsets in our physical, mental and emotional well-being.

The highly knowledgeable ancients of India discovered the tremendous import of right breathing through meditation, deep insights and research. They developed an amazing number of techniques of breathing that could help the vital breath eliminate the blockage and penetrate any sheath of the body, curing and rejuvenating it. This science of breathing is the true 'Pranayama'.

It is also through our breath that the Primeval Energy, the 'Prana Shakti', conjoins matter to Consciousness. It conjoins our body, which is matter, and each of our cells to intelligence and awareness, which is Consciousness. That is how we are aware of our body and, in the higher states of consciousness, of each cell and its activity. If the flow of energy is prevented from reaching any part of the body, that part becomes numb and loses consciousness and sensation.

Such is the power of the Prana Energy. She is there to endow us with her power and strength. Let us become aware of new vigour with every breath we take.

One night I had a vision. There was this little girl, no more than six perhaps, walking by her mother's side. A big toy animal clutched her endearingly from the back, its arms around her neck and its long legs snugly girdling her waist. The girl held in her hands a big doll. The look in her eyes told that the three, she and her two toys, constituted her world of trust, warmth and camaraderie. Suddenly the girl lifted the doll high up and pushing her head deep in the doll's tummy gave it a prolonged kiss. She then gently lowered the doll, gave it a tight hug and pressed her own head tenderly against the doll's. Ecstasy flowed through her as she closed her eyes and gave a beatific smile. The love they shared for each other was supernal.

It was clear that the doll was not just a toy for the girl, but a live entity. The tenderness and gentleness was for a living loved one, who she was sure was aware of this love, appreciated it, and even reciprocated it. It was pure love there, no make-believe, a real world of genuine emotion, no drama. A crucial human need of loving and being loved was being fulfilled.

I knew at once how divine love is. It makes one's life rich, makes one feel wanted. There is assurance in love, comforting and soothing. Tenderness, compassion and sensitivity well up naturally in one who loves. To give and receive love with no room for doubt is an aspect of pure love. Such love is singular and intimate.

Toys fulfil this essential aspect of life in childhood. On a wider scale, pets and family ensure its completion. Happiness is derived from each other's company. Loving and living for each other becomes a way of life. In a later phase of life, a couple brings to each other love, tenderness and a unique companionship. They immerse themselves in each other, experience fullness and completion in each other. Many a long-married couple are living examples of their oneness, to the extent of even resembling each other physically and in having similar behavioral patterns. At an even deeper level, it is 'bhakti' or devotion for God that generates such profound love in one. 'Bhakti' is the ultimate, unconditional love felt towards God. Steeped in the sweet intimacy of the chosen deity, God is never apart. Now every object vibrates with divine force, and an active presence of the deity is felt everywhere.

When one finally goes further, beyond attachment and questioning, beyond the world of senses, one finds this surge of love welling up from within oneself, continually, without an external cause or source. Such love gives total fulfilment. This love flows from our Atman, our very own Self. Such total satiation is a facet of 'Parama Ananada'. This bliss is the Ultimate's true nature. It is our own true nature too, when untouched by our ego and desires, hate and prejudices, anger and discontent.

I find that besides the main 'chakras', that is, centres of psychic energy along the spine, chakras of different sizes are positioned all over the body even in the most unexpected places. I discern the differences in their size by the area that is covered by a sensation of swift gyration. For example, there are minute chakras inside the eardrums, along the ridges of the ears, the tips of eyes, right along the lip-line, on finger-tips, under the nails, along the eyebrows, and even in between them (not to be confused with the crucial 'ajna chakra', which is large and slightly higher up on the forehead). There are slightly larger ones on the soles and the tips of the toes, on the heels, in the armpits, inside the bones, in the knees. Even on the tip of the tongue and along its edges, on the cheekbones, the temples, and inside the teeth. In fact, no area is neglected. Chakras are also subtle centres of Consciousness that govern the areas around them. As the Kundalini rises and spreads her dynamic influence, she energizes the chakras, and makes the energy flow freely through the subtle channels. She is the Universal Energy within us to correct us, to bring about our spiritual progress, take us through spiritual wonders, and even unite us with the Ultimate.

Kundalini in her Universal form creates the universe. She creates us too. After she brings about the conception, embryonic development, and the birth of an individual, she rests in a dormant state in the 'Mooladhara chakra' at the base of our spine. Once awakened, she works her way up through the body to influence both the body and the mind. She takes the mind progressively to higher rungs of Consciousness, refining it, till we reach divinity and find bliss and total fulfilment from within. As Kundalini moves up, and spreads her influence deeper, she systematically sets right the different sheaths of the body, the mind, the senses, and finally piercing the veil of Maya, brings about our divine union with the Ultimate.

As the purity of the mind of an individual improves, or when he actively embarks on any prescribed spiritual endeavour and dedicatedly follows the time-tested practices, or through pure bhakti, or by the grace of a guru, Kundalini slowly awakens and gradually or speedily gets dynamically activated. This could also be an unexpectedly sudden process in some cases, and in some others, so gradual and subtle that it is not even felt.

Chakras could be partially or wholly dormant, depending on the physical, mental, and spiritual condition of the individual. The main ones are situated along the spine, starting from the base, going all the way up to the crown of the head. This topmost chakra is called the 'Sahasrara Chakra', a splendorous, thousand-petalled spiritual lotus, which is the seat of Consciousness. This is the abode of Parama Shiva within our subtle body.

Once aroused, Kundalini moves upwards through the main yet extremely subtle channel called the Sushumna, to meet her Lord, Shiva, thus spiritually uplifting the individual. She penetrates the chakras stationed on the way, gushing through them, cleansing them and setting them to whirl and vibrate freely. She removes any blockages or obstructions there might be, releasing the spiritual energy enshrined there. The individual ascends spiritually. The purity of his mind increases the removal of the spiritual cobwebs therein. The dynamism of Consciousness lodged in the chakra too is enhanced resulting in the bestowal of the prowess of the particular chakra on the individual. The individual benefits tremendously as the Kundalini rises higher and systematically activates more and more complex Chakras. Though usually the Kundalini's progress is linear, from the lowest to the highest, however in some persons she might initiate her action on any chakra out of turn. The Illuminating power of Consciousness reveals progressively more and more knowledge from within, giving glimpses of the Divine within.

As the purity of the mind of the individual increases, different chakras bestow different powers to the individual. All sorts of creativity, arts, knowledge, literature, verses, or music, etc might come to the surface and express itself in the most extraordinary way.

Kundalini finally penetrates the Sahasrara Chakra. Gushing round this chakra, setting it vibrating and pulsating, she enters the inner sanctum sanctorum and meets her Lord enthroned deep within. The ecstatic union takes place and the individual receives the highest state of bliss. He experiences Shiva Himself. He experiences the highest state of 'being', the grand oneness with the Lord, with the cosmos, and with the Entirety. The individual self becomes the Universal Self.

This oneness opens up unlimited vistas of Knowledge, inviting unimaginable heights of bliss. The vast, previously unknown potentialities of the Universal Consciousness are laid bare in steady progression. Thus does the blessed individual realize the truly limitless potential within, that of the Absolute Itself.

There is no one specific path or spiritual discipline to evoke her grace. Any endeavour to bring goodness of being in oneself, purity of mind, pure faith and dedication to God, any prescribed spiritual discipline, any endeavour to reach divinity, is good enough to please her. She is a spiritual Goddess, Universal Mother, love and compassion incarnate, our guide and mentor. All she wants from us is to look within and find her there. All she is waiting for is our gaze within.

The most wondrous aspect of this divine Energy and Consciousness is that they are all-pervasive. They reside in every entity, thus in every human. It is everyone's birthright to receive their grace and experience the Knowledge, the perennial bliss, the peace, the feel of well-being and of fulfilment that I have been personally blessed with. It is a marvellous state of Beauty and Grace to be in, and I would recommend everyone to strive for this state which is everyone's birthright.

Glossary

Abhinaya	Different forms of expression.
Abhisheka	Ceremonial bathing of an idol, accompanied by chanting of mantras.
Agnikunda	A vessel for holding sacrificial fire.
Ahamkara	Ego.
Aishvarya	Resplendence.
Alta	A red liquid to beautify women's feet, like henna for hands.
Amrut	Nectar.
Ananda	Bliss divine.
Antardnyani	All-knowing.
Arati	Worshipful waving of lights to a deity or a holy person.
Arghya	Devotional offering to a deity.
Asana	Seat, yogic posture.
Ashrama	Hermitage.
Atmadnyana	Knowledge of the Self.
Atman	The absolute Reality in man.
Atmasakshatkara	An 'experience' of the Reality.
Aum	The sacred seed-word, the primal sound.
Aum Ganeshaya Namaha	Salutations to Lord Ganesha, the deity.
Avatara	Incarnation of God.
Avastha	Psychic, spiritual state of a seeker at any given moment.
Bhagavad Gita	The song celestial, as expounded by Lord Krishna to Arjuna.
Bhagya	Prosperity, luck, fate.

Bhakti	Intense devotion to the Lord.
Bhava	Mood of exalation.
Bhavani	Consort of Lord Shiva; the primal energy.
Bhava Samadhi	Samadhi with exaltation.
Brahma	The creative aspect of the Lord.
Brahmadnyana	Knowledge of the Supreme.
Brahmakamala	The thousand-petalled psychic lotus situated in the crown of the head.
Brahman	The supreme Entity, together with its manifestation or expansion that unfolds into the divine triad, the gods and demigods, the spirits and mankind, plants, animals and energies, and all the universes, born and unborn. The Entirety. The Almighty.
Brahmavastha	The state of identity with the Absolute.
Chaitanya Shakti	The cosmic force.
Chakras	Extremely sensitive psychic nerve centres.
Chit	Knowledge, Awareness.
Darshan	To be enabled to see an idol or a highly respected religious personality.
Dhyana	Meditation.
Diksha	Initiation.
Diksha Guru	He who initiates.
Durga	Another name of the consort of Lord Shiva.
Ganapati	The Lord Ganesha, the elephant-headed presiding deity for wisdom, well-being and protection; son of Lord Shiva's consort.
Ganesha Stuti	Invocation to Lord Ganesha.
Gayatri Mantra	The holy incantation to the Sun, as the giver of life, intelligence and energy.
Guru-Parampara	Spiritual linkage in the succession of a series of gurus and disciples.
Indriyas	Organs of sense and those of bodily functions.
Jada	Gross.
Japa	Repeating Lord's name or a mantra, for concentration.

Japa-Diksha	Initiation through japa.
Japa-Mantra	Mantra for meditation.
Jiva	An individual, an entity.
Jivatma	Atma covered by an individual identity.
Kamasutra	A treatise on the sensual enjoyment considered as one of the vital elements in the true appreciation and fulfilment of life.
Karma	Action.
Karta	Doer.
Kavacha	Protective cover; armour.
Kriya	Bodily activity, happening of its own, with advancement in yoga or meditation.
Kuladevata	The presiding deity of a family or a clan.
Kundalini	Semi-dormant cosmic power, Shakti, in every individual, lying coiled at the base of the spine.
Krishna	Incarnation of Lord Vishnu. Propounder of Bhagavad Gita.
Lakshmi	Goddess of wealth; consort of Lord Vishnu.
Law of Karma	The law of deeds; 'As ye sow, so shall ye reap.'
Laya	Pause; rest.
Linga	The columnar support of creation. A symbol of the Shiva aspect of the duality inherent in life as Shiva-Shakti, male-female, positive-negative.
Lotus Pose	A meditative pose.
Maha Aishvarya	The highest grace.
Mahan Avastha	A great spiritual or psychic state.
Maha Vishnu	That aspect of the Lord that sustains and enjoys this creation.
Mantra	Potent incantation, made up of seed-words and the Lord's names.
Math	Hermitage.
Maya	The spell of illusion or delusion.
Meditation	Directing the senses inwards.

Mudra	Stylized movement or gesture of the hands or fingers; expression on seeker's face; pose assumed by the seeker's body.
Nadi	Subtle nerve.
Nadi Shastri	One who can, by touching the pulse, predict for or know about a person.
Nama	Names of the Lord.
Namaskara	Salutation.
Navaratri	The nine auspicious days of worship dedicated to Goddess Durga.
Nirvana	Freedom from misery; liberation.
Nirvikalpa	Oneness with the divine, there being a total loss of individual identity; a merger with the divine, resulting in a non-dual state, where there is no admittance to otherness, a second or a duality. Mind uncentred on a deity or a mantra.
Omkara	The deep hum of AUM, the primal sound of the universe.
Om Namah Shivaya	Salutations to the Lord Shiva.
Para Brahma	The Absolute.
Parama Purusha or Purushottama	The primal Being whose two aspects are the Prakriti and the Purusha.
Paramatman	The Supreme Being as the soul of the universe.
Parvati	Durga, Bhavani - the consort of Lord Shiva.
Pradakshina	Circumambulation, around a personality, a temple, a deity, a holy place.
Prakriti	Divine Mother, giving birth to everything in this creation; personified force or energy of the Supreme in creation.
Pralaya	Dissolution.
Pranayama	The science of breath.
Prasada	Food or flowers, sanctified through having been first offered to the deity or holy personality.

Puja	Ritual worship.
Purusha	Cosmic soul, cosmic father, the cause.
Purushaartha	The divine valour or prowess.
Radha	The aspect of duality in an individual, yearning to merge with the Infinite. The spiritual or mystical consort of Lord Krishna.
Rakshasa	Of demonic nature.
Rikshawala	The driver of a rickshaw.
Rishi	Sage.
Roopa, Rupa	Looks of a person; forms attributed to the Lord.
Sadguru	Spiritual Guide.
Sadguru Tattwa	The principle of knowing.
Sadhaka	A seeker engaged in spiritual practices.
Sadhana	An endeavour towards a goal, generally a spiritual practice.
Sahaja	Of itself; happening without any effort or volition.
Sahaja Samadhi	Spontaneous meditation, happening of itself, without disturbing the tenor of everyday life.
Sahasrara chakra	A thousand-petalled, very sensitive psychic nerve centre at the crown of the head.
Sakshi	Witness.
Samadhi	Deep meditation; directing the senses inwards, thereby centring the mind on the Self.
Samskaras	Indelible marks left on the subtle mind, even through innumerable births.
Saraswati	Consort of Brahma; the goddess of speech, learning, arts and music.
Sat	Pure existence; a throb of life running through the cosmos.
Savikalpa Samadhi	Mind centred on a mantra or a deity, or on an outside agency, admitting duality.
Shakti	Shiva's consort; the primal energy of the cosmos.

Shavasana	The posture of body in death. Yogic posture of total relaxation.
Shishya	Disciple.
Shiva	The re-absorbing-unto-Himself aspect of the Lord.
Shiva Mantra	Potent incantations to receive the grace of Lord Shiva.
Shloka	Mystic couplets in Sanskrit.
Shree	Sacred seed-letter in Sanskrit.
Shri Rama	Incarnation of Lord Vishnu.
Shunyata	Void.
Siddhi	A supernatural power or faculty acquired through yogic or mystic advancement.
Sindhoor	A vermilion mark made with red lead, to indicate auspiciousness.
Spanda	Vibration.
Sthirata	The sublime equipoise.
Sthiti	Being, state.
Stuti	Praise.
Sudarshana Chakra	The divine discus of Lord Vishnu.
Sukshma	Subtle.
Swamiji	An honorific for a yogi, a saint, a sannyasi, the head of a religious sect.
Tantra	Treatise or formulae or rituals for specific forms of worship or yoga.
Tapas	Spiritual force; spiritual penance.
Ten Arms	An aspect of the divine mother, Durga, having ten arms, each arm bearing a divine weapon to destroy evil and give protection to the good.
Tilak	A vermilion mark on the forehead.
Turyateetha	When the mind is stabilized and no more flits from state to state; beyond the Turya.
Turya, Turyavastha	The fourth state, beyond the other three, those of waking, dreaming and deep sleep.
Upanishads	Ancient philosophical treatises.

Vairagya	Renunciation.
Veda	The sacred books of knowledge in India.
Vighna	Obstacles.
Vishnu	That aspect of the Lord that sustains and enjoys His creation.
Vishwarupa	The cosmic, visible aspect of the Lord.
Yoga	Unity, connection.
Yoga Mudra	An expressive gesture, a posture, a movement in yoga.
Yogasana	Posture in yoga.
Yogi	One conversant with yoga; a practitioner or someone adept in yoga.
Yoni	A place of birth or origin; the generative cause; the generative organ.